The Politics of Psychoanalyis

Also by Stephen Frosh

THE POLITICS OF MENTAL HEALTH
(with R. Banton, P. Clifford, J. Lousada, J. Rosenthall)

P. Kirby
Liverpool St
Aug/Sept '93.

The Politics of Psychoanalysis

An Introduction to Freudian and Post-Freudian Theory

Stephen Frosh

YALE UNIVERSITY PRESS
New Haven and London

First published in Great Britain in 1987 by Macmillan Education Ltd.
First published in the United States in 1987 by Yale University Press.

Printed in Hong Kong.

Library of Congress catalog card number: 86–51354

International standard book numbers: 0–300–03801–1 (cloth)
0–300–03803–8 (pbk.)

10 9 8 7 6 5 4 3 2 1

To Judith

Contents

Acknowledgements

Several people, including the students who have attended my course on psychoanalysis at Birkbeck College over the years, have helped with the ideas in this book. I would particularly like to thank Tricia Bickerton, Sarah Hampson, Wendy Hollway and Julie Kitchener for reading drafts of some of the chapters, and Danny Miller for his detailed comments and for the many lunch-time discussions around which the book took shape. I would also like to thank Steven Kennedy for his editorial advice and support.

Stephen Frosh

Introduction

Psychoanalysis, a product of the culture of late nineteenth-century Europe, has been one of the strongest influences on twentieth-century thought, its impact comparable only to that of Darwinism and Marxism. Much that was new in psychoanalysis has become accepted wisdom in our culture and has been absorbed even by people who have not read Freud's works: several decades of technical writing, popular literature and therapy have made the concepts of repression, sexual desire and the unconscious familiar, often implicit in ordinary 'common-sense' understandings of ourselves and each other. As many commentators have observed, influential theories of human nature have their own way of becoming true; thus, our awareness of psychoanalysis creates us partly in its image, so that our dreams, neuroses and resistances are comprehended in a Freudian frame. On the other hand, Freud's writings continue to be a source of challenge and controversy, as much now as when they first appeared sixty and more years ago. There is nothing in psychoanalysis, from its most general principles to its most specific observations, that can be said to be universally accepted. Analysts themselves, belonging to the various schools and institutions that have grown up in the wake of Freud, diverge markedly on crucial issues; the non-analytic world has been as scornful as it has been intrigued. The stunning virtuosity of psychoanalysis lies in walking on water: a tremendous speculative energy and certainty of theorising balanced on a foundation that half the world denies. Denies, but cannot ignore; for psychoanalysis, whether right or wrong, challenges all traditional modes of thought on human nature, and with that challenge poses questions for psychological, social and political theory.

Fundamentals of psychoanalysis

What is psychoanalysis? Originating with Freud, still awed by his work and nominally obedient to his principles, the psychoanalytic movement has expanded and diverged significantly since his time. It has been institutionalised nationally and internationally, it has developed formal and elaborate training programmes, it has infiltrated social and literary thought as well as its main area of activity – psychotherapy. It has produced, along the way, a number of different schools of thought with their own theories that in many cases vary in crucial respects from Freud's own ideas. All psychoanalytic theories do, however, have their origins in Freud's work and all share some common assumptions and affiliations. The most important of these concerns the existence of the dynamic unconscious – the idea that in each of us there is a realm of psychological functioning which is not accessible to ordinary introspection, but which nevertheless has a determining or at least a motivating influence on the activities, thoughts and emotions of everyday life. The exact structure and content of this unconscious arena is a much debated topic; for most analysts, however, it is made up of the residues of infantile experiences, possibly alongside certain kinds of instinctual impulses, particularly sexual ones. In addition, all psychoanalysts agree that children develop by passing through certain stages, leading to increased complexity of psychic structure; in all theories, the experiences of early life (up to four or five years of age), primarily with parents, are of crucial significance for the whole of later life. There is, however, considerable disagreement on the details of the developmental process, which is in some cases at the heart of differences between various psychoanalytic schools. Psychoanalysts also fairly universally agree on the significance of Freud's basic *approach*: that through the intense examination of psychological and cultural phenomena of virtually any kind (dreams, slips of the tongue, works of art, neuroses) the underlying 'dynamics' of mental life can be unearthed. For most analysts, the therapeutic situation is the place where this all happens most clearly, as well as being the appropriate setting for operation of the 'talking cure'.

There are shared bases to all approaches, then, but there is also a wide variety of theories that may be termed 'psychoanalytic', often differing greatly in their basic concepts and implications. Sometimes, indeed, different theories are directly opposed to one another on particular issues, making general references to psychoanalysis spurious. Despite this, analytic concepts are frequently employed out of the context of the specific theory from which they arise, a procedure which obscures their significance or makes them lose their sense altogether. An alternative, but equally common, failing is to take only one psychoanalytic theory and to treat it either as the whole or as the only correct approach. It is still the case that Freud's own ideas are sometimes used in this way, as if there had been no developments since he founded psychoanalysis, and also as if there are no contradictions within his own work. More recently, Lacanian ideas have been employed in a wide variety of cultural discussions as if they hold all the progressive prospects for psychoanalysis. In addition to neglecting the complexity of analytic thought, which stretches across a wider area than is encompassed by any one theory, this procedure misleadingly presents the discipline as coherent when in fact it contains numerous contradictions, some of them potentially highly productive.

In this book, the focus is on those major traditions that most clearly bring out differing aspects of psychoanalytic theory, especially as it relates to social thought. Each of these approaches is introduced in Part II in the context of what it has to say about the role of instincts in psychology (something that bears on notions of 'human nature') and about the influence of social experience in the development of the finished human 'subject'. In addition to the work of Freud himself, described in Part I, the approaches selected for consideration are 'classical' ego analysis, object relations, Kleinian and Lacanian theory, and – in Part III – the variants of these approaches that have developed when psychoanalysis has been applied in political contexts. This list is not fully comprehensive: not only are there other positions within psychoanalysis, but there are important related schools outside the psychoanalytic movement itself, for example those of Jung and Adler. However, the selected approaches are the most important in the current analytic pantheon, and they present the full range of serious theorising on most topics that are germane to the central debates within psychoanalysis. Ego analysis grew out of Freud's later work, was strongly influenced by Anna Freud's ideas and codified particularly by Heinz Hartmann and his colleagues in the United States. The focus of this school, as its name implies, is on the functioning of the ego, the core of intelligent activity which modifies and controls unconscious impulses and ensures that they are expressed only in ways that are compatible with the requirements of functioning in the ordinary social world. This approach attempts to combine a biological view of the individual with an understanding of social processes by exploring the enculturation of the child during the socialisation period; that is, its concern is with the way the individual's needs and desires become adapted to particular social demands. Consequently, ego analysis is similar in its general position to Freud's own views, for example his belief that instinctual renunciation is necessary for the maintenance of society.

Object relations theory has mainly British origins, deriving from writers such as Fairbairn, Winnicott and Guntrip, but it has in recent years become increasingly important in the United States in a variety of forms, for example in the work of Otto Kernberg. Whereas Freud places sexual and aggressive instincts at the centre of mental life, object relations theorists emphasise the *relational* context of development. For them, the crucial point in considering individual psychology is not the biological 'drives' that underlie behaviour, but the quality of relationships that are available to a person, and have been available during the formative period of very early life. These early relationships are understood to lay down basic psychic structures and internalisations which provide the template for later relationships; the quality of the early environment is thus crucial for the future conduct of a person's life. Object relations theory, with its emphasis on the importance of the interpersonal environment, presents a more 'open' view of individuality than do the classical theorists: that is, it is more accessible to the idea that the individual is best understood as part of an interpersonal 'field'. Because of this apparently social emphasis, object relations theory is at the centre of most of the debates outlined in this book.

Kleinian theory is closely related to object relations views, even being included under that heading by many writers. It is distinguished from the object relations approach here because of significant differences on some points that are crucial when considering the politics of psychoanalysis, both in basic theory and in attitudes towards therapy. The most important of these differences revolve around the Kleinian insistence on the existence of instincts that 'drive' the individual, and also on the way phantasy[1] is seen as central to psychological functioning. The result is an approach that, while stressing the importance of the 'object world' of other people for development, focuses away from the real world concerns of object relations theory and towards an internal world marked by phantasy, splitting and various complications of process and structure. Interestingly, the Kleinian emphasis on the complexities of internal life and their links with the equally complex and contradictory external world raises many important questions and provides some intriguing possibilities for attempts to construct a 'dialectical' theory of development. It also supplies some instructive concepts for use when considering therapy. To some extent, Klein's work is a bridge between classical and object relations views; but it is also distinct from both positions, and has forged a unique and powerful vision that undermines any neat categorisation of psychoanalysis' social theory.

Finally, Lacanian theory is linked to a different tradition from that of the others, that of structuralism as it has been worked out in philosophy, linguistics and cultural studies, particularly in France. Lacan's own claim was that his work represented a 'return to Freud' armed with the new tools provided by structural linguistics; others have suggested that his main achievement was to polarise analytic practice and obscure analytic theory. What Lacanianism does provide is a radical opposition to any adaptationist politics, a celebration of the subversive possibilities of psychoanalysis and, more concretely, an account of the way the individual becomes formed in the structures of language and culture. Despite some lines of agreement with Klein's work, Lacanianism is basically distinct from, and at odds with, all other forms of psychoanalysis in its relentless insistence on the impossibility of any human structure that is not bound up in, and constructed as part of, culture. This insistence has led to some of the most interesting new developments in the social application of psychoanalysis, particularly by feminists, even if they sometimes end up opposed to Lacan.

Evaluating psychoanalysis

All the issues mentioned above will be explored more fully in the discussions that follow. However, the description of the various analytic theories raises a point that must be addressed here. This concerns the evaluative criteria that can be employed to differentiate between theories and to assess the importance and validity of the psychoanalytic enterprise itself. The first aspect of this relates closely to the notion of politics employed in this book, and will be discussed below. There have, however, been numerous critiques of the whole project of psychoanalysis, the main lines of which are worth mentioning briefly. First, there is the empirical question, that psychoanalysis is 'unscientific', its theories based on no legitimate base of observation or experiment, and having the status only of speculation. The behaviourist Hans Eysenck has been a prime propagandist for this view, in numerous articles and books over three decades. His argument rests on two straightforward principles: that the veracity of psychoanalysis is testable through traditional empirical means, and that in all areas where such tests have been carried out, psychoanalysis has failed.

> We are left with nothing but imaginary interpretation of pseudo-events, therapeutic failures, illogical and inconsistent theories, unacknowledged borrowings from predecessors, enormous 'insights' of no proven value, and a dictatorial and intolerant group of followers insistent not on truth but on propaganda. (Eysenck, 1985, pp. 201–2)

Eysenck's evaluation of Freud's intellectual status is no less sweeping:

> He was, without doubt, a genius, not of science, but of propaganda, not of rigorous proof, but of persuasion, not of the design of experiments, but of literary art. His place is not, as he claimed, with Copernicus and Darwin, but with Hans Christian Anderson and the Brothers Grimm, tellers of fairy tales. (Ibid., p. 208)

That psychoanalysis has been attacked so frequently by positivists such as Eysenck for its neglect of what they claim as fundamental scientific principles (falsifiability, the provision of quantitative evidence, use of adequate controls – see Eysenck and Wilson, 1973) is a fairly substantial irony, as is the defence of psychoanalysis offered by some of its defenders in terms of its messages or general concepts or moral stature. Freud's aim certainly was to construct a new 'science', fusing biology and psychology, the body and the word; in the terms of the unpublished 1895 manuscript which influenced all his later psychoanalytic work, it was to develop a 'Project for a Scientific Psychology'. 'Science' signified for Freud the distinction between the insights of philosophers and mystics on the one hand and, on the other, the careful, uncompromising and impartial attempt to uncover the governing rules of the mind that was his image of psychoanalysis. For Freud, the basic elements of psychoanalysis were its observations, upon which 'facts', collected under the controlled conditions of the analytic situation, irresistible theorems could be posited. When he speculated, he was clear about it: in *Beyond the Pleasure Principle* he warns,

> What follows is speculation, often far-fetched speculation, which the reader will consider or dismiss according to his individual predilection. It is further an attempt to follow out an idea consistently, out of curiosity to see where it will lead. (Freud, 1920, p. 295)

But even when his ideas were at their most uncertain, Freud still felt them to be scientific in essence, unclear and available to reorganisation as they might be. Freud was particularly impatient, in this connection, with those who complained that he kept altering his ideas:

> Only believers, who demand that science shall be a substitute for the catechism they have given up, will blame an investigator for developing or even transforming his views. (Ibid. p. 338)

Whatever Freud was doing, it was not, to his mind, to be confused either with poetry or philosophy.

It is not just behaviourists and reactionary philosophers who have criticised psychoanalysis for its lack of an empirical base. Farrell (1981), in an exposition that is basically symphathetic to psychoanalysis nevertheless notes that, 'The impact of psychoanalysis on the West cannot be justified on the grounds that it contains a body of reasonably secure or established knowledge about human nature' (p. 190) – on the contrary, he finds relatively little evidence that supports the validity of psychoanalytic theory, and bases much of his defence of it on the lack of support for alternative approaches, psychoanalysis being a 'premature' theory rather than necessarily a totally wrong one. Wittgenstein, too, while exhibiting considerable interest in the project of psychoanalysis, argues against its empirical standing: 'Freud is constantly claiming to be scientific. But what he gives is *speculation* – something prior even to the formation of an hypothesis' (Wittgenstein, in Cioffi, 1973, p. 79). And Timpanaro, in one of the most extensive and honourable critiques of psychoanalysis to have originated from within Marxism, makes a sustained attack on 'the captious and sophistical method, resistant to any verification, quick to force interpretations to secure pre-ordained proofs' that he sees as characteristic of the Freudian approach (1976, p. 14). Whereas Wittgenstein suggests that much of the problem lies in Freud's desire to find laws of thought and behaviour when in fact there are none, Timpanaro accuses him of overlooking those obvious explanations which reside in material circumstances and class divisions, relying instead on finding something 'unknowable' and mysterious behind every phenomenon. Timpanaro (1976, p. 178) comments that,

> while the accusation of pansexuality often levelled at psychoanalysis is largely wide of the mark, the charge of psychologism is . . . much more accurate. The preferred explanation is always the most tortuous and complicated, and thus the most 'misanthropic'.

The criticisms presented in this work are not always easy to answer. Although the excesses of positivism are fairly obvious (too rigid a view of science, too limited a notion of human behaviour and experience, cavalier treatment of experimental data to suit their own theories, and so on), the empirical arguments that derive from progressive critics are more robust. Timpanaro himself supplies part of the answer in a quotation from Trotsky that compares the apparently 'materialist' work of Pavlov with that of Freud.

> Pavlov's method is that of experiment, Freud's that of conjecture . . . in Freudianism we have an instance of a working hypothesis which can, and indubitably does, allow for the development of deductions and conjectures along the lines of a materialist psychology. (1976, p. 207)

This is in line with Farrell's (1981) idea that psychoanalysis is a 'premature science', pronouncing on issues of significance for human experience but without the technology that makes verification of these pronouncements possible. Psychoanalysis under this view provides a direction for research and practice, always available to alteration or liable to be surpassed – an idea not dissimilar to that held by Freud himself. But another line of defence which has been taken up by many psychoanalytic apologists is that presented most forcefully by Habermas (1972), who suggests that psychoanalysis is an instance of a particular kind of science, a 'hermeneutic' approach which is 'the only tangible example of a science incorporating methodological self-reflection' (p. 214). The focus of the psychoanalytic enterprise in this view is on the unravelling of distorted 'texts'; that is, it is a form of interpretative activity, a kind of literary criticism of everyday life. As such, its project is to make sense, to find meaning in material and hence to allow for a more complete self-reflection than might otherwise be possible. Whatever the merits of Habermas' specific theory, the general argument that psychoanalytic knowledge is knowledge of a different order from that accessible by means of the experimental sciences is a strong one, however unpalatable it might have been to Freud. The object of psychoanalytic knowledge is subjectivity, the flowing, changing, productive and disjointed experience that each of us has of ourselves and the world, and the pattern of linkages that this subjectivity has with external events. The criteria for evaluation of the correctness of theories in this area cannot be solely empirical or observational, because such approaches operate on the wrong level to conceptualise or measure subjective experience. Other criteria that deal with personal *meanings* are the appropriate ones, for instance investigating the persuasive and conceptual power of psychoanalysis, its 'hermeneutic' energy. This does not mean that all psychoanalytic theorising is acceptable: as Timpanaro demonstrates, there are many examples even in Freud's work of distorted or tendentious thinking in which the material is made to fit pre-existing ideas and in which alternative positions are equally, or more, persuasive. But there is a need for a broader view of what constitutes knowledge than that available from experimental psychology – something which can speak to our experience and ideas as well as to our eyes. Limiting our concepts of ourselves and others to those that are based on simple observational measurements or laboratory experiments is a path towards complete ignorance of all internal states – of the core of psychology itself.

The politics of psychoanalysis

The final issue to be raised here is central to the concerns of this book. It begins with another common criticism of psychoanalysis, that it is by nature a bourgeois discipline, opposed to radical activity. In part, this argument derives from practice: from the dismissiveness with which analysts have sometimes greeted political action, from the moralism implicit or explicit in psychoanalytic therapy, or from the use made of some analytic theories apparently to explain away oppressive practices, for instance father–daughter rape (see Ward, 1984). Brooks (1973) supplies a shriller and more extensive critique by arguing that 'Freudianism is not a basis for a Marxist Psychology' because it systematically obscures the social base of human life, and also because it depersonalises the individual, depicting 'human behaviour as the manifestation of the play of forces of the unconscious and id, ego, super-ego, rather than as a meaningful act revealing the world' (p. 334). It will be argued later in this book that this is, in fact, the precise opposite of what psychoanalysis at its best does: psychoanalysis offers a means of understanding how the world can be 'revealed' and expressed in the experiences of every individual. But the Marxist critique cannot be dismissed so lightly when it is more carefully formulated. Once again, Timpanaro (1976, p. 12) is a guiding light here. He articulates the 'Marxist objection that psychoanalysis is a bourgeois doctrine, and to that extent incapable of seeing beyond an "ideological" horizon delimited precisely by the class interests of the bourgeoisie', a critique which stresses the tendency of Freud to regard his society as the only possible one, and to view repression as its necessary consequence. Timpanaro goes on to point out the idealist tendencies in Freud and his complete neglect of Marxist theories of the family (something 'really scandalous'), and to conclude that,

> with the exception of some inspired but fairly restricted conquests, psychoanalysis is neither a natural nor a human science, but a self-confession by the bourgeoisie of its own misery and

perfidy, which blends the bitter insight and ideological blindness of a class in decline. (p. 224)

Timpanaro does recognise some virtues in Freudianism, particularly in the early concentration on hedonism (for example, in the *Three Essays on Sexuality*), but in the main he sees it as a portrayal of bourgeois decadence. Once again, this is not wrong but it is also not the whole story. The details of the riposte to this argument are implicit in the whole of the rest of this book, but the general point is as follows. Psychoanalysis does often reveal individualistic and retrograde tendencies, and some psychoanalytic theories are wholly in this mode. But it also contains the possibilities for an approach that analyses the mechanisms by which the social world enters into the experience of each individual, constructing the human 'subject' and reproducing itself through the perpetuation of particular patterns of ideology. This is analysis of the bourgeois condition, but potentially of other conditions as well – of all conditions under which personality is formed. As such, psychoanalysis can be more than a portrayal of 'a class in decline'; it can also provide insights into how we may be constituted under changed circumstances, and possibly into how those changes may be brought about.

It is arguments such as that given above that make the juxtaposition of the terms 'psychoanalysis' and 'politics' meaningful. Workers in a number of social science disciplines now recognise the importance of people's subjectivity – their ideas, beliefs and emotions – in directing or influencing their social behaviour and perceptions of themselves and others. This recognition has led to a renewed interest in the origins and nature of subjective experience, something which has in turn led to psychoanalysis, the body of psychological theory and practice which focuses most insistently on subjectivity, dealing specifically with the workings of unconscious perception, emotion and desire. In addition, in its formulations on development and on the significance of particular interpersonal encounters, psychoanalysis offers insights into the mechanisms by which individuality becomes constructed within a social context – something that needs to be understood if the politics of subjectivity are to be accurately portrayed. Thus, in sociology, literature, film studies and philosophy, as well as in Marxist and feminist theory, there has been an enormous burgeoning of interest in psychoanalysis in recent years. In mental health practice, too (though less so within the confines of traditional psychology and psychiatry), renewed attention is being paid to variants of psychoanalysis or psychoanalytic psychotherapy, following a decade or so of humanistic or 'growth' psychology.

It is against the backdrop of these trends in contemporary thought that the politics of psychoanalysis becomes a matter for serious consideration. 'Politics' here is being used in a broad but reasonably precise sense, to refer to the positions taken up with respect to the power relations that exist between people and that are embedded in the major structures of society. These positions can be of various kinds, ranging from legitimisation of existing power relations by appeal to their biological 'naturalness', to the oppositional stance that attempts to subvert these relations by revealing the vested interests and social construction processes that lie behind them. In this context, there are two distinct strands to the 'politics of psychoanalysis' that will be dealt with in this book. (A third possible strand, dealing with the manoeuvrings of groups and individuals for power *within* the psychoanalytic movement is more properly the province of sociology or journalism – see Turkle (1978) and Malcolm (1982) for examples.) The first of these concerns the politics inherent in psychoanalytic theories, the implications of psychoanalytic ideas and assumptions for notions of individuality and society, and for programmes of personal and social change. A pertinent question here, for instance, is whether the Freudian emphasis on the existence of biological instincts (or 'drives') at the root of psychic life dooms psychoanalysis to being a reactionary approach arguing for the unchangeability of 'human nature' and the inevitability of social inequalities. Again, there are questions to be raised about the recognition given in psychoanalysis to the place of social influences in development – are these influences basic to the construction of the psyche, or are they seen as having simply a meliorative role, marginally affecting an already determined organism? Freud's own views on instincts and psychic structure are described in Chapter 1, while Part II takes up the political issues that arise and considers them in the light of post-Freudian theories. Particular attention is paid to the different theories' accounts of the importance of instincts and of the links between experience and psychic structure; the debates that surround these issues go to the core of the problem of how that which is social and that which is individual combine to form the experiencing human 'subject'. Because of this, the discussions of Part II are basic for all the later explorations of the book, which in some ways represent a working out of the implications of the various positions there encountered.

The second strand of the 'politics of psychoanalysis' concerns the application of psychoanalysis to wider political questions. Although there are innumerable ways in which this might take place, and psychoanalysts and fellow travellers have not been particularly wary of pronouncing upon anything and everything, there are two fundamental issues which have dogged psychoanalytic social theory from its earliest days and which reveal most clearly its limits and its productivity. The first of these relates most closely to the concerns of traditional socialism: the relationship between social (or state) structures and individuality. At issue here is Freud's belief, described in Chapter 2, that the repression of individual desires is *necessary* for the well-being of society, that society and the individual are unavoidably in conflict. This offers a deeply pessimistic view of the possibilities for radical social change, a point which has not escaped Freud's critics. The second social issue is that of femininity, a 'social' concern because it holds within it some of the crucial arguments concerning the impact of ideology and social structure (in this case, that pertaining to patriarchy) on the personality and experience of individuals. Freud's views on femininity are also described in Chapter 2, while Part III provides an account of some major post-Freudian attempts to use psychoanalysis to enrich socialist and feminist debate, from the efforts of so-called 'Freudo-Marxists' to the recent spate of feminist psychoanalytic criticism.

The final test of any theory is, of course, the practice to which it gives rise. The internal politics of psychoanalysis and its application to wider political questions in many ways come together in its consideration of the purposes and techniques of therapy, the area of psychoanalysis' specific practice. Here, in considering the possibilities for personal change and the means by which it might be brought about, psychoanalysis reveals its own ideological underpinnings and its views on how to produce transformations of experience and consciousness – a quintessentially 'political' task. Measures of psychoanalysis' politics can be found here in the extent to which the importance of social conditions is recognised in its pronouncements on possibilities for individual change, and in the aims that it espouses – for instance, whether they are couched in terms of adaptation to social mores, or subversion of them. The views of analysts on their own position as agents of change is relevant to this: the difference, for example, between those who obscure the power relations that operate in therapy and those who examine it is an important one in considering the expression of analysis as a political activity. Freud's views on these matters, specifically the possibilities for 'cure' and the mechanisms through which therapy operates, are presented in Chapter 3, while Part IV describes and analyses a range of post-Freudian positions that demonstrate both the underlying assumptions and the political possibilities of psychoanalytic therapy.

It is now possible to return to the question of the evaluative criteria employed here to discriminate between different psychoanalytic theories. The notion of politics used in this book takes for granted the existence of power relations that are linked with basic social structures and that are involved in the construction of each individual. Hence, the criteria employed for assessing theories are neither empirical in a traditional scientific sense, nor neutral in a political sense. The potential value of psychoanalysis for people concerned with politics lies in its ability to provide an account of subjectivity which links the 'external' structures of the social world with the 'internal' world of each individual. In the search for a socially oriented psychoanalysis, the coherence of each theory's account of how social relations become inscribed inside each person during development is an important guide to how the theory should be evaluated. More generally, theories differ in their view of how basic the social is to our understanding of 'human nature', with more progressive approaches deconstructing the latter notion to reveal how the two terms of the traditional individual–social divide actually interpenetrate one another in an indissoluble way. Again, the various theories hold different implications for practice, both in the area of therapeutic and of political change. A progressive psychoanalysis requires an approach that locates all forms of change in an appropriate social context, thus avoiding the temptation to see salvation in therapy while also spelling out the contribution that analytic help can make to wider social struggle.

In summary, this book has a dual purpose: to introduce a complex range of psychoanalytic thought, and to do so in a manner that reveals and assesses its political significance. It will be argued that only some elements of psychoanalysis are politically progressive and that even in their case the limitations of analysis have to be recognised: that it describes and acts upon the individual 'subject' without tackling the wider social structures which must also be the target for activity if change is to come about. That this is a genuine limitation, however, does not reduce the value of what psychoanalysis does have to offer. Without a theory of subjectivity, of how the individual's experience becomes organised, there can be no complete approach to politics. Psychoanalysis, with all its retrogressive tendencies and complex contradictions, offers the most provocative and persuasive prospects for the development of such a theory that are currently available.

Part I
The Freudian Base

There is no other place to start in psychoanalysis than with the work of Sigmund Freud. This is by no means an onerous duty, because the quality and provocativeness of that work still remains breathtakingly high. It is also, of course, enormous in quantity, and no brief introduction can cover all its aspects. In Part 1, some of Freud's basic notions are described thematically, selected for their relevance to the central concerns of this book – to uncover the internal politics of psychoanalysis and the potential for its application to external political questions. Chapter 1 deals with Freud's ideas on the nature of the unconscious, the role of instinctual drives in mental life, and the structure of the mind. In Chapter 2, Freud's attitude to society and its impact on each individual is described, as is his version of feminine psychology. Finally, Chapter 3 presents Freud's views on the potential impact, and mode of action, of psychoanalytic psychotherapy. The tone of Part 1 is less critical and more expository than in the later sections of this book; its purpose is to introduce the base upon which all contemporary psychoanalytic debates are built.

1 The Discovery of the Unconscious

If psychoanalysis can be thought of as characterised by any particular 'project', it is not to bring about a therapeutic transformation in the lives of individuals. Instead, psychoanalysis aims at producing a certain kind of knowledge, providing explanations of human conduct and experience by revealing the mental forces that underlie them and that are not dealt with by any other intellectual discipline. In Freud's words, 'We do analysis for two reasons: to understand the unconscious and to make a living' (Jacoby, 1975, p. 124). Increasing the complexity of psychological understanding by providing explanations for otherwise inexplicable or only partially comprehensible phenomena, especially by revealing meaningful motivations and conflicts at the base of apparently irrational and meaningless material, was at the heart of Freud's particular enterprise. Despite the increase in 'therapeutic zeal' shown by many post-Freudians, and the institutionalisation of psychoanalysis as a form of treatment for psychological distress, the central element in psychoanalysis remains its body of knowledge, its ability to interpret human experience in a way that makes it coherent. This is where psychoanalysis poses a major challenge to other forms of psychology: whereas academic psychology specialises in the description of microscopic elements of behaviour – part functions, one might call them – psychoanalysis attempts to supply explanations for the entire gamut of personal and interpersonal activity. These explanations are of a particular kind, which differentiates them from the descriptive focus of other approaches (for instance, behaviourism) and which aims to increase our understanding of psychological *processes*. According to Brown (1959), it is the depth of explanation embraced by Freud that supplies the crucial element in his search for a new psychology, entailing a particularly thorough approach to the uncovering of personal meanings.

> Meaningfulness means expression of a purpose or an intention. The crux of Freud's discovery is that neurotic symptoms, as well as the dreams and errors of everyday life, do have meaning, and that the meaning of 'meaning' has to be radically revised because they have meaning. (Brown, 1959, pp. 3–4)

Detailing the precise nature of Freudian 'meaning' requires an elaboration of his basic concepts that is the subject of this chapter, but, as noted in the Introduction, psychoanalysis was never intended solely as a philosophical or hermeneutic system. Rather, Freud makes clear in several passages his admiration for biology and his determination to root psychoanalysis in biological science. The origins of psychoanalysis reside, it seems fair to say, in the *Project for a Scientific Psychology* that Freud wrote in 1895, in which he tried to account for the whole of mental functioning in terms of the transmission and inhibition of various forms of energy. Twenty-five years later, his adherence to the possibilities available from biology was no less pronounced. In the defence of science at the end of *Beyond the Pleasure Principle* he states,

> The deficiencies in our description would probably vanish if we were already in a position to replace the psychological terms by physiological or chemical ones . . . Biology is truly a land of unlimited possibilities. (Freud, 1920, p. 334)

The notion of Freud as biologist is a central component of Sulloway's (1979) book, in which he claims that Freud's theories 'became *more* biological, not less so, after the crucial years of discovery' (p. 391). But it is also important to realise that Freud's claim to scientific status does not rest on his allusions to biology or his propensity towards the language of physics and physiology. His scientific status resides in his method and in his discovery: the method is observation, speculation and formulation of what has been observed in terms of general theories; his discovery was of the origins, motives and processes of mental life. In this respect, as Greenberg and Mitchell (1983) suggest, there is no clear distinction to be made between psychoanalysis as a natural science and as an interpretative discipline: in presenting an account of the mechanisms of psychological functioning, Freud was also explaining the meaning of psychological events. Above all, his concern was with conflict, between the individual and the world and, perhaps more powerfully and more poignantly, within the various strata of the individual's mind. Freud's creation was a dynamic psychology, of 'source, aim and object', of motivation and intention – a fully human science. And his major building-block, 'the foundation stone on which the whole structure of psychoanalysis rests', was the doctrine of repression.

Repression and the unconscious

Two of the most uninhibited writers on Freud and culture begin their major books on Freud with the assertion that the crux of Freudian theory is repression. For Norman Brown (1959, p. 3), in *Life against Death*,

> The Freudian revolution is that radical revision of traditional theories of human nature and human society which becomes necessary if repression is recognised as a fact. In the new Freudian perspective, the essence of society is repression of the individual and the essence of the individual is repression of himself.

Marcuse (1955), in *Eros and Civilisation*, is more succinct: 'According to Freud, the history of man is the history of his repression' (p. 11). In these quotations, Freud's frequent failure to distinguish between the generality of defence mechanisms and the specifics of repression is being followed. Whereas in his more careful moments (such as in *Inhibitions, Symptoms, Anxiety*), Freud was clear that repression was just one of the defences used to protect the psyche against unpalatable material, he frequently applied the notion of repression to any psychological process which prevents unconscious material becoming conscious. In the metapsychological paper *Repression* (1915a), he states that 'the essence of repression lies simply in turning something away, and keeping it at a distance, from the unconscious' (p. 147). For radical Freudians, as will be discussed in Chapter 6, 'repression' generalises still further to connote social as well as endopsychic processes. By a sleight of hand, the internal splitting introduced into the psyche by the exigencies of ordinary life are converted into a parable of the whole of social existence. The extent to which this is a justifiable process is a matter of serious dispute.

In the reference to the prevention of unconscious material becoming conscious lies the reason why the view of Brown and Marcuse concerning the centrality of repression does not really contradict the more general remembrance of Freud as the 'Discoverer of the Unconscious'. Freud himself emphasised the intimate links between repression and the unconscious. In part, this is a statement of practical observation, in the sense that it is the analysis of the various resistances displayed by clients when facing disturbing material that reveals the presence of the unconscious. From observations of resistances in analysis, plus the evidence derived from hypnotic suggestion and hysterical symptoms, Freud concluded that there had to be in existence mental phenomena which were not available to awareness, but which nevertheless had a powerful influence on psychological life.

> We have found – that is, we have been obliged to assume – that very powerful mental processes or ideas exist . . . which can produce all the effects in mental life that ordinary ideas do . . . though they themselves do not become conscious. (Freud, 1923, p. 352)

Conceptually, too, Freud stresses the necessary connection between repression and the unconscious: it is precisely the mark of the Freudian revision of theories of the mind that there cannot be one without the other. 'The repressed is the prototype of the unconscious for us', he states (Freud, 1923, p. 353), highlighting in this remark the radically new perception that is brought to bear by the theory of the dynamic unconscious. It is not so much that he recognised the existence of an area of mental functioning lying outside consciousness: many workers, before and after Freud, have done this, and there can be very little debate over the position that our mental contents are broader than that which is immediately accessible to consciousness. Freud's new contributions lie in his recognition of the relationship between repression and the unconscious, in his description of the functions of unconscious material, and in his detailing of the contents and form of unconscious life.

Freud (1915a) distinguishes between two types of repression. The first is 'primal repression', in which the mental representation of instinctual desire is denied access to consciousness; this representation therefore remains unconscious. Secondly, there is 'repression proper', which Freud refers to as an 'after-pressure', in which material which is available to consciousness *becomes* repressed because of its association with the already repressed mental representative of the instinct. In this way, material is denied access to consciousness not only because it is too threatening to awareness, but also because of the attraction of material that has already been repressed:

> it is a mistake to emphasize only the repulsion which operates from the direction of the conscious upon what is to be repressed; quite as important is the attraction exercised by what was primarily repressed upon everything with which it can establish a connection. (Freud, 1915a, p. 148)

The importance of this notion is that it suggests that repressed material does not remain static in its unconscious state (the more everyday use of the term 'unconscious', as in 'he is unconscious'), but has a life of its own, 'vicissitudes' to use a term favoured by Freud's translators. Freud notes that, if anything, unconscious material develops apace, more vigorously than material which is governed by the constraints and reality-testing of conscious experience. However, this is not to say that what he calls the 'proliferation in the dark' demonstrated by unconscious material cannot be charted. The maps are obtained primarily through the analysis of dreams, but also from parapraxes and the symptomatology of neuroses; they give rise to a vision of the unconscious as an entity (the 'Ucs.') in which all is wish, impulse and drive, where reality has no place and there are no constraints upon desire.

> The nucleus of the Ucs. consists of instinctual representatives which seek to discharge their cathexis; that is to say, it consists of wishful impulses . . . There are in this system no negation, no doubt, no degrees of certainty. (Freud, 1915a, p. 190)

That the unconscious is mostly describable in terms of what it does not have – a sense of time, of contradiction, or of reality – is no fault of Freud's, for the unconscious is the primary negation, the opposition to the world of order and common-sense, the great subverter of everyday life. As Freud notes earlier in the paper on *The Unconscious*, if we look hard and long at ourselves, the recognition is forced upon us that we are aliens, that our actions are only explicable when we refer them to 'another site' than consciousness, when we abjure the claim that we have some special private knowledge available to us about our secret process, when we treat our 'acts and manifestations' as if they belonged to someone else.

What, then, is the difference between conscious and unconscious material? Dynamically unconscious ideas have (i) been repressed, and are (ii) kept from consciousness by continuing pressure (Wollheim, 1971, p. 161). This distinguishes them from 'preconscious' ideas which can be admitted to consciousness with ease and which are more akin to the common-sense tradition of the unconscious as a library or storehouse of ideas or memories. Because repressed ideas lie outside consciousness they cannot easily be controlled, but instead are the source of many behaviours and experiences which do not have the character of being willed by the self. In this way, repressed ideas are dynamic not simply in the sense of having to be held back by an opposing force, but also in the sense of being causal, of having a motivating effect on human psychology. Freud's notion is that the emotional energy of repressed desire becomes split off from the conceptual part of that desire (the idea) and invested in something else – dreams or symptoms, for example. It is only through the recovery of the concept that the driving energy of the desire can be identified and, if necessary, rechannelled. In all this, words are crucial: not only is psychoanalysis, as will be seen, fairly dubbed 'the talking cure', but language is introduced right into the heart of the deep mystery of the unconscious. Thus, from an insightful discussion of schizophrenia, Freud generalises that

> We now seem to know all at once what the difference is between a conscious and an unconscious presentation . . . (T)he conscious presentation comprises the presentation of the thing plus the presentation of the word belonging to it, while the unconscious presentation is the presentation of the thing alone . . . A presentation which is not put into words . . . remains thereafter in the Ucs. in a state of repression. (Freud, 1915a, p. 207)

Words make consciousness of impulses possible; when the correct connections are made, they bring unconscious material through into the half-light of preconscious activity, and thence to the full glare of recognition. In this statement there can be found a provocative argument for the role of language in governing consciousness, and a major rationale for the therapeutic activity of psychoanalysis.

Freud's account of the unconscious is an explanatory one. The activities of desire, condensed or displaced by the machinations of repression, make sense of the seemingly inexplicable, tell us more about ourselves than we might wish to know. Behaviour is motivated, but the motivations are in some way dangerous and unacceptable, and therefore become hidden. Implicit in this formulation is the notion that the state of reason, of informed and conscious control over one's psychological 'self', is not a state of nature, but of culture – that is, it has to be striven for and constructed. This is one of the sources of the subversive impact of psychoanalysis: it overturns the western view that the distinguishing mark of humanity is reason and rationality. In the Freudian version, the true sources of being lie not in the 'cogito', but in desire – the unacceptable and hence repressed impulses towards sexuality and aggression which hold unrecognised sway over what we usually perceive as the central elements in our personality. The illusion of individual integrity and a unified self hides an awareness that pervades our dreams, of instinctual energy held back by repression. This is one focus of dissent amongst post-Freudian writers: the possibilities for full human autonomy and integration so central to humanistic psychology are undermined by the Freudian unconscious, according to which we are, in Deleuze and Guattari's (1977) phrase, 'Desiring Machines'.

Instincts and their vicissitudes

When considering the requirements for a complete theory of psychoanalysis, a 'metapsychology', Freud distinguished between topographical, economic and dynamic points of view, all of them necessary. The topographic view is that which we have already encountered, the distinction between conscious, preconscious and unconscious material. The economic viewpoint was basic to Freud's psychological perceptions from early on; the economy being referred to was the psychic economy, the balance of energy within the mind. Although Freud's ideas changed over the years, the economic approach became, if anything, more important, reaching its apotheosis in the theory of the Death Instinct. Two points of significance require emphasis here. First, Freud's concept of energy was employed to explain the activity of the mind – he used a 'hydraulic' model which expressed the source of activity as some movement or shift in energy from another part of the system. Secondly, he viewed the aim of the system as the restoration of peacefulness: the 'Principle of Constancy' held that,

> the nervous system is an apparatus which has the function of getting rid of the stimuli that reach it, or of reducing them to the lowest possible level; or which, if it were feasible, would maintain itself in an altogether unstimulated condition. (Freud, 1915a, p. 116)

On this premise, that what we do is forced upon us by the quest to restore our ease, much of the Freudian account of motivation depends.

As the nervous system does not in itself generate activity, there must be sources of energy or tension which impinge upon it to wake us from our sleep. Freud distinguishes two such sources: external stimuli, which we can turn away from or control with some other form of motor action, and internal drives or 'instincts', from which there is no simple escape. It is in tracing out the variable course of instinctual activity that the 'dynamic' point of view appears, and in this resides the major considerations of motivation and conflict that appear in Freudian psychoanalysis. It is not that Freud was uninterested in social phenomena nor that he failed to recognise the role of the social world in influencing behaviour; as will be described in the next chapter, Freud had much to say on both subjects. It is rather that Freud was interested in the universals of human experience, in what underlies all psychology – which to his mind meant the underlying biological determinants of human nature. In Rieff's (1959) words, 'A science that recognises the instincts is a basic science, examining not this social system or that but the system of civilisation as a formed thing in itself' (p. 339).

However, this approach is founded on a number of assumptions which direct attention away from the actions of the external world and towards the internal determinants of activity – something which, along with the sheer inaccuracy of a view that neglects the manner in which people characteristically seek out stimulation, has led to the unpopularity of the constancy principle with post-Freudians. Chief among these assumptions are that the individual is the appropriate focus of study, a 'closed system' as Greenberg and Mitchell (1983) call it, which can be considered in terms of inputs and outputs without concern for the specifics of the world outside. This leads in turn to neglect of 'objects' or, rather, to a generalised image of them as anything that satisfies desire; there is no necessity to conceive of any inherent embeddedness of individual in culture, a characteristic assumption of most progressive political philosophies. Explanation of behaviour is provided by the vicissitudes of the instinct; the environment is only relevant to the extent that it supports or opposes satisfaction. This marks a distinction between classical Freudian theory and 'relational' or 'object relations' approaches which argue that it is impossible to separate the individual from her/his interpersonal context and which hence appear, on the surface at least, to be more immediately social in orientation. It is worth noting, however, that Freud's approach has often been energetically defended by political radicals; for example, some suggest that by detailing the basic biological drives which structure the possibilities for the human psyche, traditional psychoanalysis creates the conditions under which it is possible to trace the course that individual potential takes in its path to actuality. In this way, it draws attention to the effects on human potential of the particular patterns of domination that restrict or enhance development – a significant political concern. As will be argued in Chapter 2, there is also something important to be said about the picture of this 'biological potential' which Freud draws: it is heterogeneous, perverse, conflicting – something subversive of the rigidities of conformist normality to which most accounts of human nature reduce.

The editors of the *Standard Edition of the Complete Psychological Works of Sigmund Freud* point out that there is an inconsistency in Freud's use of the word *trieb*, translated as 'instinct'. In *Instincts and their Vicissitudes*, Freud defines an instinct as,

> a concept on the frontier between the mental and the somatic, as the psychical representative of the stimuli originating from within the organism and reaching the mind. (Freud, 1915a, p. 118)

Thus, 'instinct' is itself a psychological concept, something mental that operates as the representative of a somatic urge. Yet, in another paper in the great 'Metapsychological' series, Freud clearly indicates that instincts are themselves physiological entities:

> An instinct can never become an object of consciousness – only the idea that represents the instinct can. Even in the unconscious, moreover, an instinct cannot be represented otherwise than by an idea. (Freud, 1915a, p. 179)

There is no way around this inconsistency, which appears to be a genuine product of Freud's uncertainty over the interweaving of biology and psychology in the new approach he was constructing. On the whole, post-Freudians, and Freud himself in his later years, appear to have taken the second definition as more functional: instincts are biological entities which are represented in mental life by certain ideas. If this is understood, then a major contribution of Freud's is to have traced out what he called the 'vicissitudes' of the ideas attached to the instincts.

Freud states that instinctual ideas have three components, source, aim and object. His early work was concerned fundamentally with source, 'the somatic process which occurs in an organ or part of the body' (Freud, 1915a, p. 119) and which is epitomised in his description of infantile sexuality. The central point here is simply that sexuality is the fundamental driving force behind the unconscious; it is precisely sexual energy and the sexual instinct that is at the source of human behaviour and intrapersonal conflict. Later on, Freud's attention extended to the aims and objects of instincts, the former being generally the achievement of satisfaction and the latter that thing through which such satisfaction can come about (hence the term 'object relations theorists' for a major group of psychoanalysts). The vicissitudes of the instincts refer to the defences used to prevent dangerous impulses being carried through in an unmodified form – they include reversal into the opposite, turning round on the subject's own self, repression and sublimation, all 'reality principle' transformations of pleasure principle desires. But it is in Freud's account of the organisation of instincts, of their contents and oppositions, that a major aspect of his originality lies; this account developed and changed dramatically over the years, from a concern with 'love and hunger' to one with 'life and death'.

Towards the end of his life, and with some amusement, Freud looked back over the development of his theory of the instincts. 'Of all the slowly developed parts of analytic theory', he noted, 'the theory of the instincts is the one that has felt its way most painfully forward' (Freud, 1930, p. 308). Freud appears to have started with an implicit fundamental postulate, that there could not be anything but a duality of the instincts in mental life, and then to have struggled to uncover the material to lend credence to this position. Its rationale arises from the dynamic viewpoint, the recognition of conflict as a pervasive characteristic of mental life, possessing all the appearance of being central to human functioning. If conflict was always present, then it is likely to be a basic state, which for Freud pointed unequivocally towards biology. Observation made him believe that there was no multiplicity of instincts – that it was merely a linguistic trick to introduce separate 'instincts' to account for the existence of every different constellation of behaviours. Logic made him believe that it was not possible for there to be merely one instinct, that conflict depends on two. Right up to the 1920 text *Beyond the Pleasure Principle*, these two instincts were what Freud called 'hunger and love', 'hunger' being the ego-preservative instincts which watch out for the safety of the individual, 'love', of course, being the terrain of psychoanalysis' outrageousness, the impulses striving after satisfaction, reaching out towards 'objects'. Although these are biologically programmed in the need for preservation of the species, psychoanalysis emphasises the amoral element in love, the activities of sexuality in the service of pleasure rather than of reproduction.

> The concept of 'sexuality', and at the same time of the sexual instinct, had, it is true, to be extended so as to cover many things which could not be classed under the reproductive function; and this caused no little hubbub in an austere, respectable or merely hypocritical world. (Freud, 1920, p. 324)

The distinction between ego-preservative and sexual instincts served psychoanalysis well and was the source of many of its early discoveries, especially in making sense of neurosis (which was regarded as the pyrrhic victory of ego over sex). But it could not survive the problems generated by observation of other psychopathological and normal states, which culminated in the investigation of narcissism and the postulation of a state of 'primary narcissism'. This makes a developmental norm of the possibility that the ego can become the object of sexual desire, invested with libidinal energy from which its wider powers develop. In the course of many important notions connected with narcissism, the crucial point was that Freud was forced to recognise that the ego (which from 1914 to 1923 he regarded as the 'original reservoir' of libido) contains sexual instincts, which might themselves be providing the source of energy for what had hitherto been seen as the separate ego-preservative instincts. Put differently, the ego could no longer be viewed as an agency separate from sex, for it was itself infused with it. Freud's whole dualistic structure, which he had defended against Jung's heretical widening of the notion of libido from a specifically sexual force to the all-imbuing motor of life, was at risk: psychoanalysis might truly reduce to that which its critics pilloried it as, pan-sexualism.

Freud's solution to the problems generated by narcissism was characteristic in two ways. It arose from detailed observations in an unexpected area, and it was eschatological in its implications. The observations were of what he called the 'compulsion to repeat': a postulate of psychoanalysis had been that of the dominance of the pleasure principle; yet, in observations of neurotic behaviour and dreams and (provocatively for the linguistic fascinations of Lacanians) the childhood play of Freud's own grandson, the reappearance of disturbing material could be observed again and again. And this was not just pain caused to the ego while being pleasurable in terms of instinctual satisfaction; it represented a 'remarkable fact', namely, that the compulsion to repeat often brings up material which can never have been pleasurable, and which 'can never, even long ago, have brought satisfaction even to instinctual impulses which have since been repressed' (Freud, 1920, p. 291). Traumatic dreams, of the kind characteristic in war neuroses, are an example of this phenomenon, and apparently contradict the well-known formulation that dreams are wish-fulfilments, making it necessary to consider whether there may be another force at work other than the achievement of happiness.

> Thus it would seem that the function of dreams, which consists in setting aside any motives that might interrupt sleep, by fulfilling the wishes of the disturbing impulses, is not their *original* function. (Freud, 1920, p. 291)

Instead, something must come before the dominance of the desire for pleasurable satisfaction, something that is more basic than, that is 'beyond', the pleasure principle.

Brooding on the implications of the compulsion to repeat and of adherence to the Principle of Constancy, that the aim of organisms is to reduce themselves to rest, Freud arrived at what in retrospect appears to be his most startling and (certainly within psychoanalytic circles) contentious idea. First, he examined how the repetition compulsion might link with what was already known about instincts:

> It seems, then, that an instinct is an urge inherent in organic life to restore an earlier state of things which the living entity has been obliged to abandon under the pressure of external disturbing forces; that is, it is a kind of organic elasticity, or, to put it another way, the expression of the inertia inherent in organic life. (Freud, 1920, pp. 308–9)

Clearly, all the observations of the sexual life of humans had revealed that there exists an instinct which aims at preserving living substances and joining them together into larger units – reuniting the sundered halves of the originally bisexual being, as Freud supposed in his more whimsical moments. Now it was also clear that there must be 'another, contrary instinct' (Freud, 1930, p. 310) seeking to dissolve these units into their original state. And what could this be, but a state of perfect rest and nothingness, a relief from all tension and unwanted stimulation?. 'The aim of all life is death' (Freud, 1920, p. 311).

The concept of the Death Instinct proposes that inherent in all organisms is an impulse to degenerate, to find an original quiescence and merger with passive forms. Life is an aberration, the whole of life's task is preparation for death – but death arising naturally from within the organism, not imposed from without. Laplanche and Pontalis (1973) suggest that what Freud was expressing here was something more than a specific drive: 'What is designated here is more than any particular *type* of instinct – it is rather that factor which determines the actual *principle* of all instincts' (p. 102), this principle being that of return. Suddenly, a whole series of problems came into perspective for Freud, ranging from the subtleties of sexual desire, notably sadism and masochism, to the general problems of war and human suffering. We are born with death in our hearts; its manifestation, directed outwards as a defence, is in aggression; it is opposed by Eros, the instinct of life. Sexuality and the ego-preservative instincts are not opposed, but are both agents of Eros; aggression is the agent of Death. These two instincts can fuse, as in sadism; indeed, they are always found in a fused state in the actuality of behaviour; nevertheless, they are separable and in the end represent the entire struggle of life.

> I know that in sadism and masochism we have always seen before us manifestations of the destructive instinct . . . strongly alloyed with eroticism; but I can no longer understand how we can have overlooked the ubiquity of non-erotic aggressivity and destructiveness and can have failed to give it its due place in our interpretation of life. (Freud, 1930, p. 311)

As will be discussed in the next chapter, this realisation supplied fuel for Freud's most comprehensive account of the problems of individuals in society.

The notion of the Death Instinct has been extraordinarily contentious in the later history of psychoanalysis. For Klein, it became a fundamental idea; for object relations theorists it is anathema, the most virulent expression of Freud's biological reductionism, the opposite of what is needed for the construction of a human science. More generally, the whole place of 'instincts' is in question: the critical argument is that Freud's reliance on nineteenth-century biological concepts resulted in the construction of an impersonal instinct theory which undervalues ego-functioning and leads to neglect of object relationships. For example, Freud's theory appears to explain links between people as the offshoots of instincts: what motivates individuals is the need to express the instinctual drives of sex and aggression, and it is in order to achieve this end that relationships with others are formed. The infant experiences certain satisfactions and frustrations of the sexual drive, eventually associating these with particular constellations of external conditions, leading to the formation of images of objects and relationships with them (see Greenberg and Mitchell, 1983, p. 41). Some of Freud's critics suggest that the direction of effect should be the other way around: an inherent tendency to form relationships with other people results in sexual desire (an expression of intimacy) or aggression (the result of frustration). At issue is not simply the viability of reductionist explanati human behaviour, but a whole series of central debates ir choanalytic discourse. The opposition between instinctual d and social relationships as explanations of human conduct gives rise to considerations of the malleability of 'human nature', the role of experience and the possibilities for alternative configurations of the human psyche – considerations, that is, of change and determinism, optimism and pessimism, politics and therapy.

The structure of the mind

From early on in his psychoanalytic speculations, Freud distinguished between the state in which an idea might be maintained (conscious, preconscious or unconscious) and the way in which these states might be organised – what he called the 'systems' Cs., Pcs. and Ucs.. The clearest discussion of the attributes of these systems can be found in the paper on *The Unconscious* (1915a) in the 'Metapsychological' series. Here it is made clear that the system Pcs. stands in a crucial relationship to the other two systems, enabling communication to occur between them and being the locus of censorship between them, as well as possessing important internal functions of its own, for example as the province of conscious memory, language, reality testing and the reality principle. Importantly, Freud argues that there may be censorship between the Cs. and Pcs. as well as between the Pcs. and Ucs.: derivatives of the Ucs. may circumvent the earlier stage of repression to reach a certain energic 'intensity' in the Pcs.; 'when, however, this intensity is exceeded and they try to force themselves into consciousness, they are recognised as derivatives of the Ucs. and are repressed afresh at the new frontier of censorship, between the Pcs. and the Cs.' (p. 198). Repression is not, therefore, a one-place phenomenon any more than it is a once-and-for-all event; rather, it is a continuous process, a constant struggle at all levels of the mind. But *The Unconscious* also contains another vital recognition, which at first sight seems to be at odds with the whole thrust of psychoanalytic investigation. This concerns Freud's statement on the relative *insignificance* of the state of being conscious or unconcious for the project of mapping the geography of the mind.

> Consciousness stands in no simple relation either to the different systems or to repression. The truth is that it is not only the psychically repressed that remains alien to consciousness, but also some of the impulses which dominate our ego. (Freud, 1915a, p. 197).

Instincts and their derivatives come from one area of the mind, and form the central core of Freud's earliest notions of unconscious phenomena; if they were all that the unconscious consists of, there would be complete identity between 'topographical' and 'structural' viewpoints on psychology. But Freud was increasingly aware of the importance of the mechanisms of defence, forces which oppose the expression of the fundamental libidinous instincts and hence must be part of the ego-preservative mechanism. i.e. aspects of the ego. The significant point about these defence mechanisms is that although they belong to the ego (or, in Freud's other terminology, the system Pcs.), they are as a rule *unconscious*. So, for mapping the mind, for a complete structural description of the human personality, consciousness cannot be the central concept, and it needs to be possible to discriminate between different aspects of the unconscious. There has to be a framework which is independent of the unconscious/preconscious/conscious distinction, which can explain how the unconscious can be set against itself. The particular framework which Freud devised was to have far-reaching implications for our everyday language and imagery of ourselves and, more narrowly, for the consideration of the social construction of the individual psyche.

Freud had long used the term 'the ego' (*das Ich*) in a fairly traditional manner, to signify the conscious self, occasionally interspersing it with a more precise notion of a specific agency (basically the system Cs./Pcs.). His notion was that the ego was an active agency, present from the beginning of life in some form; as late as 1920 he was arguing that 'the ego is the true and original reservoir of libido, and . . . it is only from that reservoir that libido is extended onto objects' (Freud, 1920, pp. 324–5). But in his 1923 text *The Ego and the Id*, in which the tripartite theory of the mind is adumbrated, Freud thought again, along lines which arose as much from a recognition of the truth of the poetic insight that we are often 'lived' by forces beyond us, as from science.

> Now I think we shall gain a great deal by following the suggestion of a writer who, from personal motives, vainly asserts that he has nothing to do with the rigours of pure science. I am speaking of Georg Groddeck, who is never tired of insisting that what we call our ego behaves essentially passively in life, and that, as he expresses it, we are 'lived' by unknown and uncontrollable forces. (Freud, 1923, p. 362)

Hence '*das Es*, the 'It' or Id, the thing inside but beyond us, the impersonal source of our unconscious desires. The id is mysterious, the home of the repressed and of fundamental instincts, but also the source of energy, the original self, fuelling the activities of the entire psychic system. But although all that is in the id is unconscious, not all that is unconscious is in the id: as noted above, consciousness and structure do not go together. Both the ego and the second new invention, the super-ego, can hold unconscious material inside them.

With the creation of the id, Freud's notion of the ego changed quite dramatically. Although its characteristics were familiar (the psychic location for external perceptions, control over motility and 'reason and common sense'), its history was rewritten. The ego is not primeval; rather, it is a precipitate of the id, formed in two main ways. First, the exigencies of the real world are the province of the ego, which is then charged with bringing it to bear on the pleasure-seeking id: 'For the ego, perception plays the part which in the id falls to instinct' (Freud, 1923, p. 364). But secondly, the ego is formed by processes of internalisation which are modelled on the somatic events with which the infant is familiar. An important point here is the notion of the ego as a *bodily* ego, representing itself to itself along the lines of the bodily sensations with which it is imbued, a 'mental projection of the surface of the body'. As Wollheim (1971) elucidates, this explains why the ego can develop through internalisation: 'In seeing itself on the model of the body, the ego sees its activities on the model of bodily activity' (p. 189)

As the growing child has to give up desired sexual objects – the first rude incursion of the exigencies of reality into her/his pleasure-seeking mind – so the ego takes them on, internalising them and in the process altering itself. The ego thus comes to be a home for lost desires and forsaken objects; its character is formed along the lines of the objects in the world which are introjected and absorbed, along with the id-originated psychic energy invested in them. This 'makes it possible to suppose that the character of the ego is a precipitate of abandoned object cathexes and that it contains the history of those object choices' (Freud, 1923, p. 368). The ego gradually becomes stronger through experience and through the libidinous investments made in it by the id, as the ego transforms the object-cathexes of the id into egoic structures.

From the description of the development of the ego, it is clear that internalisation is seen as a routine way in which structural differentiation occurs. This is also the principal way in which the third psychic structure is formed, the super-ego. In part, all that happens is that some of the internalised objects are set up as 'ego ideals'. But at some point in development, there occurs such an intense internalisation of the parents, couched in such ambivalent terms, that it has the power to set up an agency of major significance within the mind. This point in development is, of course, the resolution of the Oedipus complex, where the child is forced to swallow her/his desires in the face of the power of the real world, and copes with this by forming identifications with both father and mother, the relative significance of each depending on the relative strength of the child's masculine and feminine sexual dispositions (children being fundamentally bisexual, in Freud's view).

> The broad general outcome of the Oedipus complex may, therefore, be taken to be the forming of a precipitate in the ego, consisting of these two identifications in some way united with each other. This modification of the ego retains its special position; it confronts the other contents of the ego as an ego ideal or super ego. (Freud, 1923, p. 373)

The super-ego, the contents of which are unconscious, operates as a carrot and a stick, an ideal and a punishment, compelling obedience to an internal authority in the same way that the child once was forced to obey an external one. The ego strives to appease it and to be loved by it, but it cannot escape the sense of guilt which arises from the demands and criticisms of the super-ego, which (in contrast to the id's immorality) is 'super-moral' and cruel.

> We see this same ego as a poor creature owing service to three masters and consequently menaced by three dangers: from the external world, from the libido of the id, and from the severity of the super-ego. (Freud, 1923, p. 397)

The immense consequences of this view of the super-ego for Freud's social theory will be dealt with in the next chapter, as will the wider significance of the concept of the Oedipus complex. But it is worth noting here the grounds for contention. For instance, many critics of Freud have taken issue with what they regard as his mechanistic approach to human functioning: in the same way that the instinct theory is criticised for being too biologistic, so the structural theory is opposed as too impersonal, the stuff of physics rather than psychology (cf. Guntrip, 1973). The id, in particular, is a focus of antagonism: how can a personal psychology be constructed out of material which places at the centre of human functioning an 'it', something outside and beyond us, *in principle* beyond control? It is certainly true that the instinct model focuses firmly on the internal motivations for action, although, as was suggested earlier, even here there is a place for the external world as nurturer or frustrator of human possibilities. But the structural model represents a different strand in Freudian thought, one which recognises more forcefully the role of external reality and pays particular attention to the manner in which external 'objects' can enter into the mind of the child and have a formative role in psychological organisation. The structural model emphasises identifications with real figures in the external world, particularly the figures of the Oedipal drama; these identifications are formative of the ego and super-ego, and hence have a major impact on unconscious as well as conscious functioning. Despite its continuing use of instinct language and of the economics of psychic energy as explanatory concepts, and alongside its metapsychology of life and death instincts, Freud's late theory of the mind makes object relations and hence social events central aspects of development. From here, it is a short step to an elaborated account of how the politics of the external world enters into the mind of the individual. This, however, is properly the subject of the next chapter.

2 Social Repression

> It is impossible to overlook the extent to which civilization is built upon a renunciation of instinct, how much it presupposes precisely the non-satisfaction . . . of powerful instincts. (Freud, 1930, p. 286)

In the Freudian system, humans are instinctual beings, the achievement of pleasure through the expression of those instincts being the aim of life. 'What decides the purpose of life,' argues Freud, 'is simply the programme of the pleasure principle' (1930, p. 263). Unfortunately, the programme of the pleasure principle also happens to be 'at loggerheads with the whole world, with the macrocosm as much as with the microcosm' (Ibid). This is for two main reasons. First, there is the problem of the nature of pleasure itself. Pleasure is a transient phenomenon, which can only come about as a contrast between tension and its reduction, tending towards but never fully achieving a state of ease, of inactivity. Prior to death, pleasure obtains in the process of tension-reduction; absolute nirvana cannot be attained because of all the internal and external sources of stimulation which impinge on the psyche. The sensations of unhappiness, on the other hand, are much less difficult to experience. All stimulation creates tension, an unpleasurable state that motivates activity of the body or mind in the search for resolution. In addition, humans are faced with real pain from three unremitting sources: the feebleness of their own bodies, the superior power of nature, and – most significantly – the activities of other people. This is the second major opposition to the programme of the pleasure principle. Pleasure resides in the attainment of the aims of the instincts; these instincts are of life and death, manifested in sexuality and aggression. But the unlimited expression of desire in aggressiveness and sexuality must lead to interpersonal destructiveness and social devastation. Thus, in one of those paradoxes so characteristic of Freudian thought, the pleasure principle threatens individuals with suffering. The possibilities for pleasure are limited, giving rise to differences between individuals ('every man must find out for himself in what particular fashion he can be saved' – Freud, 1930, p. 271) and to the dominance of the reality principle, mostly reducing to a recognition that the avoidance of pain is a more fruitful target for life than the achievement of pleasure. 'In general,' writes Freud, 'the task of avoiding suffering pushes that of obtaining pleasure into the background' (1930, p. 264): the reality of the world is that we must seek carefully for protection rather than arrogantly for love.

There are a number of possible ways of avoiding the worst aspects of the destructiveness of the instincts and the painfulness of reality. For instance, instincts that are suppressed by psychic defences instead of being openly experienced are less clamorous when unsatisfied; against this, the controls exerted on them reduce the possibilities for enjoyment available to the psyche. Alternatively, one can take refuge in fantasy, the arena of wish fulfilment which remains exempt from the demands of reality and which enables us to take our revenge on the world. For Freud, fantasy is an alternative to the satisfaction of desires in the real world; it is a way of coping with the impossibility of living according to the pleasure principle. At times, in normal people as well as psychotics, fantasy is so much preferable to the agonies of ordinary living that external reality is denied and its image forced into the shape of our desires:

> each one of us behaves in some respect like a paranoic, corrects some aspect of the world which is unbearable to him by the construction of a wish and introduces this delusion into reality. (Freud, 1930, p. 269)

In Freud's view, while this defensive strategy is understandable, it also represents the antithesis of the psychoanalytic project, which is the production of knowledge, a braver if also humbler and more difficult facing up to the real pressures of living. Wish fulfilment is escape, 'consolation', an inability to see things as they are and hence a regression to infantile methods of surviving. But although psychoanalysis focuses closely on the internal mechanisms by means of which individuals distort or deny reality, in Freud's view the main defence against the power and pain of the world and our desires is social: the formation of 'civilisation'. For protection and out of fear, through the reality principle and not through desire, individuals form together in groups; society is constructed to curb individual instinct. Here is another paradox: civilisation, often considered the highest expression of human existence, is built on the denial of everything that we really want.

Freud has a very broad view of 'civilisation', as

> the whole sum of the achievements and the regulations which distinguish our lives from those of our animal ancestors and which serve two purposes – namely to protect men against nature and to adjust their mutual relations. (Freud, 1930, p. 278)

On one thing he was very clear and specific, however: that civilisation is no gift to the individual. Rather, it produces misery and is opposed to individual desire; its aim is to unite individuals against the threats posed by nature and by their own inclinations. Hence, while the level of civilisation can be measured by the degree of mastery over nature, its central dynamic lies in regulation of the relationships between people through modification of intrapersonal psychological structures. Before society there is only the unremitting and potentially calamatous libertarianism of the instincts; as soon as these instincts become bridled, society is formed. The essence of society and the essence of individuality stand opposed to one another: society is a process of control and limitation, of coercion of the individual in the interests of the group. Hence Brown's (1959) suggestion that 'man is the animal that represses himself and which creates culture or society in order to repress himself' (p. 9); history, in the sense of the development of human collectivity, *is* neurosis.

The theory that society is ineluctably opposed to individuality is one of the most pessimistic strands of thought associated with the bourgeois era. For Freud, the passions of the individual were primordial and dangerous, the work of civilisation being to control them – a justifiable work in the interests of the perpetuation of human existence. The conservatism of this view is obvious: social organisation is not only essential but is also inherently oppressive; presumably, the only differences between societies lie in the exact way in which these oppressions are distributed. Little scope here, apparently, for the ebullient utopianism of some post-Freudians, from those who believe society can be perfectly regulated to provide satisfaction for its individual members, to those who peer into the mists of revolution to create the perfect playground for desires. Such images, for Freud, were 'consolations', similar in scope to the illusions and wish-fulfilments that underlie religion. Human life is to be lived in the face of misery, with society as a necessary evil. However, as with much else in Freudian thought, the complexities of his detailed argument actually encompass what on the face of it are opposing arguments: the grand sweep of the theory postulates a conservative preservation of the world against the individual; the intimate detail of the account given of the developmental vicissitudes of the instinct reveal how society enters into the heart of individuality and constructs it around a social kernel – a proposition of the most radical kind. Both these trends can be observed in the confused network of ideas which lead from the Freudian account of phylogenesis (the development of the species) to that of ontogenesis. Ironically, Freud was substantially more radical in his dissection of the individual psyche than in his grander, more overtly social works.

Phylogeny and ontogeny: renunciation of the instincts

One of the most revolutionary aspects of Freud's characteristic investigative style was his search for origins, his location of explanation in the science of *how things come to be*. As shall be seen, in his account of ontogenesis, this philosophy paid enormous dividends and rescues his work from the opprobrium of essentialism into which most other theories of the human mind fall (cf. Banton *et al.*, 1985). His description of phylogenesis, however, was not so happy, reading now like an embarrassing piece of amateur speculation when compared with the enormous expansion in empirical anthropological knowledge that has come about this century. *Totem and Taboo* (1914) is the main culprit, its deficiencies so glaring that even Freud was forced to apologise for it as a 'just-so story', although he retained an attachment to its hypotheses throughout his later social works (cf. Hirst and Woolley, 1982, for a sympathetic critique). In *Totem and Taboo*, Freud postulates that there was once a 'primal horde' dominated by a powerful father who possessed all the available women. In rage and frustration, his sons ('the brothers') banded together to kill and devour him. However, because of the ambivalent structure of the instincts the brothers felt not only hate for their father, but also love; this returned to haunt them in the post-murder world and encouraged them, out of guilt and remorse, to set him up as a 'totem' and to incorporate his terror within them. Thus, as with the development of the individual's super-ego, what had been an external authority was incorporated internally as a sense of guilt, more powerful and unassailable for all that. In addition, to prevent a repetition of the primal situation, the brothers, under the shadow of the totem, imposed certain structuring rules on themselves, to regulate their relations and restrain their passions. These rules marked the beginnings of culture (although some rudimentary linkage was present in the primal horde) as the point at which natural desire is regulated by social necessity; their centre is the taboo on incest.

It is not necessary to spell out the defects in Freud's prehistory of civilisation – even sympathisers such as Marcuse (1955) are forced to interpret this part of his theory metaphorically, finding its value in the way 'it telescopes, in a sequence of catastrophic events, the historical dialectic of domination and thereby elucidates aspects of civilisation hitherto unexplained' (p. 60). There are, nevertheless, some important points of interest. First, Freud locates the beginning of culture in the construction of incest taboos: Hirst and Woolley (1982) even suggest that, in *Totem and Taboo*, 'Freud is explaining the origins of the incest taboo, *not society*' (p. 152). The primal horde was itself a form of social organisation in which the desires of some members (the brothers) were unattainable; what differentiates it from civilisation proper is that the latter is characterised by the internalisation of taboo, that is, by the complicity of each individual in the repression of her/his own desire. 'Civilization begins when the paternal taboos are self-imposed, when repressions are implemented in the interests of the group' (Reiff, 1959, p. 197).

Secondly, Freud bases his version of the origin of the totem on feelings of guilt brought into play by the murder; that is, the potentiality for guilt does not need to be explained, it is there in the pre-existing ambivalent structure of human psychology. Aggression and love are inextricably intertwined; acting on, or fantasising, the former leads inevitably to regret over the latter and hence to guilt. As will be described in Part 2, this became the kernel of Klein's account of psychological development and has substantial implications for social theory. Thirdly. Freud believed that some residue of these original events was passed on throughout the generations, that it continued to influence the Oedipus complex (perhaps explaining its supposed universality) and that it infiltrated the unconscious of latter-day individuals. This does not mean that the exact content of the unconscious is inherited, as Jung might have it, nor that Marcuse (1955) is wholly correct in his more limited view that 'the crime is re-enacted in the conflict of the old and new generation, in revolt and rebellion against established authority – and in subsequent repentance' (p. 69). Rather, Freud's account stresses the way the universality of primary process functioning demands universal constraints and modes of organisation shared by members of all cultures, posing similar problems and encountering comparable obstacles.

Freud's hunt for a phylogeny reflects his enduring need for an account of the father that satisfactorily explains the turbulence of development. In his 'just-so story', the account has such a tenuous hold on possibility that its conservative elements might be happily overlooked, were it not for the fact that they influenced Freud in many of his other writings. For instance, they result in a legitimising of social repression that is familiar from many approaches which hypothesise a basic opposition between individual and society: 'human nature' is so destructive that it must be curbed by strong controls. In addition, Freud's attachment to the primal horde story reveals a peculiar and general characteristic of his understanding of the past. Freud's liking for Lamarck and his view that the events surrounding the killing of the primal father are passed down in some coherent fashion across generations is in line with his general disregard of the possibility of developmental change through evolution. The past lives on unchanged, in the species as in the individual; murder of the primal father and aggressive wish towards the real parent are parallel in this respect. In fact, the 'archeological' practice which Freudian psychoanalysis takes as its model actively accentuates the significance of the long-ago: the further in the past an event, the more it dominates the present, producing a conservative, repetitive tendency of eschatological proportions. Because of the nature of the instincts, certain scenarios will always be replayed, with a universal, repressive result. How odd, then, given this conservatism and pessimism, that when Freud traces the way the individual's instincts are actually organised, he comes up with what might be seen as a prototypically social account.

As will be discussed below, the problem of the control of aggression is seen by Freud as crucial for the maintenance of society. However, it is the problem of love which exercises his theoretical interest most fully, and which gives rise to some of his most radical and enduring insights. At first sight, this is a surprising issue for consideration in the context of a hypothesis of society – individual opposition: it might seem that erotic love could be exploited in a relatively straightforward way by society to provide a compelling basis for ties between its members. Indeed, in *Group Psychology and the Analysis of the Ego* (1921), Freud argues that groups such as armies or the Church are sustained by erotic ('libidinal') ties, which are played upon by leaders to give these groups their coherence. But love (which for Freud is either the same as, or an aim-inhibited derivation of, sexuality) is not built to be social: being an element of the instincts, it is greedy, self-serving and hostile to the interests of the group. For one thing, sexuality is an exclusive phenomenon, whereas society depends on the formation of multiple links:

> sexual love is a relationship between two individuals in which a third can only be superfluous or disturbing, whereas civilization depends on relationships between a considerable number of individuals. (Freud, 1930, p. 298)

To the criticism that love need not be exclusive but can be extended to others – the 'love thy neighbour' exhortation – Freud replies that this is the antithesis of love, brought about by a manipulation of the Death Instinct on the part of society as a means towards the forced internalisation of restrictions on violence. It has nothing to do with love:

> A love that does not discriminate seems to me to forfeit a part of its own value, by doing an injustice to its object; and secondly, not all men are worthy of love. (Freud, 1930, p. 291)

Love has its prototype in the earliest exclusive bond with the parent, it is not some air freshener to be sprayed around, a sanitised mist reviving optimism and fellow-feeling. It cannot, therefore, be used unaltered in the interests of civilisation, because it is always threatening to break up that civilisation into smaller units. Parenthetically, this is one of the subversive aspects of women's role in the Freudian world-view: women represent the sexual impulse; more prosaically, they are always trying to reclaim their menfolk from the clutches of the work of building culture (which forces men to 'carry out instinctual sublimations of which women are little capable' – Freud, 1930, p. 293) into their isolated family units. Hence, civilisation opposes women by the same principle that it opposes love. But more of that later: the main point here is that love is doomed because society requires multiple, sanitised relationships, and because it needs the energy that might be put into sex to be diverted instead to the task of building culture. The story of how this doom is lived out, how society organises human sexuality, is the heart of psychoanalytic theory and its most radical assertion.

'Freud's definition of sexuality,' writes Brown (1959), 'entails the proposition that infants have a richer sexual life than adults' (p. 26). This is because of their 'polymorphous perversity'; that is, the nature of the sexuality of children is that it is formless, it spreads in all directions and can embrace all objects and bodily parts, it is purely and simply about *pleasure* with no thought for propriety or procreation. If there is an 'essence' to the individual, it is that before being human s/he is an unorganised mass of libidinal instinct. The child is thus a sexualised being from birth, but this sexuality possesses the peculiarly unsettling characteristic of being uninhibited, of not being channelled in any particular direction. Were it not for the fact that there is no substitute for sex as a means of propagating the human race, society would seek to wipe out all traces of the child's desire; even so, the sexual life of humans 'sometimes gives the impression of being in the process of involution as a function' (Freud, 1930, p. 295). But given the realities of biology (at least in Freud's day), society contents itself with restricting the possibilities present in the child to what can be tolerated:

> The child, far from being an asexual innocent, begins life as a demanding, narcissistic and auto-erotic animal who is gradually forced to accept the existence of others, and certain socially sanctioned organisations of its sexual needs. (Hirst and Woolley, 1982, p. 141)

In culture as diagnosed by Freud, this 'socially sanctioned organisation' is that of genitality, epitomised in the organisation of sexuality around family life and the creation of aim-inhibited eroticism (friendship); that is, heterosexual genitality is not a *natural* organisation of the sexual instinct, but a channeling of, or restriction on, potential to be found in the child. The infant may be polymorphously 'perverse', but the adult is respectably crippled.

Freud thought that the repression of infantile sexuality was justifiable from the point of view of society: how else would it be able to cope with the destructiveness inherent in the unbridled expression of adult lusts? But this accedance to reality, grudgingly and perhaps ironically given, does not reduce the seditiousness of his account of how that repression takes place. Our 'normality' is *not* biologically determined; it is constructed as civilisation makes the animal child into the social adult; this means that alternatives are envisionable. Freud himself, who believed in the inevitability of sexual repression, acknowledged that its severity may vary with the economic structure of society (cf. Freud, 1930, p. 293), and the radicals that followed him have always taken heart from the notion that sexuality is not fixed and that those parts of it that are not expressed in heterosexual genitality may still reside, repressed but timelessly alive, in the unconscious (see Chapter 6). But even more important than this raising of possible alternatives to dominant organisations of sexuality is the recognition that what Freud describes is the way society enters into the essence of the human individual, organising the instincts where usually we consider that we are most privately ourselves. This does not happen smoothly, however: repression is a painful phenomenon, fraught with crises; pleasure is not easily overcome by reality. Indeed, the trauma of sexual restriction is one which lives on inside through the whole of life, generating what we know as 'normality' and what we experience as neurosis.

If human desires are automatically opposed to human society, the maintenance of the latter must depend on the possession of a powerful mechanism for channelling and controlling desire so that the instinctual aggression and sexuality of the individual can be harnessed to the work of culture. In the Freudian scheme, the mechanism which brings society into the individual's mind is not simply an external one such as the 'conditioning' of children to behave in certain acceptable ways; this would assume the existence of an already established individual consciousness which could then be shaped by the operations of social interaction. Instead, psychoanalysis emphasises the unconscious and *formative* function of social construction: the individual's psychological organisation comes about through encounters with sociality which have a governing effect on experience and on the positioning of the individual with respect to her/himself and to relations with others. For example, the 'precipitation' of the ego through perceptual experiences and through the introjection of lost objects occurs in the context of a specific set of social relations, themselves only available because of the particular ideological structures that dominate within a society. Psychoanalysis, focusing firmly on the immediate developmental context of the child in western culture, has always envisaged these significant social relations in family terms, according to the structure of the Oedipus complex.

There has been a great deal of criticism of the Freudian concept of the Oedipus complex, either in terms of its universality (or lack of it), or because it is seen to neglect the significant involvement of other factors (e.g. class conflicts) in social determination. But as an account of the perpetuation of patriarchal ideology it remains worthy of serious attention; as will be described in Chapter 7, it has been used by feminist theorists to extend importantly the psychoanalytic view of the construction of gender identity. For Freud, the Oedipus complex is a necessary concept, providing an explanation of the pattern of human development that is unavailable otherwise. It becomes, in psychoanalytic thought, a touchstone of orthodoxy: anthropologists seek to find it everywhere, or to deny psychoanalysis by the discovery of societies in which Oedipal conflicts are unknown; revisers of Freud's theories claim allegiance to the notion of Oedipus if they wish to remain in the fold, even if their use of it – like Klein's – is substantially modified. There are several reasons why the concept has been given such importance, but the main one is that it suggests a mechanism whereby Freud is able to address a central question about development, neglected in other psychological approaches. If the distinction between infant and adult lies in the ordering of desire along specifiable and predictable lines, how does this come about? How is it that the deepest recesses of the mind can be reached by social events, can be affected by the limits imposed upon desire by the dominance of 'civilisation'? In other words, the theory of the

Oedipus complex provides a description of some possible mechanisms by which social structures are incorporated into individual consciousness and have a formative role on the ordering of the psyche.

The starting point for the Oedipus complex is the taboo on incest, viewed by Freud as the defining element in the promulgation of culture, the point at which the unbridled lusts of individual desire become constrained by non-biological forces. For the incest taboo is *not* natural, despite its apparent universality in one form or another; it is, in fact, incestuous desire that is natural, because it reflects the free play of the pleasure principle, operating without consideration of the conventions that determine what is or is not an acceptable sexual object. In fact, it is the universality of incestuous desire that creates the need for universal taboos. So what the incest taboo represents is the materialisation of the contradiction between the total instinctuality of the infant and the demands of society; in other words, the structuring of desire into a socialised form. The taboo, along with its associated power relations, is experienced by the child at the point where s/he becomes aware of the existence of potential love objects outside the self, who can offer more than the narcissistic pleasures characteristic of oral and anal stages of development; given the structure of children's lives such a love is almost bound to be incestuous and hence forbidden. Thus, 'so long as the community assumes no other form than the family, the conflict is bound to express itself in the Oedipus complex' (Freud, 1930, p. 325). Under this complex the male child's desire for the mother (see below for a consideration of feminine development) is contradicted by paternal authority backed up by the punitive force of the castration threat. The child's obedience to this threat – that is, his terror within the 'castration complex' – results in him renouncing (repressing) his passion and identifying with the father.

This is the model for all the individual's encounters with society: desire opposed by authority, authority internalised and made one's own. Thus, the father in the Oedipal structure is not just (or even) the child's real father, who may be threatening or appeasing, appalling or absent; he is the symbol of patriarchal authority and hence of all social authority under patriarchy, he stands in the position of the originator of culture and of sexual difference, of what is male and female, allowable and forbidden. Referring to the way the castration complex terminates the Oedipus situation by enforcing the repression of the child's desire, Mitchell (1982) states that it 'governs the position of each person in the triangle father, mother and child; in the way it does this, it embodies the law that founds the human order itself' (p. 14). For Laplanche and Pontalis (1973), the Oedipus complex describes the triangular configuration 'constituted by the child, the child's natural object, and the bearer of the law' (p. 286). The real father slips away in this; what emerges instead is a description of the impossibility of interpersonal relationships (child with object) that are not already structured by something outside them, the 'law' by which society operates.

The Oedipal matrix is thus a symbolic matrix, not something that can necessarily be observed in the surface interactions between parent and child. It is the realisation by the child of the sexual and power structures of reality, of how the world is organised. What makes human society human, what makes the child human rather than animal, is just this realisation. As Hirst and Woolley (1982) put it, human society is founded on the symbolic structurings of kinship and property, rather than on the biological ones of procreation; through her/his encounter with these symbolic structurings and the defensive identifications which result from it, the child incorporates not only social controls, but a whole network of possible and taboo social relationships, resulting eventually in the dominance of genitality and the construction of men and women 'who can in turn stand in the places of this symbolic system' (p. 148). Sexuality, from being polymorphous and perverse, is channelled into genitality and an ego-ideal modelled on family functioning, procreation and aim-inhibited libidinal excursions into friendship. Society drives the most personal parts of us – our desires – into deeply protected guerrilla positions, whence they continue their sniping into everyday life. 'The infantile conflict between actual impotence and dreams of omnipotence', writes Brown (1959), 'is also the basic theme of the universal history of mankind' (p. 25).

The instincts are not, of course, confined to sexuality. In terms of the preservation of human society, control of the Death Instinct, in its manifestation as aggression, is at least as important. Humans are not simply lovers: as we have seen, that would be bad enough. They are also haters, of themselves and of one another:

aggression is seen by Freud, in his later work, as an 'original, self-subsisting instinctual disposition' in people, as such constituting 'the greatest impediment to civilisation' (1930, p. 313). Society is perpetually threatened with disintegration under the force of this urge, with its unlimited and eventually triumphant energy, waiting to smash everything to pieces in an orgy of destructiveness. Hence the full ingenuity of social controls has to be employed to so channel the aggressive instinct that it supports rather than threatens the preservation of the social world. Certain fairly obvious moralistic techniques are employed in this, such as the commandment to love one's neighbour as oneself, but more importantly a series of subtle manoeuvres are instituted which have the effect of making the individual turn her/his aggression inwards, where it acts as a control over behaviour rather than as an incitement to violence.

> Civilization . . . obtains mastery over the individual's dangerous desire for aggression by disarming it and by setting up an agency within him to watch over it, like a garrison in a conquered city. (Freud, 1930, p. 316)

In Freud's later work, this manoeuvre was canonised as the formation of the super-ego.

In the previous chapter, the generation of the super-ego was outlined: how it appears at the culmination of the Oedipus complex, when the prohibitions and symbolic violence of the father is internalised by the child as part of the new series of identifications that are brought into play by the castration complex. (Once again, this is an androcentric account, with femininity dealt with below.) Two aggressive elements combine here. First, there is the aggression with which the child feels her/himself threatened: the violence of the castrating father, itself at least in part a projection of the child's Death Instinct. Second, there is the aggression that the child feels against the father, an aggression generated by the paternal prohibition and repressed because of the child's fear of retaliation and also because of ambivalence: the child cannot bear to destroy with hatred the father who is also loved (as the brothers of the primal horde discovered to their cost). This internalised aggression is experienced as guilt, the most obvious price of the march of civilisation; guilt which does not depend on actions, but which arises directly from the clashes in the instinctual furnace.

> Whether one has killed one's father or has abstained from doing so is not really the decisive thing. One is bound to feel guilty in either case, for the sense of guilt is an expression of the conflict due to ambivalence, of the eternal struggle between Eros and the instinct of destruction or death. (Freud, 1930, p. 325)

Guilt arises as the external threat of punishment and is internalised and given structural permanence in the super-ego, where it is free to judge wishes with the same sadistic vigilance with which it would previously have judged actions. Nothing can be hidden: the real aggression of the world and the projected aggression of the Death Instinct are now part of the psyche set against itself, hedging in the thoughts and behaviours of the individual with proscription and punishment. Thus guilt has two origins, first a fear of authority, second a fear of authority internalised, the super-ego. Of these two, it is the latter that is more destructive to the happiness of the individual:

> The first insists upon a renunciation of instinctual satisfactions; the second, as well as doing this, presses for punishment, since the continuance of the forbidden wishes cannot be concealed from the super-ego. (Freud, 1930, p. 319)

Ironically, the super-ego is an escalating phenomenon: created by instinctual renunciation (of Oedipal desire), it demands more and more renunciation as its aggression is turned virulently against unconscious wishes; the stronger the repressions, the stronger the sense of guilt. Society needs this to happen, according to Freud: obeying an erotic compulsion to form people together to protect them against nature and each other, it demands a renunciation of exteriorised aggression and its replacement with this internal agency of control. The second part in the cultural taming of instinct is thus complete: just as sexuality is channelled into genitality, so aggression is mastered by incorporation into the punitive super-ego. Once again, civilisation advances at the expense of individual happiness. Once again, Freud develops a theory which asserts the essential negativity of instinct, the way in which what we bring with us threatens to destroy the things we need in order to survive, a philosophy too pessimistic for many of his more hopeful followers. And once again, almost despite himself, Freud's account focuses on the manner in which impulses or feelings that seem so much part of our 'selves' that one assumes they are basic, in-born consequences of being human, are actually products of our immersion in the social world.

Femininity, misogyny, patriarchy

Freud's ideas on female development have come under fire from feminists throughout the history of psychoanalysis, for understandable reasons: they value women negatively, they exclude women from the work of culture, and they appear to assert that all this is biologically determined in the little girl's lack of a penis. Philip Rieff, always a sympathetic critic of psychoanalysis, makes no bones about Freud's misogyny:

> Not only does Freud aver that girls *feel* biologically at a disadvantage, inferior, because they do not possess a penis; he affirms that they *are* in the grossest sense something less than boys. (1959, p. 174)

Freud regards women as arrested in development, unable to reach male potentials:

> He contrasts the job of psychoanalysis with male patients – to *develop* their capacities, sexual and otherwise – with the more limited aim, in the case of women patients, of *resigning* them to their sexuality (Ibid, p. 175)

The 'marks of womanhood' listed by Mitchell (1974) in her pro-Freudian text *Psychoanalysis and Feminism* are 'masochism', 'passivity', 'vanity', 'jealousy' and 'a limited sense of justice'. And the sources of this in Freud are clear: despite acknowledging the howls of anger that are liable to come from feminists and female analysts, he unceremoniously asserts the fundamentally unwholesome nature of womanhood. For example, towards the end of one of his most substantial analyses of femininity – the 1933 *New Introductory Lecture* on the subject – Freud makes the following sweeping and unhappy statement:

> The fact that women must be regarded as having little sense of justice is no doubt related to the predominance of envy in their mental life . . . We also regard women as weaker in their social interests and as having less capacity for sublimating their instincts than men. (Freud, 1933 pp. 168–9)

Earlier, in the 1925 paper, 'Some Psychical Consequences of the Anatomical Distinction between the Sexes', Freud suggests that it is because of the relative weakness of the female super-ego that women never possess as developed an ethical awareness as do men. Finally, Freud's anti-feminism is made explicit in the context of his speculative anthropology. In his last completed work, *Moses* and Monotheism (1939), Freud struggles to articulate the experience and origins of the Jewish people, producing a fragmented and unusually convoluted text which stands as a monument to the self-questioning and personal dislocation brought about in him by the rise of Nazism and his own consequent exile. In the course of this moving and deeply felt work, Freud develops the argument that the transition from matriarchy to patriarchy which supposedly occurred at some period in human history was an important advance of intellect over the senses.

> But this turning from the mother to the father points in addition to a victory of intellectuality over sensuality – that is, an advance in civilisation, since maternity is proved by the evidence of the senses while paternity is a hypothesis, based on an inference and a premise. Taking sides in this way with a thought process in preference to a sense perception has proved to be a momentous step. (p. 361)

This is also why, according to Freud, it is correct for children to bear their father's name rather than their mother's: paternity, being unprovable, is related to the intellect rather than to the senses, and hence is superior. Ironically, it is precisely this point that is taken up by some feminist psychoanalysts to suggest the absurdity of the male claim to power, because it rests on the word of the woman.

In the face of evidence that Freud has not in some simple manner been misread, and that his anti-feminist views were both widespread and influential in his theorising, is psychoanalysis defensible as a progressive system combating sexist assumptions, or should it be viewed as just another straightforward ideological product of patriarchy? In the followers of Freud, both tendencies are evident, as will be seen in Chapter 7; but Freud's own position is more subtle than the statements presented above might suggest.

There are a number of possible ways of rescuing Freud's account of women from the doldrums of ideological sexism. For example, it is relatively easy to uncover support in his writings for a biologically reductionist feminism that makes women 'naturally' superior to men. Just as some modern feminists argue that women have special nurturative capacities which men lack, or that women's 'mothering instincts' would lead to a beneficial reconstruction of the world were they to take over, so Freud identifies the female principle with something closer to nature, less sublimated, less diffused through repression, less displaced. For Freud, 'women are erotic hoarders in the male economy of culture' (Rieff, 1959, p. 183); they are the representatives of pleasure, of emotion and sensuality. In Freud's view, this is mostly a negative attribute, given the necessity for society to overcome pleasure in the interests of survival, but the possibility is clearly there for a feminist revaluation of the material – in opposing culture, women also oppose neurosis. But the typically patriarchal image of women as mothers and seducers does not lose its conformist impact by a simple rereading of its political valency; it is conformist in its reductionism, its assertion of the biologically determined distribution of psychological attributes and their consequences for social life. It makes no fundamental difference whether emotion is evaluated as good or bad if it is assumed that the distribution of emotion between sexes is something biologically determined, for in the end one is left with no possible recourse to social change: social structures do not play an essential part in development, patriarchy is not to be understood in terms of any complex process of internalisation of the axes around which the social world is built, but as a simple choice of how an inborn difference is to be valued. If Freudian thought is to be used in a more radical manner, one has to look elsewhere for a starting point.

As usual with Freud, it is in his search for the genesis of 'normality' that his most profound challenge to ideology inheres. Where common sense takes as natural that which can be observed (e.g. that women and men have different social roles and possibly different psychological characteristics), Freud asks, 'how does this come about?' – how do people become what they are? In the area of sexual politics, his answer is an important one, however dubious some of its details. Women and men become what they are through a series of identifications and defences which build upon an initially bisexual base and which diverge at a relatively late stage in development, the phallic stage at which the Oedipus complex comes into play. (As will be seen in Chapter 7, feminist psychoanalysts tend to place the divergence much earlier, possibly at birth, but do not challenge the essential argument that sexual divergence is a consequence of developmental and social processes.) As the boy's Oedipus complex has been described above, the Oedipal development of the girl will be the focus here.

The girl's Oedipus complex is not a simple parallel to that of the boy – hence Freud's rejection of Jung's term 'Electra complex'. Rather, it is a more difficult version of the boy's development, which has two additional tasks to achieve and which in one crucial respect reverses the order of events. The two additional tasks are, first, that the girl must give up her phallic, male centration on her own 'penis', the clitoris, and, secondly, that she must transfer her desire from the mother to the father. The reversal is that whereas for the boy the castration complex brings the Oedipus situation to a close, for the girl it starts it off. All three of these factors are intertwined.

Despite his affinity for biological determinism, Freud knew that something difficult happened to women, that the question of female development was worth asking even if the final result was due to biology. In the context of his belief that women were bound to live out a particular trajectory for themselves, Freud's version of this question is a limited one, but it is worth asking nevertheless:

> how does a girl pass from her mother to an attachment to her father? or, in other words, how does she pass from her masculine phase to the feminine one to which she is biologically destined? (Freud, 1933, p. 152).

Until entry into the phallic phase, there is little divergence between male and female development, as children of both sexes are attached to the mother and both boys and girls experience similar oral and anal vicissitudes. Most significantly, both are bisexual: that is, they contain the potential for masculinity and feminity, in differing proportions due to biological variations (but differing within members of the same sex as well as between the sexes) but nevertheless present in both. But the accedance to the phallic stage creates new problems. The centre of erotogenesis for the boy shifts from the anus to the penis, his desire becoming that of penetration and possession of the mother, of getting her with child. For the girl, the leading erotogenic zone is the clitoris. But, according to Freud, it cannot remain so: 'With the change to femininity the clitoris should wholly or in part hand over its sensitivity, and at the same time its importance, to the vagina' (Freud, 1933, pp. 151–2). Parenthetically, this quotation demonstrates some characteristic elements in Freud's moralism: the development of femininity is a change from masculinity ('the little girl is a little man' up to this point – not the boy a woman) and Freud, partially identifying femininity and the vagina with passivity, takes as self-evident the necessity for its acquisition. What he believes he is describing is the state of affairs under nature; what feminists have taken up is the possibility that it is in fact the state of affairs under patriarchy. In any case, the chain of events according to Freud is the following. The little girl, dependent on her clitoris for sexual stimulation becomes aware of its inferiority as an organ, and feels a mixture of damaging emotions: a general sense of her own inferiority in the world, her distance from power, a hateful rage at the mother for having created her like that, in her own image, and a passionate envy of the real thing, the penis possessed by father and brother alike. The girl thus shifts from mother-love to father-love because she has to:

> No phallus, no power – except those winning ways of getting one . . . The girl's entry into her feminine 'destiny' is characterised by hostility to the mother for her failure to make her a boy; it is an entry marked by penis-envy, that in its turn must be repressed or transformed. (Mitchell, 1974, p. 96)

The castration complex – that is , her recognition of herself as already castrated – pushes the girl into the Oedipus situation, in which her desire is to displace the mother in order to get for herself a share in the father's power. Hence the virulent reproaches that

Freud supposes young girls to feel against their mothers; hence also that change in sexual object which marks the accession to femininity and which can, under adverse emotional and constitutional circumstances, result in female homosexuality or neurosis. Finally, the desire for the penis must itself be renounced and replaced by the desire for a baby, 'in accordance with an ancient symbolic equivalence'; in another moment of tremendous misogyny, Freud suggests that the mother's happiness 'is great if later on this wish for a baby finds fulfilment in reality and quite especially so if the baby is a little boy who brings the longed-for penis with him' (Freud, 1933, p. 162). No simple factor of society valuing boys more than girls for economic or ideological reasons is sufficient for Freud: the extra valuation of boys is understandable in terms of the way boy children supply what women really want, a desire which may be repressed but which is never lost, a penis the same as a man's. Taken in conjunction with his failure to attend to pre-Oedipal development, Freud's downvaluing of feminine and maternal attributes (the maternal urge is displaced from the desire for a penis) sets major limitations on the coherence of his account of female development.

There are some startling implications which derive from this disturbing tale of female psychosexual development. Freud's emphasis is on the effects that the female Oedipus complex has on later development, particularly concerning the super-ego. In the case of the boy, the castration complex forces a tremendous repression of incestuous desire and a strong identification with the father, giving rise to the punitive and powerful internalised conscience, structured into the super-ego. No such mechanism operates for girls: they remain in the Oedipus situation for a relatively long time and leave it (through a process never clearly specified) only incompletely and with difficulty. They consequently have much weaker super-egos, producing the character deficiencies described above. Secondly, passivity is encouraged in the girl: with her recognition of the inferiority of the clitoris she gives it up (at least as an object of masturbation, a claim that most feminists have challenged) and thus also gives up a more active stance towards her sexuality. As Mitchell (1974) puts it, the dominance of passivity enables a transition to occur 'from the active wanting of her mother to the passive aim of wanting to be wanted by her father' (p. 108), a classic formulation of what is supposed to be women's role and difficulty in intimate relations. But it is a more complex point that has provided the basis for a feminist reading that is sympathetic to Freud. This takes up his notion that girls experience themselves as inferior but interprets it in cultural rather than biological terms. What is symbolised in penis envy is the girl's growing realisation that she is cut off from the sources of power in society, that her only hope lies in wheedling her way around a man and eventually producing a son who can achieve all her forcibly forsaken desires. Freud's symbolism of male power – the famous 'phallic symbol' sanctified by appearance in a multitude of coffee-table magazines – is read as a description of the real world under patriarchy but not 'in nature'. A major defence of Freud that follows from this is that his description is not necessarily sexist (although his personal valuation of women is); rather, it is an accurate portrayal of a sexist world. Not that all feminists accept this position: Chodorow (1978), for instance, argues that there are stringent limitations on the extent to which Freudian psychoanalysis can be understood as descriptive rather than prescriptive for patriarchy, and advocates a rereading of psychoanalytic theory which will be described in Chapter 7. But the project Freud identifies forms the basis even for such positions: that one cannot simply 'explain' femininity by an appeal to nature, but that, instead, it is necessary to devise a description of how what appears to be natural comes about – how, that is, masculinity and femininity are constructed. Psychoanalysis may yet, therefore, provide some tools for changing the sexism of the social world by adding to our understanding of how it is perpetuated.

The prospects for change

It is clear that, whatever his own liberal sympathies, Freud did not hold out much hope for any radical change in social affairs. His basic postulate of the opposition of society to individual desire would be enough to settle that matter, although he does explicitly allow that different social organisations may produce somewhat different experiences of repression, with the most advanced civilisations producing the most. In addition, Freud writes off most radical hopes as a search for 'consolation', 'for at bottom that is what they are all demanding – the wildest revolutionaries no less passionately than most virtuous believers' (Freud, 1930, p. 339). Socialism has some accurate insights, but is mistaken in central respects: the accuracy is in recognising that a 'real change in the relations of human beings to possessions' would alter social relations positively, the mistake is in the idealism with which socialists view human nature, neglecting the ambivalent structure of the instincts from which all else follows. This ambivalence produces the confrontation between individual and society, with its resulting repression, and it also ensures the repetitive nature of political life: how history, however ruptured by revolutions, cyclically reproduces the same results, the brothers internalising authority after having murdered it. Finally, although this has been more a fault of post-Freudians than of Freud himself, revolt is psychologised: revolutionary motivation is reduced to individual psychology, is potentially an indication of pathology.

All this makes psychoanalysis an apparently dubious ground for radical critiques of society to venture upon. Yet, as will be argued in detail in Part 3, what in some ways is most reactionary in psychoanalysis also holds the seeds of a truly critical practice. Here, all that needs mentioning is that several areas of political debate have arisen from Freud's social account. The first concerns the inescapability of social repression: is it genuinely the case that all social configurations depend on the submergence of fundamental desires, and do they all do so to the same extent? Freud's own answers appear to be 'yes' to the former question and a qualified 'no' to the latter: the principle is that for society to survive individual desires have to be contained. Others have disputed this: for instance the libertarianism of Marcuse and Reich is based on the premise that non-repressive societies, allowing free play to the sexual instincts, are imaginable. A second issue concerns the immersion of individuals in society. Freud's formulation seems to balance precariously between a description of the individual as a biological entity with her/his essence residing in specific drives, and a complex account of the social construction of that individuality through the exposure of the human to particular social and interpersonal structures – an uncovering, that is, of the social bases of what is usually taken to be 'natural'. Thus, on the one hand, sex is an 'instinct'; on the other, a person's sexuality is ordered through a certain set of experiences with external 'objects' or people, notably the Oedipus complex. It is perhaps in this arena that feminist psychoanalysis has most to offer. Thirdly, there is the issue of social change, about which, as described above, Freud is extremely pessimistic. Some workers have argued that this is due to his neglect of social factors in his theory of the unconscious; others have suggested that his pessimism is belied by his own concepts, for example that the idea that the child's original 'polymorphous perversity' becomes channelled through repression into socially acceptable modes of expression implies the continued existence in the unconscious of seditious, politically revolutionary alternatives to the social order. However, the strongest defence of Freudian theory must be in its power to *analyse,* to display the unconscious roots of personal and social action, to make this material open to awareness and hence to make ideology open to inspection and change imaginable. It is because of this that psychoanalysis has at various times, including the present, had a profound hold on the radical imagination. Many radicals have employed Freud's theory to enrich their understanding of the necessary conditions for change: for some (e.g. Reich) removal of sexual repression is crucial; for others (e.g. feminists) the integration of personal and political change is the essential condition for real progressive advances. While Freudian theory is rife with unexamined assumptions and retrogressive elements, it has to be engaged with seriously by all workers aware of the need for an account of the way in which the structures of the social world enter into individual consciousness and influence perceptions, feelings and actions. In other words, as the significance of subjectivity is more fully recognised in radical thought, so psychoanalysis moves once more to centre stage.

3 Analysis

Freud's pessimism over change, so obvious in his views on the future of society, extends to his account of the prospects for cure of individual distress. His formulation of the aims of therapy does not include the loss of all pain; instead, it focuses on the necessity of living with ones's ailments. In one of his earliest psychoanalytic works, Freud describes a challenge from an imaginary patient:

> Why, you tell me yourself that my illness is probably connected with my circumstances and the events of my life. You cannot alter these in any way. How do you propose to help me then?

Freud's reply confronts all movements arguing for the possibilities of salvation – religious, political and therapeutic:

> No doubt fate would find it easier than I do to relieve you of your illness. But you will be able to convince yourself that much will be gained if we succeed in transforming your hysterical misery into common unhappiness. (Breuer and Freud, 1895, p. 393).

Such a formulation not only supplies a rebuff to those who attempt to evaluate psychoanalysis on the narrow grounds of its success at removing symptoms, but it also contains a subtle political formulation: that the 'common unhappiness' of normal living is different only in degree from 'hysterical misery', and that both are connected with the 'circumstances and events' of life. Analysis cannot change this: its sphere of operation extends no further than making misery more obvious and hence, hopefully, more manageable; it does not act directly on social conditions. If many post-Freudians have aspired to promise more to their patients, or have attempted to pronounce intelligently on the appropriate conditions for a mentally healthy society, it has usually been at the expense of the recognition of the differing roles available to therapeutic practice and social action. None have described more succinctly and accurately than Freud the limited possibilities for individual change within a repressive environment, nor have they always appreciated his insight into the significance that even this amount of change may have. To understand the origins and implications of this position, it is necessary to examine Freud's ideas on the nature of psychopathology, particularly conflicts, anxiety and symptomatology.

From anxiety to defence

Freud's views on anxiety undergo an important modification during the latter part of his career, with a reasonably satisfactory position not being worked out until as late as 1926, with the publication of *Inhibitions, Symptoms and Anxiety*. Previous to this, the notion is that anxiety is a product of repression, caused by the failure of instincts to achieve release. As such, it is a purely quantitative phenomenon, produced by undischarged excitation, the original lack of discharge being due either to a real interference with sexuality (the 'actual neuroses') or to early psychological events and repressions ('psychoneuroses'). This is a straightforward matter of psychic economics: the idea is that, 'in repression, the instinctual representative is distorted, displaced and so on, while the libido belonging to the instinctual impulse is transformed into anxiety' (Freud, 1926a, p. 263).

Interestingly, in this version of things psychic conflict is not produced so much by the ambivalence of the instincts themselves as by the impossibility of life according to the pleasure principle; that is, anxiety is a pure product of the clash of instinct with reality. However, with the reformulation of psychoanalytic metapsychology that takes place in the 1920s, Freud is driven to look again at the problem of anxiety, making particular re-analyses of his published case studies, 'Little Hans' and the 'Wolf Man' (Freud, 1926a, pp. 258ff). Most significant here is his analysis of the sources of repression in these instances – sources which turn out to be closely linked with the presence of anxiety. The new structural theory of the mind had created a clearer disjunction between conscious, preconscious or unconscious ideas, and the structures in which these ideas could be contained – id, ego, super-ego. In particular, it was more firmly stated that mechanisms of defence such as repression are aspects of the ego, even though they are unconscious: they must be so, because their function is to protect the ego from the damaging consequences of instinctual eruption. When the question is raised as to why the ego should have to ward off material arising from the id – i.e. why repression is necessary – the answer from the analysis of case material comes back: to deal wih anxiety. The *reason why* the instincts are intolerable to the ego is that they threaten to overwhelm its fragile manoeuvers in the real world through the urgency of their fantastic demands; this creates anxiety in the ego and makes repression of the instincts necessary. Thus, instead of anxiety being the result of repression, it is now revealed to be its source: 'It was anxiety which produced repression and not, as I formerly believed, repression which produced anxiety' (Freud, 1926a, p. 263). Anxiety no longer is thought to arise from repressed libido; instead, the ego's anxiety (for it is the ego that is now recognised as the seat of anxiety) sets repression going and is thus the primary cause of neurosis.

The recognition that repression is caused by anxiety raises more forcefully than before questions concerning the exact nature and source of this anxiety – the details of the precise fears experienced by the ego. Otto Rank (1924) had addressed this problem and argued that all anxiety has its origin in the birth trauma; the task of analysis was therefore to return the patient to the position where s/he could relive the trauma, integrating and overcoming its terrifying elements and hence renouncing contemporary anxiety. Freud took issue with this, asserting that there is no justification for assuming 'that whenever there is an outbreak of anxiety something like a reproduction of the situation of birth goes on in the mind' (Freud, 1926a, p. 245); he could not believe that a child could retain the memory of birth in a form which could haunt the exact content of her/his fears throughout life. Nevertheless, he was willing to allow a certain function for the birth trauma, that of giving the affect of anxiety 'certain characteristic forms of expression' (Ibid.), a way of indicating distress and danger which may become more sophisticated but not different in kind during development. (Incidentally, this marks a shift away from Freud's earlier notion that anxiety symptoms mimic the experiences of the sexual act; now they mimic birth.) Arising from the critique of Rank's theory, Freud proposes two closely related sources for anxiety. First, anxiety may be a response to a traumatic situation in which the ego experiences a feeling of helplessness in the face of an excitation with which it cannot deal. Birth is the first such circumstance, hence its implications for the form anxiety takes later on, but all situations of extreme non-satisfaction give rise to anxiety of a similar kind. Secondly, anxiety is a signal of *danger*. Such dangers are usually concerned with losses or separations, because it is these which might place the individual in a position in which s/he experiences unsatisfiable desire. Again, the first such separation is that of birth, but there are others that occur predictably throughout development, from loss of the mother as an object, to the threat of castration or (in the case of girls) the recognition of it, to 'social anxiety' when the super-ego is formed: 'what the ego regards as the danger and responds to with an anxiety-signal is that the super-ego should be angry with it or punish it or cease to love it' (Freud, 1926a, p. 297). Finally, there comes fear of death, which is but 'fear of the super-ego projected onto the powers of destiny' (Ibid.). The aggression of the super-ego represents as much of a threat to the ego as the libidinal demands of the id. More basic than repression, then, is the source of repression: anxiety. More basic than anxiety is the experience of separation and loss, the threat to the organism always being that it will be overwhelmed and annihilated. And given the presence of the instinct of death, this is indeed its eventual fate. Birth is unavoidable, the loss of the mother is unavoidable; the castration complex is universal, as is fear of the super-ego. Anxiety, therefore, is unavoidable, and with it the whole paraphernalia of repression and symptom-formation.

Symptoms are inextricably linked both with anxiety and with the mechanisms of defence, of which repression was for Freud the most important. Anxiety is the cause both of symptoms and of defences: the purpose of the mechanisms of defence is to ward off dangers; the particular defences that are characteristically chosen by any individual (a choice probably determined by heredity – Freud, 1933) determining the kind of symptomatology that s/he is likely to show. Repression is the distinctive character of hysteria, the original psychoanalytic neurosis, while regression and reaction-formation are associated with obsessive–compulsive neurosis.

In fact, it is often hard to differentiate between the concept of a defence mechanism and that of a symptom: the function of symptoms, too, is to avert danger, and in many respects they operate in the same way as defences, both to redirect the energy of unconscious material and to give it some form of substitutive expression. More formally, however, symptoms are to be seen as a substitute for something that has been held back by defences; as such, it is really an instance of failed repression, a 'return of the repressed'. Certain instinctual wishes have been repressed by the ego because of anxiety, however, the repression has partially failed either because it has been inappropriately applied or because of the strength of the wish. The instinctual impulse finds a way through into expression by employment of a substitute that gets round the defence; unfortunately, because this substitute is a very much reduced and inhibited version of the original impulse, it is incapable of supplying real satisfaction. Hence, the ego loses on two counts: it suffers because the instinct is achieving partial expression, and it suffers because that expression is only partial.

> In this event the position, generally speaking, is that the instinctual impulse has found a substitute in spite of repression, but a substitute which is very much reduced, displaced and inhibited and which is no longer recognisable as a satisfaction. And when the substitutive satisfaction is carried out there is no sensation of pleasure; its carrying out has, instead, the quality of a compulsion. (Freud, 1926, p. 246)

Symptoms thus possess an *expressive* function, revealing the unconscious desires which are being defended against, albeit in a displaced fashion. Hence Freud's (1917) castigation of psychiatry for not having anything interesting to say about psychopathology other than a 'diagnosis and prognosis – uncertain in spite of a wealth of experience – of its future course' (p. 290). Symptoms, as a substitute for something that has been repressed, have a sense, which is dependent on a detailed examination of the patient's experiences for its elucidation. Analysis of the form of the symptoms and the experiences that they are linked to will reveal this sense, which must reside in some formulation involving conflict, loss and anxiety, and the defence of the ego against the overwhelming awareness of these things. It is a major strength of psychoanalytic practice that it takes seriously the *content* of disturbance in order to find clues to the underlying conflict: somewhere in the obsessional thought that a person has lies an indication of the precise nature of the underlying difficulty, and not just of the fact that s/he is an 'obsessional neurotic', the end-point of psychiatry's description.

The problem for the ego in all this has become quite complex. Previously, it was struggling against a danger which in some fashion came from the demands of instinctual material. Now, with the formation of the symptom, some of these demands are being expressed in a distorted but nonetheless damaging fashion. The ego therefore has to turn its attention to a new struggle, against the symptom, while ensuring that the original impulses are not freed from repression. The way the ego attempts to manage this is by adapting to the symptom and making it part of its own organisation, whilst concurrently defending against its continual renewal of the demands for instinctual satisfaction. The situation would only be eased by total success at repression, or by complete and uninhibited absorption in the unrealistic demands of the id – these states being not alternative means to mental health, but characteristic of either neurosis (ego sides with reality) or psychosis (ego sides with the id) respectively. One of the pessimistic elements inherent in Freud's position is thus the avowal that there is no way that a balance can ever be fully achieved; nor can suffering of this form be permanently avoided or removed from the psyche. It is an inevitability, given our constitution and the structure of our minds, that instinct will clash with reality, that the ego will have to fend off the demands of the id and the super-ego, and will hence have at times to restrict its organisation and acquiesce in the formation of symptoms. It is not just that the world is a hard and nasty place; it is also that the structures which give rise to anxiety and symptoms are permanent elements of the human mind.

The prospects for cure

Freud's pessimism over the possibilities for cure, expressed in his dictum that all that can be hoped for from psychoanalysis is the conversion of 'hysterical misery' into 'common unhappiness', prevented him from fully espousing any particular model of mental health as a positive aim for therapy. Instead, he constructed an approach, a practice defined by its process rather than its product. In Rieff's (1966) terminology, the distinctive attribute of Freudian practice is the adoption of an 'analytic attitude' which exposes contradictions and defences but leaves it to the individual to choose the particular direction s/he will take. The result might not, in fact, amount to much:

> Our impression is that we must not be surprised if the difference between a person who has not and a person who has been analysed is, after all, not so radical as we endeavour to make it and expect and assert that it will be. (Freud, 1937, p. 329)

Freud's comment here acknowledges and side-steps the criticisms of psychoanalytic practice that have bedevilled the entire history of the movement. Psychoanalysis is itself one of the three 'impossible professions' doomed to producing unsatisfactory results, the other two being the bringing-up of children and the governing of nations (Freud, 1937, p. 352). This is for two reasons. First, psychoanalytic practice is immensely laborious, expensive and time-consuming, so that most analyses are doomed to be incomplete, and very few people can ever expect to benefit from one. 'Poor ourselves, and socially powerless,' laments Freud, psychoanalysis can never be introduced at a level which will produce mass changes in consciousness (1917, p. 483). More significantly, psychoanalysis is the wrong kind of practice for the production of deep-rooted change. Although Freud frequently compares analysis to 'surgery', and asserts that it is a *relatively causal* approach to the solution of psychological difficulties, he retains a persistent admiration for the biochemistry of the psyche, regarding the manipulation of that as the only truly causal approach. Because psychoanalysis cannot intervene on the chemical level, it is only partially causal, preferable to other treatment methods because it does not restrict itself to the treatment of symptoms. But suppose, Freud suggests,

> that it was possible by some chemical means, perhaps, to interfere in this mechanism [of psychic energy], to increase or diminish the quantity of libido present at a given time or to strengthen one instinct at the cost of another – this then would be a causal therapy in the true sense of the word, for which our analysis

> would have carried out the indispensable preliminary work of reconnaissance. (1917, p. 487)

Thus, psychoanalysis' claim to credence is not as a therapeutic system; as described in Chapter 1, Freud emphasises its status as science, to be commended for the insights it brings on the nature of human psychology, rather than for any quick or simple results.

The second source of Freud's pessimism lies in his view of the intractability of psychological structures and dynamics, and of the possibilities for the avoidance of suffering. The expectation that neurotic phenomena might be curable comes itself from a vague and romantic feeling that neuroses are in some way unnecessary (Freud, 1933, p. 153). Psychoanalysis, of course, has revealed the inevitability of neurotic conflict in the contradiction between internal desire and external constraints. Life is lived in pain: there is necessarily conflict between what may be desired and what may be achieved. Hunting for happiness is not a project that psychoanalysis can accede to, because it is itself the most radical critic of the foundations of such a project.

> One feels inclined to say that the intention that man should be 'happy' is not included in the plan of 'creation' . . . our possibilities of happiness are already restricted by our constitution. Unhappiness is much less difficult to experience. (Freud, 1930, pp. 263–4)

Repression is a fact of life, essential for survival in a social world; this interacts with the demands of psychic energy to produce the impracticability of life according to the pleasure principle. Freud's location of psychic distress within a philosophical context making conflict an essential ingredient of human existence forms an irreducible limitation on the possibilities for the psychotherapeutic process. The aim of psychoanalysis might appear to be to liberate the individual from determination by unconscious conflicts, but there are not really any escapes from such conflicts, all apparent escapes being illusions. The analytic attitude can be applied to all solutions, all systems holding out promises of happiness or cure, from religion to revolution. Make choices, certainly, but only in the knowledge that all of them are determined, that, like 'free association', everything is chained to the relentless exhortations of desire.

This is Freudianism at its harshest: no real solutions to conflicts are available, all choices can be analysed, no solutions are worthwhile. However, there is another theme in Freud's writings on cure, apparent more and more in his later works, which seem to hold out a firmer hope for change, and which expresses reasonably clearly what might be taken as at least an intermediate aim for psychotherapy. It may be that Gabriel (1983) is correct in supposing that this represents a compromise position which Freud is forced into by his recognition of the impossibility of real cure, and that this is reflected in a growing sacrifice of the goal of 'self-understanding' in the interests of strengthening the resistances and making life more livable. Nevertheless, the particular approach taken by Freud has provided more explicit guidance for his followers than his broader speculations on the limitations of human possibilities; in particular, this is true of the approach that might in general terms be called 'siding with the ego'.

Freud provides a clear account of the aims of therapy in the *Introductory Lectures* (1917). The 'pathogenic conflict' in neurotics, he notes, is between two powers operating at different levels of consciousness, one preconscious or conscious, the other unconscious. For this reason, 'the conflict cannot be brought to an issue; the disputants can no more come to grips than, in the familiar simile, a polar bear and a whale' (p. 484). The 'sole task' of psychoanalytic therapy is to make such a meeting possible, to bring the elements of the conflict together on to a terrain in which they can battle out their contradictions. Such a moderate aim is congruent with the position described above in that it sets analysis no more of a task than to reveal conflict, and offers no particular direction in which it should be resolved. But it also suggests a more optimistic view of what can be achieved by this: a 'true decision' between the conflicting forces might be reached once they are placed on common ground. As, following the metapsychological works of the 1920s, Freud becomes more concerned with the analysis of the ego, so there comes about a subtle development in his thinking on the relative value of, and appropriate direction of effort for, psychoanalytic practice. In the *Introductory Lectures,* the focus is upon revealing unconscious conflicts, but the task of analysis is also expressed operationally, as 'overcoming the resistances, lifting the repression and transforming the unconscious material into conscious' (p. 489). The 'unconscious to conscious' theme becomes increasingly dominant in later works, with its most famous formulation being that of the *New Introductory Lectures* (1933), where the purpose of psychoanalysis is given as,

> to strengthen the ego, to make it more independent of the superego, to widen its field of perception and enlarge its organisation, so that it can appropriate fresh portions of the id. Where id was, there ego shall be: it is a work of culture – not unlike the draining of the Zuider Zee. (p. 112)

And in *Analysis Terminable and Interminable* (1937), Freud describes the 'essence' of the analytic situation as the alliance that the analyst forms with the ego of the patient, an alliance which enables the latter to 'subdue certain uncontrollable parts of his id, i.e. to include them in the synthesis of the ego' (p. 337)

These are still cautious passages, but they incorporate an unmistakable siding with the ego and, alongside this, with the reality principle against the pleasure principle. Despite the goal of life being the attainment of happiness, in analysis it is the achievement of control over instinctual desire that is aimed at. While Freud at various points, notably in *Civilisation and Its Discontents,* contests the repressive rights of society, he is not hopeful that gratification of desire is an attainable end for therapy. Society is necessary for perpetuation of humanity; hence, given the fundamentally antisocial nature of the instincts, repression has to continue and frustration is bound to be experienced. The only legitimate aim for psychotherapy under such circumstances is to 'strengthen the ego', allowing more successful negotiations between the individual and the world, but also strengthening the defences against the instincts, thus in a way creating more alienation from unconscious desire. This idea has been contested in various ways, on the one hand by theorists who question Freud's view of the inherent destructiveness of the instincts, and on the other hand by those who denounce his view of society as fundamentally opposed to human desire. This debate, of course, is along the same lines as that surrounding the general pessimism of Freud's social theory.

Given the equivocations surrounding the purposes of therapy, what can be hoped for from an analysis? Freud is at times very clear on this matter: on the surface at least, not much. Not only does psychoanalysis sometimes turn out to serve only to raise resistances, but even where it is relatively smooth and complete its 'total result' is only that the patient 'has rather less that is unconscious and rather more that is conscious in him than he had before' (Freud, 1917, p. 486). But this, Freud goes on to say, is in fact really a great deal, for it represents the patient coming into her/his heritage, becoming what s/he might be under the best possible conditions. Similarly, in *Analysis Terminable and Interminable,* Freud refuses to commit psychoanalysis to the normalisation of the patient or to the

> demand that the person who has been 'thoroughly analysed' shall never again feel the stirrings of passion in himself or become involved in any internal conflict. The business of psychoanalysis is to secure the best possible psychological conditions for the functioning of the ego; when this has been done, analysis has completed its task. (Freud, 1937, p. 354)

The caution of this position is striking: no comment is made on the acceptability or otherwise of the various 'passions' and conflicts that might stir inside the analysed person. Simply, analysis endeavours to help in self-control, to make difficult feelings tolerable and to enable the ego to get on with the business of negotiating everyday life. The achievement of increased ego control is not easily attained, however, and raises more specific, technical questions concerning the point at which analyses can be regarded as complete. On the face of it, any increased egoic control is advantageous, with analyses that end at different points all being potentially beneficial. But such is not quite the analytic experience: analysis can be broken off too early (in fact, Freud ascribes all therapeutic deteriorations to clumsy work or analyses too soon terminated), and improvement can be too sudden. Freud's own criteria for recognition of progress are more stringent and in a sense 'objective', in relying neither on the reports of the patient on her/his subjective state, nor on simple changes in symptomatology. For one thing, the 'obscurities of the case' have to be cleared up: the sources of the current difficulties, the underlying reminiscences and conflicts have all to be brought into the open, the detective work has to be complete (Freud, 1917, p. 506). This is in line with popular views of analytic practice which overemphasise intellectual 'interpretation' and the discovery of traumatic but forgotten events. But it is the second criterion that is more significant: that the libidinous energy which has become attached to the symptoms should be freed and put at the disposal of the ego, so that it can be once more (or for the first time) put to good use in the work of culture and of everyday living. Neurosis is produced in the conflict between social reality and instinct; it is resolved if this conflict and its historical roots are unearthed (the detective task) and if the energy of instinct is put at the disposal of the ego, instead of being wasted in the prodigality of symptom formation. Thus, the removal of symptoms *is* an important element in the analyst's appraisal of whether an analysis is complete: although psychoanalysis does not operate directly on symptoms, it also does not ignore them. The important addition, which separates psychoanalysis out from symptomatic treatments such as behaviour therapy, is that the analyst must also investigate the widespreadness of the changes in the patient's internal libidinal economy, and must evaluate whether her/his reality orientation is sufficient to maintain a relatively symptom-free existence.

Psychoanalysts, beginning with Freud, have always recognised their failures in practice, to be separated off from the essential failure of any therapeutic approach to conquer the reality of the human experience. To some degree, these failures have been explained by the necessity to experiment with different kinds of patients, only some of whom are suitable for analysis. Thus, Freud had to learn from experience that psychotic patients, suffering from what he termed the 'narcissistic neuroses', were unsuitable for his therapeutic art, mainly because of issues concerned with transference. But there are additional reasons for treatment failures, apart from the obvious encroachments of therapeutic incompetence amongst inexperienced or incompletely analysed analysts. One of these is the reliance of analysts on making an alliance with the patient's ego. This requires the ego to be relatively normal; but as Freud (1937) notes, a normal ego is, 'like normality in general an ideal fiction' (p. 337). The abnormal ego, on the other hand, is a regular state of humanity; all that distinguishes people from one another in this respect is the extent of that abnormality, with the fragmented ego of the psychotic being the extreme case, unable to form the kind of alliance and allow the type of synthesis necessary for analysis to proceed smoothly. Thus, the degree of 'modification of the ego' may play an important part in determining the potential for successful therapy. Again, given that all egos have some modification in them, the degree to which these act defensively to oppose therapy is a crucial factor in determining its progress. The ego has an investment in symptoms, in that they avert the prospect of something worse; therefore therapy, which is geared mostly to the uncovering of unconscious id material, has also to work on the operations of unconscious ego defences, appearing as resistances of various kinds. This is not just so that the id can be brought into the light of day, but also because these same defences will be used to oppose recovery:

> The crux of the matter is that the mechanisms of defence against former dangers recur in analysis in the shape of *resistances* to cure. It follows that the ego treats recovery itself as a new danger. (Freud, 1937, p. 341)

The outcome of therapy depends importantly on the strength of these oppositional defences; given the limited power of analysis, it is not surprising, in Freud's view, that it is the defences that so often win.

Another factor determining the impact that therapy may have concerns the 'constitutional' strength of instinct by which the ego is opposed. Just as the pre-existing strength and integrity of the ego is important, so is the power of the id. Analysis aims, to use the extension of the 'Zuider Zee' analogy that Freud takes up in *Analysis Terminable and Interminable,* to remodel the old dams against instinct put up in the childhood of the individual. As the adult ego is stronger than that of the child, and as it also has the support of the psychoanalyst, the new dams can be expected to be made of stronger material, making it less likely that the derivatives of desire will trickle round them in the form of symptoms. The problem is that no solution is absolute, no dam proof against all forces; the quantitative strength of the instincts will set an absolute limit on the extent to which analysis can successfully support the construction of new defences. And as analysis has only a meagre, finite power, the final result is not always that much different from the original, symptomatic situation. This, parenthetically, is one reason why neuroses with traumatic onsets are more easily dealt with: here it is not, on the whole, an internal passion that has had to be repressed, but an external event that has proved too painful or threatening to be integrated. Analysis does not, therefore, have to contend with the continuing pressure of instinct in unravelling the defensive configurations that have developed to protect the infantile ego and have become habitual in adult life.

So psychoanalysis, however moderate in its aims, can be thwarted in many ways. In the end, even given totally successful analyses of defences and instincts, and given a complete working alliance with the patient's ego, there are matters about which it can do nothing. Freud (1937) locates the male fear of castration and the female demand for the penis as the bedrock of analysis, the biological point beyond which psychoanalysis cannot go ('The repudiation of femininity must surely be a biological fact, part of the great riddle of sex' – p. 357); more generally, his view of life and death instincts places limits on the possibilities for real progress. All who have followed Freud have reconsidered his drawing of the therapeutic line, and have done battle over the extent to which the forces of darkness can truly be overcome. One answer to them must be that too simple an optimism makes for a will o' the wisp, not true light. However, the harshness of Freudian pessimism has social as well as individual consequences, and it will be necessary to consider the extent to which it is determined by a confused and conformist social outlook, rather than by the realism upon which Freud prided himself so much. The misogyny of the quotation bracketed above is suggestive in this respect. But before moving on to the wider extensions of the psychoanalytic debate, it is necessary to turn briefly to the internal determinants of the therapeutic situation: what happens between analyst and patient.

The mechanisms of therapy

The mechanisms of therapy are crucial for psychoanalysis. This is despite the fact that, as Gabriel (1983) has noted, Freud consistently refers to therapy as an 'art', to be distinguished from the science of psychoanalysis, implying that it is impossible to lay down hard and fast rules for its progress. Nevertheless, especially in his more ego-oriented work, there are some relatively clear guidelines which have formed the basis of all later therapeutic activity by analysts. According to Freud, analysis has as its two principal stages the search for repressions and the removal of those resistances which maintain them (1917, p. 488); over time, the analysis of resistances is emphasised as Freud's attention turns to the question of how to increase the ability of the ego to cope with unconscious conflict. The 'correction' of defences so that they become more appropriate to the task in hand is made possible by means of the here-and-now analysis of resistances as they occur in the treatment situation. In fact, Freud (1914b) argues that it is by means of the working through of resistances that most change comes about in patients, and that it is this process which distinguishes psychoanalysis from treatments such as hypnotherapy, that operate purely by suggestion. The medium for all this is, of course, talk: the 'fundamental rule' of analysis is that the patient relinquishes her/his power to censor thoughts and, instead, 'free associates', saying everything that comes into her/his mind, however apparently trivial or embarrassing. Not that such relinquishing of censorship is actually possible; Freud avers that in every instance free association breaks down, and it is precisely at that point that the analyst knows that significant material is to be found. The patient agrees to the rule, but finds it impossible not to attempt to maintain some places of asylum within the mind, because of the preciousness of the knowledge available to her/himself and the threatening consequences to the defences if it should come to light. In a telling analogy, Freud locates the hidden impulse that provokes this anxiety in the realms of criminality.

> Suppose that in a town like Vienna the experiment was made of treating a square such as the Hohe Markt, or a church like St. Stephen's, as places where no arrests might be made, and suppose we then wanted to catch a particular criminal. We could be quite sure of finding him in the sanctuary. (Freud, 1917, p. 329)

Analyis operates through talk, but listens to the slips and silences that infiltrate the associations of the patient, viewing them as leverage points to begin the process of shifting the great mass of resistance. Resistance penetrates throughout the therapeutic encounter: in a paper on 'Beginning the Treatment', Freud (1913) lists a range of initial resistances which can only be dealt with by gradually winning the trust of the patient; later, all the 'chance events' that occur in a person's life can be made into reasons for interfering with or breaking off the analysis. The symptoms are, after all, serving a purpose, and there is a considerable amount of pain involved in giving them up.

The analyst's communications, too, are not simple ones. Making interpretations is a subtle procedure, requiring not just an awareness of what might be happening inside the patient and in the interaction with the analyst, but also an ability to choose the correct moment to communicate this knowledge. Too quick an interpretation can leave the patient cold or, worse, increase the power of the resistances; the vital skill is to be able to assess when the patient has come 'so near to the repressed material that he has only a few more steps to take under the lead of the interpretation' (Freud, 1926b, p. 134). There are certain rules that can help in this: for example, the analyst's counterpart to the fundamental rule is the method of 'evenly suspended attention', by which s/he takes note of everything the patient says or does. The analyst maintains an emotional distance – a kind of surgical coldness – which protects both parties by making it possible to evaluate the patient's communications dispassionately and assess her/his emotional state. Most importantly, the analyst enters upon a special kind of relationship with the patient, special in a way that goes further than its surface idiosyncracies and allows a peculiar kind of emotionality to surface and bring about change. The central element in this special relationship, which enables emotional restructuring to occur in the apparently unpromising land of the encounter between a patient and an analyst who is a stranger to her/him, is that of transference, recognised in some of Freud's earliest writings and raised increasingly to the apex of psychoanalytic practice. In the *Fragment of an Analysis of a Case of Hysteria* ('Dora'), Freud describes transferences as

> New editions or facsimiles of the impulses and phantasies which are aroused during the progress of the analysis; but they have this peculiarity, which is characteristic of their species, that they replace some earlier person by the person of the physician. To put it another way: a whole series of psychological experiences are revived, not as belonging to the past, but as applying to the person of the physician at the present moment. (Freud, 1905, pp. 157–8)

First noted by Freud in relation to the resistances of patients to treatment, transference has increasingly come to be seen as the central element in the psychoanalytic situation, encouraged by the passivity and 'blank screen' behaviour of the analyst. The general notion is that our earliest relationships, real and fantasised, lay down inside us general tendencies, repeated in all our relationships with other people. We relate to others not just in terms of their 'reality', but in line with unconscious expectations and fantasies of our own. This is a normal process, bringing about normal difficulties and distortions ('misrecognitions') which can become pathological under certain circumstances. Thus, in the context of the relationship with the analyst, the patient reproduces her/his impulses, fantasies and desires which are directed towards other current and past objects. From the moment the patient meets the analyst, transference is present, operating initially to oppose progress but gradually taking on the dual role of resistance and expression of the patient's personal history. Distinctively when compared with some later theorists, Freud argues that although transference is experienced by the patient as real and as referring to the person of the analyst, it actually has nothing to do with current interactions, but is totally a reconstruction of infantile feelings, hence usefully revealing to the analyst the 'kernel of [the patient's] intimate life history' (Freud, 1926b, p. 141). This allows a curious 'as if' quality to infiltrate the analytic session (Langs, 1976): the patient behaves as if her/his feelings were legitimately directed towards the analyst, while the latter interprets them as displacements, whose appropriate objects belong to the past. On no account must the analyst live up to the transference: in a paper on 'Transference Love', Freud (1915b) warns that gratifying the (female) patient's desire will only enhance the infantile elements in her love, continuing her inability to achieve gratification in the real world; in addition, every departure from analytic distance and the pure pursuit of truth supports the patient's resistances and makes the analytic work more difficult. Transference, at least for Freud, is thus an intense set of feelings experienced by one partner in the therapeutic encounter, but revolved and interpreted by the other.

There are three things which differentiate the analytic situation from the normal one. First, transference is encouraged by the structure of analysis, the dependency it generates and the withdrawal of the analyst from full presence; this prevents the kind of reality-testing which occurs in ordinary life and which enables people to modify their experiences of one another. Secondly, the behaviour of the analyst is different from that of people in ordinary settings. Not only is the analyst passive and obscure, refusing to reveal anything of her/himself and yet expecting the patient to talk in detail about the most personal and embarrassing concerns, but s/he also engages in the peculiar business of *interpretation,* uncovering the primal roots of fantasies and emotions and making their affective content available for 'working through'. The link with transference also clarifies the source of the power of interpretations, which at their best do considerably more than provide a straightforward kind of intellectual knowledge. Our commonest image of psychoanalytic practice is of the analyst offering interpretations of material produced by the patient; this always raises the problem of how this kind of cognitive procedure can bring about therapeutic results – whether self-knowledge is the same as change. The posing of this problem is based on a neglect of the central position of transference: the whole emotional power of interpretation resides in its contextualisation in a highly charged relationship, which in turn draws its energies not just from current concerns, but from repetition of the past. Any statement of analyst to patient is read through the miasma of transference, so that it can sometimes even be converted into its opposite; the patient's response is then taken up and reinterpreted, a looking-glass regress forcing realignment of psychic material. Recognition of the centrality of transference was a major source of Freud's pessimism over the possibilities of work with psychotics, where the capacity for transference is severely impaired by the splitting of the ego, so that patients treat the analyst only with indifference and cannot work through their feelings in the analytic context. Other workers, notably Klein, have been more optimistic, viewing psychosis as based upon the same projective and introjective mechanisms which they claim are the foundations of transference.

A third distinctive characteristic of the analytic situation resides in a special kind of transference that occurs in therapy, the 'transference neurosis', in which 'all the patient's symptoms have abandoned their original meaning and have taken on a new sense which lies in a relation to the transference' (Freud, 1917, p. 496). An 'artificial neurosis' is created which not only mimics the real illness, making it visible to the analyst and hence susceptible to her/his interpretations, but also removes the investment of energy from the original symptoms to those appearing in the therapy.

Thus, the stages of therapy that occur in psychoanalysis are as follows (Freud, 1917, pp. 507–8). First, 'all the libido, as well as everything opposing it, is made to converge solely on the relation with the doctor'. Because of this convergence, the symptoms are divested of energy, and the transference neurosis appears. This is already an advance, because the various unreal objects to which libidinal energy has been attached now become unified into one, albeit still unreal, object – the imaginary presence of the analyst, imaginary because there is no way in which her/his real attributes can become known by the patient. Next, the analyst interprets the transference, suggesting meanings for the phenomena being experienced and observed, gradually allowing the mental conflict between ego and instinct to be fought out and settled without recourse to fresh repression, until 'the alienation between ego and libido is brought to an end and the subject's mental unity is restored'. Finally, the libido is released from its 'temporary object', the analyst, and returned to the disposal of the ego. This whole process is particularly facilitated by the way the analyst sides with the patient's ego, making it stronger and hence more ready to give some licence to libidinal impulses without having to resort to the extreme defences that were previously used.

In all this, the most striking factor is the absolute presence of the analyst. Apparently non-directive and passive, interpreting only the material that the patient brings, often silent, never giving advice, avoiding unnecessary contact, the analyst nevertheless has total control, is at the centre of all the feelings and of all the power that resounds around the consulting room. This centrality is not actually dependent on any particular pattern of behaviour by the analyst: it is built into the structure of any therapeutic encounter and would have to be actively subverted if it were to be changed. But the mystery of the analyst's person, her/his avoidance of self-disclosure and use of an interpretative stance reflecting all emotions back on to the patient, emphasises the power imbalance in the situation and also aligns the analyst with pervasive cultural images of the healer as an expert who acts on the essentially passive body of the patient/sufferer (see chapter 1 of Banton *et al.*, 1985, for a discussion of the overlapping images of doctor and psychoanalyst). Freud was aware of how significant the person of the analyst is, and devoted considerable attention to the question of who should be an analyst, instituting the requirement of a training analysis, and warning that the analyst's personality might prove to be as much a source of obstacles to therapeutic progress as that of the patient. The whole notion of 'counter-transference', the feelings engendered in the analyst by the specific characteristics of her/his patients, is an attempt to deal with the difficulties of describing and utilising the impact of the analyst's personality. In Freud's view, counter-transference was something to be reduced as far as possible: the analyst should be neutral and realistic, free from feelings of her/his own which might interfere with the pursuit of the truth of the patient's pathology. Whatever the intention of this injunction, its effect is to accentuate the asymmetry of the analytic encounter by exaggerating the difference between the patient (full of neurotic emotions) and the analyst (distant, patient and calm).

For many people, this asymmetry is linked to a central political question concerning the practice of analytic therapy. Not only does psychoanalysis explicitly avoid attempting to influence the conditions under which a person's life is lived, thus opening it up to accusations that it privatises distress and suggests that non-social solutions are attainable. It also accentuates the power of the therapist to such a degree that it appears to validate authoritarianism: the analyst is present but unavailable, critical but unchallengeable, the object of many desires but the gratifier of none. The real distress engendered in the patient by the experiences which s/he has undergone are taken up into the person of the analyst so that all reality is lost and everything is understood in terms of the transference relationship – an astonishing piece of megalomania, if nothing worse. Finally, the power of the analyst is both accentuated and denied: an unreachable expert, yet supposedly a neutral helper. Foucault (1967), presents this critique at its most provocative, encapsulating both the strength and danger of the Freudian position, and placing it in its cultural perspective:

> all nineteenth-century psychiatry really converges on Freud, the first man to accept in all its seriousness the reality of the physician–patient couple, the first not to look away or investigate elsewhere . . . Freud . . . exploited the structure that enveloped the medical personage: he amplified its thaumaturgical virtues, preparing for its omnipotence a quasi-divine status . . . The doctor, as an alienating figure, remains the key to psychoanalysis. (pp. 277–8)

This argument will be taken up again in Part 4, where it will be suggested that the psychoanalytic focus on the encounter between analyst and patient not only emphasises the power relations present in therapy but also provides some tools for altering them. In this way, the apparent authoritarianism of analysis can turn out to be more progressive and 'subversive' of internalised authority than do the more apparently egalitarian efforts of many of Freud's opponents. In any event, all those who have followed Freud have fought over the role of the analyst; in this fight are encapsulated many of the issues of politics and power, therapy and cure that are thematic for the whole of this book.

Part II
Repression and the Unconscious

One of the central components of the project that psychoanalysis has set itself is to identify the fundamental building-blocks of the human psyche and to describe the developmental sequence in which psychological organisation takes place, including a relative weighting of the roles of biological and social influences. Much of the recent interest in psychoanalysis centres on this attempt to construct an account of individuality and of subjectivity that recognises their importance and complexity, while also dealing with their links to the social world. Different psychoanalytic theories, however, vary considerably in the particular accounts that they present, and the divergencies between them reveal a good deal about the political assumptions and possibilities of psychoanalysis in general. In the next two chapters, four theoretical 'schools' that all offer something of significance are outlined and discussed, with particular consideration to the stance that they take up on the significance to be attached to biological 'drives', and on the role that social or environmental events play in the construction of each individual person. The four schools are those of ego psychology, object relations theory, Klein and Lacan; these also provide the foundations for the discussion of the applications of psychoanalytic theory later in the book. The thrust of the two chapters taken together is to question any simple polarisation of psychoanalytic approaches into politically acceptable non-biological, and unacceptable biological, camps, and to attempt to draw out those elements in each theory that hold most promise for a 'social' psychoanalysis.

4 Instincts and Objects

The view that each individual possesses a fundamental core of selfhood from which all her/his attributes arise is a dominating notion in Western perceptions of what constitutes basic humanity. In a general way, it is reflected in the philosophy of the 'cogito' ('I think therefore I am'), that at the centre of being is a rational source of meanings (wishes, desires, attitudes, etc.), an idea that is common in religious formulations of personal responsibility and which is also found throughout mainstream psychology. It is precisely in challenging this notion of the existence within each of us of a central, directing consciousness that the psychoanalytic revolution inheres. Freud's formulation of the unconscious makes all human behaviour and experience comprehensible only through reference to 'another site' than consciousness. In Freudian terms, not only is thinking a complex phenomenon which must itself receive explanation (the concepts of primary and secondary process being of relevance here), but it is also illegitimate to assume that psychological functioning is unified in any meaningful sense. Psychoanalysis argues that behind the experience that we may have of ourselves as coherent psychological beings there exists a basic split in the psyche, reflected in the way some ideas are conscious or preconscious while others are radically unconscious. We may think we choose what to say, select what to do (the 'we' here being our conscious, articulated selves), but in fact we are chosen, or at least our choices are constrained by forces which lie outside of conscious control or easy access. It is only through recognising the existence of such unconscious forces and using them as explanatory items that human behaviour and experience become at all plausible; knowing that they exist does not, however, make us easily able to control or even recognise them in ourselves.

The formulation presented above would, by and large, be acceptable to most schools of psychoanalysis; acceptance of the concept of the dynamic unconscious can in many ways be taken as a *sine qua non* for a psychoanalytic theory. But dissension surrounds various aspects of the Freudian tale, dissension which revolves around two distinct but related points: first, what is it that is contained 'in' the unconscious, thus providing the motivation for behaviour and perhaps indicating the form of 'human nature'; and, secondly, how does the characteristic structure of the psyche come about? The first question is a familiar one in psychology as it deals with the issue of 'nature versus nurture', in this context the problem being the extent to which one can accept a biological 'instinct' theory as an explanation of the sources of repression and the contents of the unconscious. It is clear from the description of his ideas given in Chapter 1, that Freud places great emphasis on the role of basic instincts or drives which are biological even when they sound metaphysical (as with the Life and Death Instincts). A large number of post-Freudian psychoanalysts have contested this point, either denying completely the importance of biology for psychodynamic accounts of human functioning, or modifying its importance. The second issue is more subtle, centring on whether humans can be construed as inherent unities, becoming split only through the effects of inadequate developmental settings, or whether our 'basic' nature is split, contradictory and fragmented. Freud appears to favour the latter view in his repeated insistence on the 'dialectics' or instinctual construction, the contradictions that are built into the psyche and that are manifested in the formation of the unconscious through the necessary processes of repression. Exactly what it is that is repressed and how strong that repression may be could vary from culture to culture and individual to individual, but in every case repression exists, and in every instance the material of desire which is repressed is predominantly sexual. At the deepest, most biological level according to Freud, lies a mighty conflict, and this determines the possibilities for psychological development.

Both the identified issues are of considerable importance for the theme of the 'politics' of psychoanalysis, for they deal in slightly different ways with the theme of the malleability of human nature, the impact of the environment on the construction of the final form of each individual. This is obviously so in the discussion of instincts, for clearly it must be the case that if human behaviour is fixed by biological drives it can only be controlled, never seen as a product of social construction. A politically progressive psychoanalysis, one might therefore assume, would begin with a denial of Freud's instinct theory and its replacement with a theory that showed how the 'instincts' themselves were socially constructed. But the political implications of the 'splitting' issue are no less important, not just because this issue involves discussion of the role of the environment in human development, but also because it allows one to debate the exact nature of any 'social construction' that may take place. In this and the following chapter, these issues are examined by means of a description of the major post-Freudian psychoanalytic traditions that bear upon them; specifically, ego psychological, object relations, Kleinian and Lacanian theories. These approaches provide the foundations for the applications of psychoanalysis that are discussed in Parts 3 and 4. It will be argued that the differences between them, both subtle and substantial, provide important insights into the varying possibilities for the construction of what might be called a 'social' psychoanalysis.

Ego and adaptation

'Ego psychology' follows fairly closely the parameters of Freudian psychoanalysis, adhering particularly strongly to its concern with the significance of biological drives and their tolerability in the ordinary social world. Anna Freud (1941) set the tasks of ego psychology and also to some extent indicated its inherent limitations right at the beginning of her major work, *The Ego and the Mechanisms of Defence*. In this she states,

> From the beginning analysis, as a therapeutic method, was concerned with the ego and its aberrations: the investigation of the id and of its mode of operation was always only a means to an end. And the end was invariably the same: the correction of these abnormalities and the restoration of the ego to its integrity. (p. 4)

While she does not go as far as to reject the concept of the id, she clearly regards the study of the ego as the true project of psychoanalysis, for scientific reasons (the ego is 'the medium through which we try to get a picture of the other two institutions' – p. 6) and in the interests of therapy. In this connection, it is of relevance to note that Anna Freud's theories developed from her work with children, where negotiations with here-and-now reality are central, and where enhancing an individual's ability to cope with a destructive environment is often the only viable aim for therapy – a circumstance which automatically leads to a greater focus on the ego. Hence her concern with adumbrating the various defence mechanisms characteristic of the ego's unconscious processing and necessarily combated in analytic work. But the quotation above is at odds with Freud père's concentration on his instinct theory: whereas some of Freud's most intense intellectual energy went into elucidating the machinations of id-impulses, for Anna Freud this was only so that the therapy of the ego might be more effective. It is this concern, too, with *therapy* that is limiting (see Part 4 for a fuller discussion): Freud was clear that his interests were those of the scientist, mapping the mind; his daughter prioritises the correctional, applied aspect of psychoanalysis and in doing so opens the way to those who would reduce it to a technology of adaptation. The critical edge of psychoanalysis, as philosophers such as Marcuse (1955) and Jacoby (1975) have argued, derives most strikingly from its theoretical concepts, which present a radical new vision of 'human nature'. Obviously, these concepts are tied up with empirical observation – the science of the consulting room – but an important source of their strength is that they are not limited to what might be usable in everyday practice. In treatment, it is truly helpful to have Anna Freud's clear list of the major defence mechanisms available, but this list does not substitute for a theory of the structure and dynamics of the mind. Placing emphasis upon the ego and therapy as the main thrust of psychoanalysis risks losing sight of its most radical vision – the notion that there may be parts of ourselves which are always profoundly at odds with other parts, and with the world.

American ego-psychologists, notably Hartmann but to a lesser extent Erikson, have concerned themselves so much with the adaptive properties of the ego that they have sometimes made such 'adaptation' a biological imperative: adjusting the demands of the instincts to fit in with what is socially possible, or acceptable, is seen as necessary for the survival of the human species. Mannoni (1971), in a brief but incisive critique of what he sees as the bowdlerisation of psychoanalysis in America, draws attention to a comment by the psychologist Hilgard in 1949, that 'the mechanisms of adjustment were the features of Freudian theory that were domesticated earliest into American psychology'. Mannoni comments,

> This is an astonishing statement, if one remembers that the theory constructed by Freud . . . did not in the slightest degree make adjustment either a basic issue or a therapeutic goal. No such word even appears in the indexes of Freud's works. (p. 182)

Mannoni suggests that Hilgard's statement should be reformulated to express the idea that Freud's theory was domesticated *by* the American psychology of adjustment, a suggestion which neatly points to the major political criticisms of this work. Poster (1978) makes a similar point in suggesting that America produced a hidden agenda for psychoanalysis, linked to the prevailing ideology of individual autonomy through social adaptation: 'Underlying ego psychology was a concern to foster personality development and to bolster democracy against the dangers of "totalitarianism"' (p. 65). Mannoni, parodying Erikson's work and objecting to the idea that one should be adapted to one's cultural environment, sees adaptation as being about social conformism: 'Everybody must be like everybody else so that we may all recognise each other as nice people' (p. 184). Thus, while Erikson removes some of the determinism from Freud's developmental theory by reinterpreting the various stages (oral, anal, genital) in terms of modes of relating to objects, he appears to suggest that each individual comes, through the adaptive abilities of the ego, to conform with the specific cultural modes of relating that are created from these possibilities by their particular society. In developing his critique of ego psychology, Poster also pays particular attention to Erikson's work, because it represents an attempt to develop a theory of character formation that attends to the significance of cultural influences. What is interesting about this theory, as Poster points out, is its focus on questions of 'identity' and in its shifting of the psychoanalytic focus away from infancy to the entire life cycle, with especial consideration of the identity traumas of adolescence. The developmental history that

Erikson produces by this means is one firmly centred on the ego: how the individual struggles with the issues presented at each stage of the life cycle and makes sense out of experience. In Erikson's formulation, cultural considerations, particularly as revealed in differing child-rearing techniques, influence the manner in which common problems such as autonomy and separation or the generative demands of adulthood are coped with, with the crucial issue being the extent to which each individual can absorb the available cultural values and internalise them to produce a set of ego functions that are at one with the surrounding society. Mental health is basically a product of successful adaptation to culture or, rather, a successful use of cultural resources to enable integration of the ego as a centre of a coherent personal identity. The difficulties with this approach are basically clear: Erikson's concern with society actually drifts into a legitimation of it; the problems that individuals experience occur because they are dislocated from their culture, not because the culture itself may be disturbed. In Poster's words, 'The focus on the individual's development leads conceptually to a wholesale legitimation of the society. For the individual to achieve "wholeness" and spiritual fulfilment social arrangements which are very suspect become advantageous' (p. 72).

Although Erikson, through the clarity and humanity of his writing, has done much to popularise ego psychology, it is Hartmann who is the central figure in this school, producing many of its most incisive ideas but also developing the concept of 'adaptation' most elaborately, making it a central goal, the aim of psychological development and the final arbiter of mental health. Hartmann takes up the notion, found in Freud, of the ego as the agency through which the demands of the id are mediated so that they can be managed in the real world. This is at the base of the distinction between the pleasure principle, which dominates the functioning of the id, and the reality principle, the alterations to desire made necessary by the social environment. Where Hartmann differs from Freud is over the development of the ego, and it is in this difference that some of the differing implications of their psychologies originate. Whereas Freud contends that the ego is gradually precipitated from the id through the frustration of desire and that the energy it has at its disposal is derived from the instincts, Hartmann's theory suggests that the ego and id have a simultaneous development from some undifferentiated origin, so that the ego also has its own constitutional base, providing it with an energy that is as primordial as that of the id. This means that the ego is a biological given; as the function of the ego is to relate to reality, the effect of this notion is to heighten the role of reality in development, making it a primary source of motivation. In addition, whereas Freud emphasises the ego's role in dealing with conflicts between impulse and reality, Hartmann, as part of a project to convert psychoanalysis into a general psychology, emphasises those aspects of the ego's functioning which are 'conflict free': for example, perception, intention, language, motor skills and many other psychological functions are held to develop outside the regions of conflict. Finally, the direct link that the psyche has with reality through the ego means that the internal economy of the mind can be affected by the external world in a way not described by Freud, and which radically alters the opposition presented by him between individual pleasure-seeking desires and the limits of toleration imposed by society. According to Hartmann, because reality enters directly into the mind it can influence what is experienced as pleasurable; in a sense, it can change the basic urges of the individual mind. Hartmann refers to this as a 'partial domestication of the pleasure principle' (1956, p. 218); in fact, it represents a profound triumph for the reality principle, as pleasure itself is colonised.

On the face of it, there is much that is attractive in Hartmann's approach for the development of a psychoanalytic theory that takes account of the impact of the external world on personal development. By making the energy of the ego into a basic building-block of development, Hartmann moves reality to centre stage, allowing it even to infiltrate the pleasure dome at the centre of the traditional psychoanalytic universe. But Hartmann also incorporates a strand of biologism into his approach which lies at the source of that eventual conformism of ego psychology criticised earlier. At the centre of this is the concept of 'adaptation'. Hartmann suggests that in the same way as humans are preordained by evolution to be able to adapt to their physical environment, so they are biologically programmed to adapt to their social environment, which is, after all, just as important for purposes of survival. The ego is the organ of adaptation whereby this struggle for survival is pursued: its energy is always oriented towards enabling the individual to fit in with the dictates of reality. And this entire process is biologically ordained: each person is born with the ability to adapt to an 'average expectable environment'; this biological urge is at the root of the individual's interactions with society. Greenberg and Mitchell (1983, p. 249) articulate the heart of this notion clearly:

> The point of intersection of the biological and social comes in the concept that adaptation to the social environment is guaranteed by innate psychic structures, at least insofar as the environment is within the 'average expectable' range. Man in this view is not quite a social animal, but he is an animal innately equipped to become part of an ecological system that has strong social ingredients.

Interestingly, in the light of his notion of the central role of external reality in governing psychological structures, Hartmann presents a rather undifferentiated view of the social world. Unlike object relations theorists (discussed below), he does not focus particularly on the details of mother–child relations; rather, he emphasises innate characteristics of the individual which allow adaptation to an essentially passive environment. What does happen, however, is that the concept of the *biological* becomes enormously extended, to include that 'average expectable environment' which is otherwise known as society. It thus becomes a biological given that each individual has to adapt to the constraints of the culture in which s/he finds her or himself. Hartmann is clear as to where this leads: 'The crucial adaptation that man has to make is to the social structure and his collaboration in building it' (Hartmann, 1959, p. 30). Mannoni (1971) points to the Darwinist assumptions inherent here: the ego, having its own biological origin, brings with it an inherited disposition to be adapted to the 'probable' reality which it will find – that is, it is biologically programmed to adapt to the social world. The conformist consequences of this view are obvious, for it makes a failure to 'adapt' an indication of psychopathology. Mannoni and Guntrip, from their widely differing viewpoints, are united in criticism here. Guntrip makes predominantly humanistic points: he dislikes Hartmann's 'systemic' concept of the ego because it is not about the *personal* self; he dislikes Hartmann's whole project because it is about the survival of the organism rather than the experience of personal development and the realising of one's 'inherent ego-potential for unique individuality as a person relating to other persons' (Guntrip, 1973, p. 109). But also he takes issue with the whole notion of 'adaptation':

> We only reach the level of psychoanalytic concern when either accepting or resisting, complying with or altering the environment, is in the service of quality of personality, not of mere survival of the organism. (Ibid., p. 110)

It is the environment, if anything, that should be called upon to adapt, to make it possible for each individual to fulfil her/his own potential. 'Adaptation' leads to conformity, the development of a 'false self'; the true self is creative as well as adjusted.

Mannoni (1971) is more forthright in his defence of the radical vision of psychoanalysis. In this view, a correct definition of adaptability would be, 'the ability to *disadapt* oneself. For man has always been adapted, in the Darwinian sense of the word. He constantly disadapts himself by modifying the environment' (p. 189). The significant issue that this quotation brings into focus is ego psychology's relative neglect of questions of the quality and structure of the environment to which people can be expected to 'adapt'. In part, this is due to the biologism of ego psychology: by extending the concept of biology to include much that would usually be regarded as social, and making biological considerations central to its theory of motivation, it risks setting up social adjustment as the principal criterion of mental health. Linked with this is the poverty of ego psychology's pronunciations on the *kind* of society to which people should be expected to 'adapt'. It provides at best a general account of social or 'cultural' influences on the internalisation of values, and tends to see the precise interpersonal mechanisms whereby social factors are influential over development as subsidiary to the general biological imperative of adaptation. The result is that although ego psychology appears to provide insights at the level of social structure, it in fact takes this structure as an inviolable given, restricting itself to an account of how individuals manage to adjust to their culture. It is this that raises the spectre of conformism over ego theory: it says little about the conditions under which individuals might best develop their potentials, or relationships might be made optimally fulfilling. Instead, it takes for granted the social world and concentrates on how people can be helped to fit in. For an adequate social psychoanalysis to develop, it is necessary to move beyond this stance to one that deals more successfully with the intricacies of personal development and the complexities of society.

The relational critique of biological psychoanalysis

Freud's concern with 'instincts' or 'drives' has often been criticised from within psychoanalysis as too biologistic or mechanistic. Perhaps the best known traditional critique is that deriving from the so-called 'culture school' of analysts such as Karen Horney and Erich Fromm. The particular contribution of Fromm to the development of psychoanalytic social theory will be described in Chapter 6, but the general argument of this group is that what Freud mistakenly viewed as biologically determined is in fact culturally conditioned, and that psychoanalysis can be reframed as an account of the way the psyche is formed within any specific society. However, there is also a focus upon current circumstances that tilts the balance away from the familiar psychoanalytic concern for the formative episodes of childhood: Horney, for example, emphasises that the cultural conditions under which a person lives will be a major determinant of the likelihood of neurosis, and of the kind of neurotic difficulties that s/he will experience. It is obviously important for any theory to take account of the impact of current stresses on psychological well-being, but the culture school tends to do this at the expense of the psychoanalytic recognition of the significance of internal events. The net result of this approach is to reduce the significance placed on the dynamic unconscious and to upgrade the importance of the regulation of consciousness through cultural patterning. Consequently, cultural school theory becomes distanced from psychoanalysis, for which the locus of concern is the internal world of the individual, formed in the cataclysmic encounters of childhood and perpetuated in the depths of the unconscious. The phrase 'culturally conditioned', used above, was chosen specifically to suggest this point: in obeying their exhortation to examine the *general* social conditions under which people live, the culture school theorists neglect the specific, 'micro-social' internalisations of social structure which produce a dynamic unconscious along certain specifiable lines and which also explain the manner in which past events can be perpetuated in, or accentuated by, present circumstances. Culture school theory, because of its focus on the way in which cultural conditions distort character, also fails to provide an account of the manner in which society penetrates individual consciousness *in the process of its construction*; instead, it implicitly postulates the existence of a preformed human individual whose capacities are developed or thwarted by the social conditions under which s/he lives. In Fromm's work, this results in a humanistic psychology emphasising the growth potential of each individual, to be realised through personal effort and change. As will be discussed in Chapter 6, this is a poor substitute for a radical theory of either psychoanalysis or society. In an important way, it lessens the specificity of the Freudian account of the manner in which unconscious desires become regulated, replacing it with a general opposition between an undifferentiated individual and an equally undifferentiated society.

The critique of Freudian instinct theory which comes from the object relations school[1] is of greater interest, because it shares in the fundamental psychoanalytic position that gives centrality to the concept of the unconscious, whilst arguing that the appropriate level of explanation to be used in psychoanalysis is psychological or psycho-social, not biological. This point about 'level of explanation' is an important one: it is not that biology does not exist, but that it is not relevant. In the words of a prime propagandist of the object relational view, Harry Guntrip (1973, p. 49), biology is only

> a study of the *machinery* of personal life, not of its *essential quality*, to use Freud's own term, a study of the mechanisms of behaviour and not of the meaningful personal experience that is the essence of the personal self.

This is a revealing quotation: with his reiteration of the term 'personal', his use of the notion of the 'self', and his concentration on the 'experience' of the individual, Guntrip aligns himself firmly with humanistic psychologists who advocate a focus on each person's potential for a meaningful existence as the true subject for psychology. Not surprisingly, given this, Guntrip (1973) argues that Freud's reliance on nineteenth-century biological and physical concepts resulted in an impersonal instinct theory which is inappropriate for a psychology that is actually about people in their relationships with themselves and others. He suggests that the instinct theory side of Freud's work should be jettisoned because it ties analysis to an overly reductionist viewpoint which only acknowledges meanings as residing in physical impulses. This provides no information when one wants to discuss humans as people whose fates are dependent on the quality of the relationships they form with others. 'Here the important concepts are needs, purposive activities, meanings and significances' (Guntrip, 1961, p. 145).

The fundamental proposition of object relations theory is reflected in its name. In the traditional psychoanalytic view, human psychology is driven by the impulse to express instinctual drives, and it is in order to do this successfully that relationships with others are formed. In object relations theory, this order of events is reversed, Freud's instincts being replaced by an assumption that humans are fundamentally relationship-seeking creatures: in Fairbairn's terms, libido is object-seeking rather than pleasure-seeking. The substance of the object relations argument is thus that the core of human essence is a drive to form relationships. Hence Winnicott's idea that there is no such thing as a baby, only a baby-and-mother field, and Fairbairn's refusal to distinguish between energy and structure to indicate that the ego is always in motion, striving to form relationships with others. Although, according to Winnicott at least, instinctual satisfactions occur, they are merely 'orgiastic' experiences, and it is the non-orgiastic activities of personal relating that form the basis of psychological development and experience. The tendency to form, or try to form, relationships is the motivating drive to which most aspects of behaviour or experience can be reduced and which gives meaning to pleasure. For Fairbairn (1941, p. 34), 'It is not the libidinal attitude which determines the object relationship, but the object relationship which determines the libidinal attitude', with maturity defined in interpersonal rather than individualistically genital terms.

The human individual's basic reality is expressed in her/his relationships, which express a fundamental need but which are very different from the instinctual 'needs' that are the stuff of Freudian theory, being concerned instead with the interpersonal conditions necessary for healthy psychological development. Thus, Greenberg and Mitchell (1983, p. 198) list the basic 'needs' implicit in Winnicott's theory as including 'an initially perfectly responsive facilitation of [the infant's] needs and gestures; a nonintrusive "holding" and mirroring environment throughout quiescent states', and so on – no mention here of feeding or the gratification of any incipient sexual impulse. Nevertheless, it is hard to envisage the origin of the drive to form relationships that object relations theorists postulate as basic, unless it is in biology: as everything reduces to this drive, and as it is the defining characteristic of human existence, it possesses a function not unlike that given to sexual energy by Freud or, perhaps, general libido by Jung. It may be that viewing libido as object-seeking is more accurate or more morally acceptable than viewing it as pleasure-seeking, and there is certainly an argument to be made from observations of infant behaviour that they are born with a fundamental affinity for social interaction which is not connected with any obviously Freudian drive gratification. However, none of this represents a complete escape from biology; it simply alters what it is that is regarded as innate. But the significance of this difference should not be underestimated, and nor should its political possibilities: whereas Freud viewed the individual as a self-contained world, comprehensible in terms of the way energy is inputted to, and outputted from, the system, object relations theory embeds each individual in a social context and suggests that there is no way of understanding the one without the other. This means that whereas classical Freudianism always views the individual as in essence separate from the social world that influences her/him (an 'essentialist' notion), object relations theory holds the potential for an account of human nature and development that makes social relations central in the construction of the self. As will be described below and in Part 3, this orientation has led to an intricate and important description of mother–infant relationships which has been extended less successfully into a general social theory.

It is sex and aggression that dominate the Freudian instinctual pantheon, so these have to be dealt with in some specificity by object relations theorists. Their general argument is that sex and aggression derive from the desire for personal relationships, the former as an expression of intimacy and the latter of frustration. As such, they are not 'mighty impulses to be mastered', but simply important expressions of the quality of object relationships that a person is currently sustaining, or has internalised from the past.

There are, however, differences between the two, which Guntrip at least regards as significant. Sex does have biological characteristics: it is an 'appetite' which, while it may be taken up in the service of personal relations (this would be the mark of a mature rather than a purely 'orgiastic' experience), always retains a concern for bodily satisfaction. Sex is thus a primarily biological phenomenon which *becomes* personal; according to Guntrip, this explains why Freud, who centred his theory on sex, thought that biological instincts are primary. His mistake was not to distinguish clearly enough between sex and aggression, for aggression is the pure culture of relationships: it does not represent a manifestation of some ineluctable 'death instinct', but is a result of frustration, or 'a personal meaningful reaction to bad-object relations, to a threat to the ego, aroused initially by fear' (Guntrip, 1973, p. 37). Aggression is thus *primarily* in the service of personal aims, although this may in the end involve self-protection; it thus operates the other way around from sex, as firstly personal and only secondarily biological. It should be noted that there is some variation within the object relations school on the exact way in which aggression is to be construed. Fairbairn's account, which pre-dates Guntrip's, is similar to that given above in emphasising the sources of aggression in frustrating experiences, but he does nevertheless note that aggression is 'a primary dynamic factor in that it does not appear capable of being resolved into libido' (1951, p. 171). Winnicott's idea that aggression is 'almost synonymous with activity' (1950, p. 204), on the other hand, sits ill with the overall object relations view. As will be described in more detail in Chapter 5, Klein's argument that aggression is, if anything, *the* basic biological drive, is in direct opposition to all these positions.

In rejecting the notion that human psychology is driven by biological instincts, object relations theory also rejects the separation of 'impulse' and 'structure' that is characteristic of Freudian psychoanalysis. Fairbairn (1944, p. 88) is clear on this point, stating that, 'Ultimately "impulses" must be simply regarded as constituting the forms of activity in which the life of ego structures consists'. Objecting to the conventional image of the ego as a rider just about managing the ebullient and energetic tumult of the id-horse, object relations theorists argue that instincts are subordinated to the whole of the 'person-ego', that they operate in the service of relationships and that they derive their energy from this fundamental drive.

> Instincts can only operate satisfactorily when they belong to a stable ego, and therefore cannot be the source of the ego's energy for object-relating. It seems more conceivable that the energy of the ego for object-relating is the primary energy; as Fairbairn put it, 'libido is object-seeking'. (Guntrip, 1968, p. 422)

There are some important consequences of this view. For one thing, it suggests that Freud's 'economic' approach (the theory of psychic energy) is no longer significant in its own right: 'energy' is simply the activity of the ego as it forms relationships with others. This also produces a drastic revision of the notions of the reality and pleasure principles. Fairbairn argues that if the infant's ego is always oriented towards forming relationships, then the psyche is to some extent determined by the reality principle from the beginning. It is only when relationships prove difficult or frustrating that the reality principle gives way to the pleasure principle, which is consequently properly to be understood as 'a subsidiary principle of behaviour involving an impoverishment of object relationships' (1944, p. 88). Similarly, Guntrip argues that true pleasure lies in experiencing a satisfying relationship to reality; when pleasure – the Freudian 'purpose of life' – is pursued for its own sake, a psychopathological condition is at hand. There is a specific disagreement here between object relations theorists and many political Freudians: whereas the former play down the significance of the pleasure principle, some of the latter (for example, Marcuse – see Chapter 6) see in the pleasure principle a revolutionary hope – a psychic realm that is fundamentally and ineluctably opposed to ordinary social reality. In valorising reality over pleasure, object relations theory appears to promote adaptation, something it is opposed to in ego psychology. However, this is not altogether a fair conclusion, because its version of the 'reality principle' refers to the quality of relationships that are formed between ego and object, between the child and other people. This concern for quality rather than just adjustment leaves open the possibility of a theory that both emphasises the importance of living in the real social world, and also allows space for a critical vision of how that world might be improved.

Another consequence of the notion that impulse and structure go together is a rejection of Freud's concept of the id, and with it his whole structural theory. This results from Fairbairn's insistence that from the start of life instincts or 'impulses' operate in the service of a relationship-seeking ego, which initially constitutes the whole of the infant's mental structure. Thus, it is not necessary to postulate the existence of a separate realm of the psyche which contains a pool of impulses that fuel psychological functioning, and it makes no sense to describe the ego as somehow 'precipitated' from somewhere else. Importantly, it is not the concept of an *unconscious* that is disputed, but its localisation in a *structure* which is somehow split off from the other parts of the mind. This is a characteristic and central point for object relations theory: that the psyche is initially a unity, a total ego which has the potential to develop into a coherent and integrated personal self. Psychic splitting is a secondary phenomenon, a derivative of something else, and signifies a distortion of optimal development. Fairbairn's claim is that the child is a whole being from the start of life, and would ideally remain whole however much her/his complexity might alter during development. In Guntrip's (1973, p. 93) gloss, 'the human infant is a unitary dynamic whole with ego-potential as its essential quality from the start'. More fully,

> Fairbairn believed that we must be aware of the fundamental dynamic wholeness of the human being as a person, which is the most important natural human characteristic. To Fairbairn, the preservation and growth of this wholeness constitutes mental health. (Ibid.)

The emphasis on *naturalness* is noticeable here, suggesting a normative view of mental health that is very similar to that of humanistic psychology and rather different from the more cautious presentations characteristic of Freud. In addition, the passage implies an identity between ego development and the creation of a true self that is representative of the use of 'ego' terminology in object relations writing. For instance, Guntrip's rejection of the concept of the id is in order to extend the notion of the ego, so that the ego becomes the whole person, suffused with its own energy and gradually enabling the organisation of all experiences within its unifying framework.

> The only escape from a dualism of radically opposed structures is to banish the term 'id', and reserve 'ego' to denote the whole basically unitary psyche with its innate potential for developing into a true self, a whole person. (Guntrip, 1973, p. 41)

The psyche should not be seen as the container of incompatible desires and impulses which operate in a way that cannot be integrated; rather, everything that exists within the psyche is consistent with its wholeness, is, in that way, all ego. Instead of the ego being formed as a precipitate of the id when desire comes into conflict with reality, object relations theory suggests that it is the unconscious that is an epiphenomenon, formed only when the 'innate potential for developing into a true self' is frustrated. Hence the fervour of Guntrip's attack on the notion of the id: it is anathema because it suggests the permanent existence of a psychic region which can never be integrated with the rest of the personality, which always belies the concept of a whole, mature self. The following is presumably meant as damning criticism:

> Thus Freud could take the term 'id' from Groddeck, who wrote, 'We should not say "I live" but "I am lived by It"'. This completely destroys the unique and responsible individuality of the person. (Guntrip,1973, p. 105)

Whether the phrase 'I am lived by It', though unpalatable, nevertheless might an accurate representation of experience, does not seem to be at issue, because the idea of an It/id smacks of biology and hence is regarded by Guntrip as reductionist and mechanistic. Greenberg and Mitchell (1983, p. 213) note that in this respect Guntrip's critique of Freud is moral rather than empirical: 'he considers drive theory degrading to mankind and, on that basis, unacceptable'. As will become apparent at other points in this book, optimism over human nature is a characteristic attribute of object relations theory and is coupled with a positive view of the possibilities for psychotherapy; the political consequences of this optimism are worthy of debate.

The maturational environment

The concern of object relations theorists with personal relationships leads to an emphasis on the type of environment available for maturational purposes. Instead of impulses originating from the id driving the individual towards certain aims and hence necessitating the use of objects, there is an ego embedded in human relationships from the start, the developmental history of which takes place in the context of these relationships. In line with this, Fairbairn replaces Freud's developmental scheme of oral, anal, phallic and genital stages, which refers to parts of the infant's body and which is therefore individualistic in its conception, with a scheme based on the quality of relationships with objects: immature dependency, transitional (latency and adolescence), mature dependency. What distinguishes the first and last of these stages is the ability of the mature dependent adult to differentiate her/himself from the parent or other object, whereas the immaturely dependent infant is in a state of 'primary identification' with the mother, unable to experience her/himself as in any way separate. The differentiations of maturity also allow for a degree of reciprocity which is unavailable to the dependent infant.

The transition from one stage, or pattern of relating, to the other is a long and potentially difficult one, but in Fairbairn's view it is fundamentally natural, a gradual unfolding of needs and potentials that take place within the context of a carefully graded pattern of separations. This idea, incidentally, has influenced workers outside the object relations school: for example, Margaret Mahler's intricate account of the phases of ego development is based around a 'separation–individuation' structure that is very similar to Fairbairn's, describing how the child's total embeddedness in the mother becomes a gradual position of separation and identity (Greenberg and Mitchell, 1983). What is distinctive about Fairbairn's account, however, is the position it takes up with respect to *internal* object relationships – the inside of the mind, as it were, which is the primary focus of psychoanalysis. For Fairbairn, the entire world of internal object relations is a compensation for environmental deprivation, for the frustrating aspects of the relationships that the infant experiences with real, external objects – predominantly or exclusively the mother of early infancy. The ideal situation is the perfectly gratifying mother, leading gradually and naturally to the perfectly poised individual at peace with the world, functioning with a whole ego and able to form totally fulfilling, mature relationships with others. Under such circumstances, psychology would consist of an exploration of the way in which people relate to real, external others. What actually happens, however, is that society interferes with the bond between mother and infant, creating unnatural separations too early, and resulting in the infant experiencing objects as depriving and frustrating ('in a state of nature the infant would never normally experience that separation from his mother which appears to be imposed upon him increasingly by conditions of civilisation' – Fairbairn, 1944, p. 109). Because it is so distressing to desire an object which is also so unsatisfying, the infant sets up substitutive ones inside – or, rather, s/he *internalises* the object in an attempt to control ('coerce') it more successfully. Thus, internal objects are compensations for the deprivations experienced in the real world: their source lies not in the biologically determined ambivalence of the instincts, but in the frustrations of maternal failure. Psychodynamics – the internal world of unconscious phantasy and mental structures, the primary material for psychoanalytic exploration – are thus the products of environmental events. Freud's notion that fantasies are substitutive satisfactions has been taken to extremes in this theory: as Greenberg and Mitchell (1983) note, all psychopathology and virtually all psychodynamic life is hypothesised to have maternal deprivation at its root.

Fairbairn's (1944) description of how the originally unified ego of the child becomes split in the face of failures in the early environment has proved seminal for object relations thought, and provides a stark contrast to the ideas of Melanie Klein, to be discussed in Chapter 5. According to Fairbairn, the first defensive manoeuvre that the infant undertakes to cope with the frustrations of the external maternal object, is to internalise it in an attempt to control it or make it palatable.[2] The unitary ego is thus faced with an ambivalent object which is the focus both of libidinal desire and hostile aggression. To cope with this painful, internal circumstance, the object becomes split into an acceptable, rewarding, 'good' object, and an unsatisfying 'bad' one. In fact, Fairbairn postulates that the unsatisfying object has two aspects: 'On the one hand, it frustrates; and on the other hand, it tempts and allures' (p. 111). To deal with this situation, the bad object is split again into its two elements, with the newly created exciting and rejecting objects being repressed as another defensive act. The crucial point here is that this process also creates a specific psychic structure. This follows from Fairbairn's fundamental postulate that ego and object only exist in relationship with one another: hence, as the object is internalised so part of the ego is redirected from the external to the internal world; and as the internal object is split so is the ego. Fairbairn describes a psychic structure organised around three ego–object pairs: between a libidinal ego and an exciting object; between an anti-libidinal ego (or 'internal saboteur') and a rejecting object; and between a central ego and an idealised object. The last of these is the residue of the healthy relationship between the original unified ego and the accepting outer world, and contains the self of ordinary consciousness; the other two pairs represent the attachment of the ego to bad objects which are nevertheless desired. The libidinal ego's attachment to the exciting object fills it with greed but also leaves it deprived, while the anti-libidinal ego's link with the rejecting object makes it the repository of destructiveness and hatred. Hence, these two ego–object pairs provide the focus of psychopathology of all kinds; they are maintained in a repressed state, and are split off from and rejected by the central ego. Thus, Fairbairn (1944) proposes that it is infantile dependence rather than the Oedipus complex that is the 'ultimate cause' of psychic organisation; more fully, it is the child's response to external difficulties with the mother that create an internal world of splitting and repression.

Although Guntrip sets himself up as simply an elaborator of Fairbairn's theory, Greenberg and Mitchell (1983) point out that he alters this theory in some important ways. These centre on his concept of the 'regressed ego', which he introduces as an addition to Fairbairn's scheme. Guntrip was impressed by observations, in himself and in his patients, of the severity of the schizoid withdrawal from relationships with objects, and the intense fear combined with neediness that such relationships could provoke. He therefore proposed that the libidinal ego undergoes a final split, leaving part of it attached to the exciting object, but hiding away another part in an even more withdrawn state, characterised by a renunciation of all objects, internal as well as external. The motivation for this withdrawal derives from early deprivation; what is novel about Guntrip's formulation is that it proposes that this deprivation is structurally embodied in the mind, as an infantile ego that longs for a return to the objectless but whole state of the womb, when it was entirely one with the mother, before frustration and rejection set in.

> Guntrip suggests that the early traumas generated by inadequate mothering are essentially frozen in time: the helpless and terrified infantile ego, overwhelmed by unrequited longings and

> dread of abandonment, remains alive within the regressed ego, in the heart of the personality. (Greenberg and Mitchell, 1983, p. 212)

Regressive longing is at the core of psychopathology; a mixture of desire for good object relationships and a fear of forming any at all. This is distinct from Fairbairn's proposal that it is attachment to bad object relations that forms psychopathology, and it also offers a new view in proposing that an objectless ego state is possible; Guntrip can even be read as proposing that 'withdrawal is primary, and object seeking is a secondary defensive reaction against the terror of regressive longing' (Greenberg and Mitchell, 1983, p. 215). But the crucial point remains the same for all object relations theorists: that the painful structuring of the psyche is a consequence of environmental failure, and in important ways embodies that failure in the structure it produces. Splitting, fragmentation and withdrawal are observable aspects of personal life, but they are not essential; given a good enough social world, they would not occur at all.

In what has been described above, the characteristic concern of object relations theorists with the early mother–infant bond is revealed, as well as their tendency to play down the Oedipus situation and find a source for all psychological conflict in failures of maternal gratification. Winnicott provides the quintessential instance of romanticisation of the possible relationship between mother and child. He suggests that the mother has the role of providing a 'facilitating environment' in which the child's inner potential to develop her/his true self can be unfolded. At birth, the infant is in an unintegrated state, unable to piece together the portions of experience that become available – a description which, incidentally, distinguishes Winnicott from Fairbairn's insistence on the *primary* unity of the neonate ego. It is the mother's role to support the infant's ego after birth by falling into a state of 'primary maternal preoccupation' in which she has complete oneness with her babe and can provide her/him with perfect 'holding', allowing the child to gain a sense of trust in the world and a security in her/himself. At first, the mother–child dyad centres on periods in which the infant is excited and the mother magically anticipates the object suitable to the child's desires, conjuring up a sense of omnipotence in the infant which serves as the basis for a solid and creative sense of a powerful self. In between these periods, when the child is quiescent, the mother provides a solid but non-intrusive presence that allows the child to feel secure in the presence of someone else – the foundation for the important capacity to be alone that once again marks the healthy ego. Gradually, as the child's sense of hallucinatory omnipotence becomes strong enough for her/his self to begin to be established, the mother has to learn how to fail gradually, to recover in stages from the 'illness' of primary maternal preoccupation, so that the child can learn the limits of her/his power and can start to experience her/himself as a separate being in a real world. In all this the mother functions as a kind of mirror to her child, mediating reality gradually, at a pace appropriate to the infant's development, geared to presenting her/him with a picture of the strength of her/his presence in the world. This is the foundation of 'good enough mothering', and if managed leads to the formation of a 'true self' as the child discovers the power of her/his own egoic desires. The mother's ability to carry off this task is rooted in biology: it is something that develops over pregnancy and is intuitive and special, qualitatively distinct from the knowledge possessed by child care experts, the naturally occurring basis for all healthy human development. Conversely, psychological problems of all kinds are 'environmental deficiency diseases', stemming from early failures in mothering.

Although, as noted above, Winnicott accepts that the newly born infant has a fragmented ego (he even allows for the existence of the id, again in contrast to Fairbairn and Guntrip), he stresses the *naturalness* of the process whereby the child's sense of integrated selfhood is formed – its requirement is simply a supportive, non-intrusive environment, and it is environmental *failure* that gives rise to internal splitting. Winnicott (1963) acknowledges the fragility of the image of perfect development that his description of good-enough mothering conjures up, and argues that it is this fragility that gives rise to a hidden aspect of the personality, a core of subjectivity held 'incommunicado' from the rest. But it is his more famous distinction between the 'true self' and 'false self' that reveals Winnicott as an exponent of the concept of fundamental psychic unity. The mother is supposed to provide her infant with the conditions under which her/his potential for selfhood can be realised. Interference with this function, for instance because of the mother's anxiety or failure to perceive the child's omnipotent desires, is experienced by the infant as an 'impingement' on the natural organisation of experience, and leads to anxiety about total disintegration. This results in a defensive hiding away of the child's spontaneous desires in the form of a secret 'true self', which avoids expression because of the danger that it will be destroyed by the inadequate environment. To enable transactions with reality a conformist 'false self' is formed, split off from the true self and protecting its integrity. The false self is inauthentic because it is built up on the pattern of the mother's desire, not the child's, hence its conformity: the child is someone else's image of her/him, acting in line with the mother's expectations and wishes so as to win her love. Greenberg and Mitchell (1983) describe how Winnicott comes to use the false self as a single diagnostic principle, 'representing a continuum of psychopathology from psychotic states, in which the false self has collapsed, to nearly healthy states, in which the false self mediates selectively and sparingly between the true self and the outside world' (p. 208).

There are some striking similarities between Winnicott's account of development and that given by Lacan, particularly in his emphasis on the 'mirroring' of the child's desire by the mother, and on the nature of the false self. As will be made clearer from the description of Lacan's views given later, however, there is a crucial difference in the use of these notions by the two psychoanalysts. For Lacan, there is no pre-given unity to the psyche; the 'mirror' that the child perceives her/himself in gives a false sense of integrity; the false self is a full description of the ego. For Winnicott, it is part of the inheritance of each individual human to become whole and unified; the false self is the product of an interference in this process, and split off from it is a bearer of the individual's authenticity, the true self which contains all her/his spontaneous desires. Ironically, in articulating the possibilities that the real world offers for perfect development, Winnicott eventually presents a theory which relegates the external environment to the passive (non-constructing) role of supporting the unfolding of an integral, unified ego that is genetically preordained.

The limits of object relations theory

Object relations theory makes some important contributions to attempts to develop a psychoanalysis that deals seriously with the impact of social factors on the development of individuals. For one thing, it formulates its understanding of basic mental structures in social terms: the mind consists of ego–object links which are the internalised representatives of external social relations. In this respect, object relations theory is 'constructivist' in outlook, arguing that the full personality is formed through a process of social encounter that consists not just in some inherent individuality being conditioned or otherwise influenced by the actions of other people, but rather that individuality itself *consists of* an amalgam of personal (ego) and social (objects) components. The emphasis of these theorists on the environment is thus not accidental: for them, there is no individual without the social, no self without the other. Again, their formulation is strikingly different from classical psychoanalysis, even though the developmental theory of the latter also deals in detail with the experiences of the child in the context of a network of family relationships. Classical analysis takes the individual as a 'closed' system of biological drives which suffer a certain fate due to social constraints (and their own inherent contradictions); each person's internal world does not, therefore, contain anything social, even though it is affected by interpersonal events. For object relations theorists, on the other hand, the internal world is set into motion by sociality (maternal deprivation), and its structure and contents are the product of a collision between internal needs and real social forms.

Despite these genuine advances in psychoanalytic theory, the object relations position has some substantial drawbacks. These centre on the way its social vision is restricted to the mother–child network, and on the notion of the basic unity of the infantile ego. There are clear conformist dangers present in object relations theory's romanticisation of motherhood and in its view that all psychological splits are introduced by frustrating experiences with the maternal object – for instance, that it implies a *biologically* determined mothering role which must take priority over all other aspects of a woman's life (see Riley, 1983, for an account of the social policy effects of Winnicott's views). There is considerable empirical and anthropological evidence to suggest that the relationship patterns that surround early infancy are socially constructed and that infant–mother links develop gradually and often with difficulty (see, for example, Rutter, 1982); approaches that prioritise mothering as much as object relations theory does neglect this data and fuel attempts to bolster traditional patterns of family life. In addition, the focus on two-person, mother–infant relations is in some ways less socially perceptive than Freud's concern with the three-person Oedipus situation. While it gives an account of the immediate interpersonal experiences of the child, it suggests that the whole of sociality can be reduced to this two-person network, failing to consider the way in which the dyad may itself be structured by something outside it – the exigencies of social structure as reflected in class, race or gender relations, for example. In the image presented by both Fairbairn and Winnicott, the external world functions only as an interference: in a perfect mothering environment, there would be but mother and babe, and nothing else. This is a conventionally asocial approach to development, suggesting that it is possible for it to occur outside society. In this respect, object relations theory represents only a limited advance on traditional psychology: although it extends the focus of the latter from the individual to the dyad, it goes on to treat this dyad *as if it were an individual*, suffering constraints imposed by wider society, but in no way inherently constituted by it. This point will be taken up more fully in Chapter 7, when the feminist work that has built on object relations theory will be discussed, but one of its effects is to limit the scope of this theory's approach to social change. At its most extreme, it proposes that social and personal distress could be overcome if we could return to that fundamental state of human nature expressed in the new-born child's loving relationship with the mother; all would be harmonious if the world were only less frustrating. This idea leads to the proposal that complete integration and happiness is possible within ordinary life, and that it depends not on a total restructuring of society, but on alterations in the kinds of relationships that parents form with their children.

The view that there is a basic unity within the psyche, which is adopted explicitly by Fairbairn and Guntrip and implicitly by Winnicott, is in some ways at odds with the constructivist orientation described earlier, because it suggests the existence of a human 'essence' which stands outside the social world, even if it needs certain environmental conditions to apply before it can be brought to fruition. Whereas object relations theory's constructivism holds the seeds of a major contribution to a more social psychoanalysis, its adherence to a whole-ego view leads it towards individualism. The political implications of this position are not invisible even to the proponents of object relations theory. Guntrip suggests that the apparently intractable 'vicious circles of deteriorating relationships' which we get into 'as individuals, classes, nations and races' can be broken to reveal the 'will to peace . . . behind all the turmoil of conflict':

> This happens on a social scale whenever negotiation ends conflict. It happens in a far deeper and more radical way when people discover that they can, through a long therapeutic analysis, outgrow their hates and fears and find a 'true self' in a positive capacity for making and maintaining good personal relations. (1968, pp. 424–5)

The issue of whether this individualistic political philosophy is a necessary consequence of the whole-ego position is an important one in considering the practical ramifications of psychoanalysis as theory and as therapy. The idea of a free or 'true' self presented by object relations theory has some enabling consequences, in that it asserts the significance of each person's experience and directs attention to the environmental blocks to personal fulfilment. This humanistic standpoint operates alongside the theory's important focus on the impact of social experiences on mental structures to supply an attractive counterweight to some other tendencies in psychoanalysis. However, the whole-ego argument also leads to an assertion of a fundamental separation of individual from society: the individual's psychic potential is pre-given, and it is the role of society simply to support that as it unfolds. Hence, the social world is reduced to a passive container of individual desires, and it is postulated that only certain kinds of social experience – frustrating ones – have consequences for psychological development. With such a set of assumptions, Guntrip's focus on individualism and regressive withdrawal becomes comprehensible. To come to grips with the interpenetration of social and individual, psychoanalysis requires a theory of how the psyche is constructed through sociality, not born outside it.

Despite its important constructivist advances, object relations theory thus provides only a limited base for a more social psychoanalysis. In the next chapter, the possibilities for advance within Kleinian and Lacanian psychoanalysis are examined.

5 Splitting the Mind

In the previous chapter, it was argued that despite the advances present in object relations theory, its potential contribution to a social psychoanalysis is limited by its adherence to a 'primary unity' view of the psyche and its description of the environment as passive and at best supportive of the child's naturally determined development. In these affiliations, object relations theory appears to go against its own constructivist premises, which make the structure and content of the mind a product of interactions with specific people. Instead, it assumes a basic healthiness or 'goodness' in the child which needs only tolerant conditions to reach fulfilment. This assumption is challenged by approaches that contest the idea that there is an inherent unity to the mind, and in particular that the ego is a whole entity at the start of life. Traditional Freudian psychoanalysis, for example, regards the ego as a developmental achievement, built on the basis of a heterogeneous unconscious which is always threatening to disrupt its precarious unity. The ego is thus a *construction*, as is the super-ego and the whole organisation of unconscious desire. Underlying the fragile ego are id impulses, particularly destructive ones, which repeatedly threaten the integrity of ego functioning. Similarly, in those post-Freudian approaches which contest the idea of a primevally unified psyche, humans are viewed as fundamentally split, the repository of desires which conflict amongst themselves and with the outside world of 'rational' control. The effect of this proposition is to make appeals to 'human nature' unavailable, at least in any simple way: if there is no particular organisation of the psyche which can be understood as the 'truth' of the individual, then explanations of individuality have to be historical, in the sense of revealing the processes whereby the individual's particular psychic structure has come to be. What then becomes the 'nature' of each individual is the history of her/his construction in the face of the demands of experience – a fundamentally social understanding of development.

In this chapter, two differing accounts that emphasise the splits to be found in the psyche are discussed. The first of these is that of Melanie Klein, which is closely linked to object relations theory (and indeed owes a fair amount to the work of Fairbairn), but which differs significantly from it in its approach to the Freudian instincts, its notions of mental structure and of 'phantasy', and its evaluation of the possibilities for the achievement of a unified psyche. Secondly, Lacan's very different approach will be presented as the most detailed and extensive account of the implications of a refusal to acknowledge the ego as a significant element in mental structure. Many of the issues raised in Chapter 4 recur here: the importance of biology, the role of environmental or social structures. The orientation of these two theories is, however, different enough from what has gone before to throw new light on these issues. In all this, the terminology is problematic, as words such as 'psyche', 'ego' and 'self' are used confusingly and sometimes interchangeably in the literature. Here, 'psyche' refers to the whole mind, however its structure is envisioned; the 'ego' refers to that agency of mental structure in which rational or reality principle processes and defence mechanisms predominate, and which may be seen by some theorists as identical with the psyche, while others see it as only part of the whole. The 'self' refers to the individual's experience of her/his consciousness, and is hence usually seen as a property of the ego, although in some views the two concepts are identical.

Envy and destructiveness

Melanie Klein's particular contribution to the debates on psychological structure and development derives from the extraordinary manner in which she employs concepts from both 'biological' and 'relationship' approaches. She does this by combining a severe instinctual bias (adopting the least popular of Freudian concepts, the Death Instinct, as her starting point) with a subtle account of psychological development through periods marked by the relative disintegration or integration of ego–object relationships. This developmental account, which focuses on the so-called 'paranoid–

schizoid' and 'depressive' positions, will be described in detail later; here, Klein's concern with instincts and with the 'negative' emotions of envy, greed and loss which form the basis of so much that is expressed in the psychoanalytic situation, will be examined. Ironically, it can be argued that this theory's focus on inborn negativity and what appears to be its neglect of the 'real' environment (e.g. the way a mother *actually* treats her child) enables it to proffer some new insights on the penetration of individuality by social construction processes. This derives in part from its account of splitting, but more generally from its fascination with the structure of relationships that the infant forms in the merger between her/his biological impulses and human environment. Klein's theory also provides an important comparison with those approaches that suggest the existence of a primordially integrated consciousness, an ego or self (depending on the theory) which is initially a unity, even if it is likely to be fragmented by the vicissitudes of experience. Klein asserts the inherently split nature of the mind, as an entity imbued with internal contradictions in its fundamental nature.

Klein assumes that at birth there exists a primitive ego, which is relatively unformed but has at least the ability to experience anxiety, use some fundamental defence mechanisms (projection and introjection) and form certain kinds of primitive object relationships (Segal, 1973). In contrast with Fairbairn's view, however, this ego does not constitute the whole of the neonate mind. In addition, there are instincts in existence from the start; these instincts are represented in mental life by 'phantasies', which are the means by which the ego attempts to ensure the satisfaction of the instincts. Thus, Klein adopts that view of instincts found in Freud which assumes the instincts themselves to be entities acting on a biological level but having representatives in mental life, by which they become known. It is at this point that Klein embarks on a deviation from Freud which is deceptively subtle and which, were it not for the tenacity with which she holds to instinct theory, would align her firmly with the object relations theorists described previously. This deviation has to do with the status of objects in the child's early psychic economy. In Freud's account, objects are the least essential aspect of the instincts, being simply those entities which the infant finds will allow satisfaction to come about. In Klein's world, however, objects exist from the start, and the instincts are *always directed towards objects*, rather than being directionless psychic urges. This raises the question of where these primeval objects come from, a question given different answers at different stages of Klein's theorising (Greenberg and Mitchell, 1983). Three particular theories concerning the origins of these objects stand out: as inherent in the instincts themselves, a kind of inherited knowledge of appropriately satisfying images based on bodily parts; as derivatives of the Death Instinct when it is 'deflected' at birth (see below); and as 'explanations' conjured up by the child to explain her/his experiences of early internal sensations. The significant point, however, is that although she postulates that at birth the infant is embedded in a total phantasy world, Klein always provides instincts with some necessary object. This moves her theory away from the closures of Freudianism to the more open possibilities of an encounter with reality that later object relations workers have focused upon; it is relationships of various kinds with objects, initially internal ones, that form the basis of psychological development for Klein. Greenberg and Mitchell outline the central significance of this perception:

> The very building-blocks of mental life in Klein's theory are different from those in Freud's. For Klein the basic units of mental processes are not packets of objectless energy, but relational units *ab initio*. (1983, p. 137).

In this way, Klein provides not just a bridge between classical and object relations theory, but also a distinctive view of development which combines biological and social outlooks in the single concept of the instinct. This has led not only to considerable confusion, but also to a great deal of light.

The first object of desire is the mother's breast, which in the child's mind becomes split into a good (gratifying) and bad (frustrating) breast (Klein, 1946, p. 2). The good object is seen by Klein as forming the core of the ego when it is taken in by the child, contributing vitally to psychological growth. In a sense, it is the child's 'aim' to incorporate the goodness of the primal object in order to facilitate the formation of a strong and secure ego. The problem is that the Death Instinct operates at the centre of the infant's experience; it is, for Klein, the source of activity and disturbance, acting through the creation of a primeval threat of annihilation. Klein takes literally Freud's polarity of Life and Death Instincts, and envisions the child as the battleground of these mighty forces. Although she is sometimes cautious in her expression of this idea, merging it with a more palatable terminology of love and hate, there can be no doubt of its role in her theory, nor of its biological underpinnings:

> In speaking of an innate conflict between love and hate, I am implying that the capacity both for love and for destructive impulses is, to some extent, constitutional, though varying individually in strength and interacting from the beginning with external conditions. (Klein, 1957, p. 180).

The early environment of the child has, goodness knows, enough sources of terror for the infant; but its capacity to destroy is increased out of all proportion by the operation of the Death Instinct internally, which presents the vulnerable and fragile neonate ego with a threat of annihilation that gives rise to tremendous anxiety. This anxiety is immediately taken up into the child's object relationships:

> I hold that anxiety arises from the operation of the death instinct within the child, is felt as a fear of annihilation (death) and takes the form of fear of persecution. The fear of the destructive impulse seems to attach itself at once to an object – or rather it is experienced as the fear of an uncontrollable, overpowering object. (Klein, 1946, p. 4)

Just as the 'good' breast is the early representative of the Life Instinct, and the child's aim is to incorporate and identify with it, so the ego copes with the threat from the Death Instinct by 'deflecting' it outwards, on to the breast. The breast is consequently felt to be aggressive and threatening to the ego, giving rise to a sense of persecution. In this way, the original fear of the Death Instinct is transformed into fear of a persecuting object (Segal, 1973); the main anxiety during this period is that this object will get inside the ego and overwhelm it. This is, it must be remembered, a description of *normal* infancy: although normal children are not consumed by anxiety all the time, they nevertheless are bound to experience it, because it begins within them, as fear of their own Death Instinct.

It is clear from what has been described above that there is a great emphasis in Klein's theory on the role of phantasy. 'Phantasy' refers to the psychic representation of instincts, but, because of the indissoluble link between instincts and objects, it is also the arena in which the child's object relational drama is experienced. This does not, however, mean that the experiences are not in an important sense *real*: 'Phantasy is not merely an escape from reality, but a constant and unavoidable accompaniment of real experiences, constantly interacting with them' (Segal, 1973, p. 14). In contrast to Fairbairn's view of phantasy as a substitutive response to external frustration, Kleinians view it as the basic stuff of psychological functioning, without which there would be no mental processes at all. The internal phantasy world has absolute primacy in this model, and all that we do, think and feel depends upon it. And because this world of internal objects exists as 'really' as the external one, the latter can never be experienced in a pure form. This is a very important point in the Kleinian argument. It is nowhere denied that the nature of the real environment makes a significant difference to the child: as will be described below, important developmental achievements are held to depend on the provision of sufficient good experiences from the environment. However, the outside world is always perceived and related to through a screen of the child's internal drives and phantasies, which may alter its impact dramatically. Even if the early environment is perfectly good, or 'good enough', in Winnicott's phrase, the child will experience anxiety and fear, and will suffer aggressive and destructive emotions. All that Kleinians can say about good experiences at this developmental point is that they will 'tend to lessen the anger' (Segal, 1973, p. 15); they will never wholly take it away. At best, the harshness of the child's initial objects, generated by the Death Instinct, may become overlaid by internalisations of the actual parents and gradually become transformed, but the initial anxiety to which they give rise will always appear – it is the starting point of psychological development, more fundamental to Klein than the sexual impulses accentuated by Freud.[1]

The effect of Klein's notion of the Death Instinct and her prioritising of the importance of the child's internal world, can be seen in the concept of envy, described in much detail in her 1957 paper, *Envy and Gratitude*. Klein (1957, p. 176) is clear on the origins of envy: 'I consider that envy is an oral-sadistic and anal-sadistic expression of destructive impulses, operative from the beginning of life, and that it has a constitutional basis.' Envy is a two-person emotion, aiming at being as good as the object; when this is felt to be impossible, however, it aims at spoiling the goodness of the object, so as to remove the source of envious feelings (Segal, 1973, p. 40). This spoiling aspect of envy contains its destructiveness, especially when, as often, it is mixed with greed – the ruthless acquirement of all the goodness that lies within an object, 'scooping out' the goodness of the breast, in Klein's words. Where greed and envy differ is that the former is primarily concerned with introjection (taking in all the object's goodness), the latter with projection (putting badness into the object to destroy it). It is this projective mode of operation that makes envy such a pure and powerful expression of the Death Instinct: whereas destructiveness is a consequence of greed, it is a motive for envy (Greenberg and Mitchell, 1983). Envy is unavoidable: whether the breast is fulfilling or not, envy ensues. If the breast is unsatisfactory, the child hates and envies what is felt to be the mean and grudging breast; if the breast is satisfactory, s/he envies its inimitable flow of goodness, wishing hopelessly to own it. Thus, when envy is intense, the perception of a good object can be as painful as that of a bad one, for the better it is the more it gives rise to envying desires. Finally, envy destroys hope, because it is directed at the sources of goodness in the child's world; its recurrence during psychotherapy is both a necessary focus for work and a profound threat to progress.

This description of envy seems to doom the child to experiences of badness and despair. The more goodness there is around, the worse s/he is likely to feel. In fact, however, it is precisely here that the Kleinians introduce the importance of environmental experiences. For although gratification does provoke envy, which is why it is impossible ever to remove it completely and why it is so persistent throughout life, other emotions are also brought about by gratification: admiration, love and gratitude. The capacity for these positive feelings derives from a deep relationship with the good object, and is advanced when the proportion of gratifying experiences is greater than that of frustrating ones. This brings about an immensely positive state, the basis of integrated development:

> If the undisturbed enjoyment in being fed is frequently experienced, the introjection of the good breast comes about with

> relative security. A full gratification at the breast means that the infant feels he has received from his loved object a unique gift which he wants to keep. This is the basis of gratitude. (Klein 1957, p. 188)

Strong envy of the feeding breast interferes with this enjoyment and hence undermines the possibilities for gratitude and also for the integration of the psyche (as positive feelings fail to predominate over negative ones, leaving the child's mental world in a threatened state). All this also influences the vicissitudes of the Oedipus complex, when it appears later in development: although by this time people are being recognised by the infant as individuals, s/he still perceives them in terms of her/his own projections. This brings about intense envy as well as the jealousy of the ordinary Oedipal rivalry, as the parents are phantasised to be providing one another with the gratifications that the child most desires. If the child's envy is not excessive, jealousy in the Oedipal situation becomes a means of working it through, because being directed at rivals rather than at the primal, internalised object, it is felt to be more manageable and less destructive. On the other hand, if early envy remains powerful, it can also destroy the possibilities for successful resolution of the Oedipal phase – as in psychotic states.

Here, then, is a powerfully biological theory taking on board the most contentious of Freud's metapsychological ideas. Nevertheless, despite its undoubted valorisation of internal processes over environmental conditions, and its reliance on much criticised concepts of instinct, it holds out a perspective for the construction of a psychoanalysis that takes account of social relations. The theory is clearly founded on the notion that the infant is riven from the start with conflicting desires, some of the most powerful of which are aggressiveness and destructiveness. As such, it is superficially less optimistic than the more humanistic orientation of object relations theory, where the emphasis is on a positive object-seeking tendency which gives rise to destructiveness only when thwarted. Yet, there is another kind of optimism in the Kleinian approach. At one level, this arises straightforwardly from its focus on negative impulses: it confronts the painful phenomenon of destructiveness and examines what can be made of it, how gratitude and other positive feelings can be constructed, how social relations can be formed and maintained in the face of envy and greed. In this way it recognises some deep anxieties that people have, and reaches out to social ways in which these might be overcome. In contrast to the tendency of object relations theorists to talk in terms of a *return* to a loss or missed state of perfect support from the mother, Klein's theory focuses on the need to take the experience of envy or destructiveness and make something productive out of it. For example, Kleinian theory's emphasis on the control of destructiveness, the achievement of gratitude and (as will be discussed in the next section) the expression of reparative urges, provides some strategic ideas on the amelioration of actually experienced negativity. Secondly, Klein shares with object relations theorists an appreciation of the relational nature of development, in her case expressed by her reformulation of instinct theory to incorporate relationships with objects (internal and external) as fundamental aspects of what appear to be biological entities. This is, in some ways, the reverse of ego psychology's tendency to impose biology where all is apparently social, making Klein's work viable as a source of politically progressive insights. Finally, Kleinian theory's concentration on phantasy, the internal world which mediates the impact of the outside world, brings into focus one of the most radical elements in psychoanalysis. It refutes a simple individualism which begins with an integrated self and then examines what the social world makes of it. Instead, the (real) social world is experienced through a conflicting screen of internal forces, which alter and shape it powerfully. As will be argued more fully in the next section, this allows the theory to become dialectical, positing contradictions within as well as between each element in the inside–outside divide.

Splitting and reparation

The thrust of Klein's developmental theory is to recognise the conflicting forces that operate within the psyche and to detail the processes by which these, in interaction with the equally conflicting forces of the external world, produce a final mental structure that can be understood in relationship terms. The clearest way into this is through a brief outline of the central elements in the theory, in particular the 'paranoid schizoid position' and the 'depressive position'.

In Melanie Klein's view, the newborn infant is not only imbued with the instincts of life and death, but also has enough ego to experience anxiety and to employ certain defences. As described above, the earliest anxiety is a product of the Death Instinct, which is experienced by the ego as a threat of annihilation. It is in order to protect itself against this threat that defence mechanisms are brought into play, and it is through the interaction between instincts, defences and the external world that the mental organisation of the infant reaches a coherent form. According to Klein, and in contrast to the view of Anna Freud, the earliest defences employed by the infantile ego are projection and introjection, with splitting being both a consequence of these processes and a defensive manoeuvre in its own right. Projection, the phantasised insertion into the external world of impulses that originate within oneself, is ontologically the earliest of these mechanisms, although introjection, which is the phantasised taking into the self of material that lies outside, is intimately bound up with it from the first moment of development. In addition, as a reflection of the Life and Death Instincts, the young ego possesses tendencies both towards integration and towards fragmentation. Although the general thrust of development is towards increasing the degree of integration of the ego, its opposite tendency towards splitting and fragmentation is a powerful one, operating both as a straightforward consequence of the early ego's lack of cohesion at birth, and as a defence against primordial anxiety (Klein, 1957). Whereas in the classical view splitting and repression are linked defences, Klein places splitting much earlier, suggesting that it is a primitive way in which intrapsychic conflicts (which, because of the ambivalent structure of the instincts, exist from the start) are coped with by simply holding them apart. Repression, on the other hand, relies on the removal of anxiety-producing material from a relatively coherent consciousness, and hence requires the existence of a stronger ego. Thus, in Klein's account not only are instincts separable from one another and opposed to each other at birth, but the consequence of the anxiety that they generate is to create immediate and inevitable splits in the infantile mind. Psychic unity is not just empirically unobtainable; it *cannot* be present because of the fundamental make-up of the child.

Before describing the postulated order of events in early psychic life, it is worth stressing that the defences employed by the ego are seen as central to development: splitting is not in itself a negative phenomenon, and nor are projection or introjection. Thus, splitting represents the first attempt to organise the chaotic contents of the psyche and hence is fundamental to processes of ordinary thought and discrimination; more psychodynamically, it allows a separation to occur between good and bad aspects of the psyche and of objects, thus preserving the existence of the good parts from the threatening, destructive fury of the bad and enhancing the security of the ego. It is only this protection that provides the context in which good ego–object relations can develop and become strong enough to allow later integration to occur. Similarly, the projection of good impulses from the self into the mother allows the formation of good ego–object relations to take place, and also preserves internal goodness until the child is able to integrate it with the equally preserved, but now relatively overcome, destructive impulses. This process will be clarified below; the general point is that these early defences (including some very extreme ones, such as projective identification, in which parts of the self are projected on to external objects and then identified with) serve normal and necessary developmental functions.

None of this is to say, of course, that splitting cannot go awry, and come to hamper development or even form the prototype for psychotic breakdowns (for it is recourse to these early defences that is characteristic of schizophrenia). Thus, Klein (1946, p. 5) suggests that 'primary anxiety of being annihilated by a destructive force within, with the ego's specific response of falling to pieces or splitting itself, may be extremely important in all schizophrenic processes'. Excessive anxiety can bring about too much of a split, leading to fragmentation of the ego which results in it being broken up into unintegratable little bits: 'in order to avoid suffering the ego does its best not to exist, an attempt which gives rise to a specific acute anxiety – that of falling to bits and becoming atomised' (Segal, 1973, p. 31). On the other hand, failures of splitting are just as destructive: for example, excessive envy can interfere with the primal split of the initial object into its good and bad aspects (the good object being attacked mercilessly by envious impulses), making the building up of a good object hard to achieve, with synthesis then becoming impossible. The defences also produce their own anxieties: for instance, projective identification, which can be a way of investing destructive or valued parts of the self in a 'safe' object, can also lead to the fear that an attacked object will retaliate, or that important parts of the self may be imprisoned, leading to a dangerous depletion of internal resources (Segal, 1973, p. 30). Importantly, there is an environmental role here: an excess of bad experiences can fail to mollify the destructive urges of the infant, making the defences more and more extreme and self-damaging.

In the ordinary course of things, the child's initial use of projective defences initiate her/him into the 'paranoid–schizoid position'. At the start of life, the infant's precarious psyche is threatened with being overwhelmed by the destructive forces emanating from the Death Instinct; to cope with this, these destructive impulses are projected outwards on to objects. At the same time, the Life Instinct is also projected outwards, in order to create an ideal object to which the ego can aspire; without this, the entire external world would be a place of harrassing destructiveness and persecution. With the duality of instincts, the child's perception is that there is a duality of objects: even though the actual 'object' on to which destructiveness and idealism are projected is one (the breast) it is *experienced* by the child as two separate objects. That is, the breast, which in fact is a single object with rewarding and frustrating aspects, is split in phantasy into the good, nurturing breast, and the bad, frustrating one. In significant respects, the ideal trajectory for development is from this split situation to one in which the ego can deal in an integrated way with the actual contradictions of the external world – can achieve, in a sense, a comprehension of dialectics.

According to Klein, the child's psychological development is dependent for a positive outcome on the presence of a good internal object which can become the nucleus of a stable and integrated self. As this good object can only derive from the external set of relations in which the child is embedded, and as these are already infiltrated by the child's projected and split impulses, the principal aim of the infantile psyche becomes that of introjecting the ideal object, something which cannot be achieved without the risk that the persecuting object will enter in and destroy it. So the good and bad parts of the ego–object nexus are separated, as a protective strategy both for the good (internalised) object and for the psyche as a whole, in that splitting can also lead to a dispersal of the destructive impulse and therefore of internal persecutory anxieties. Hence, in order to be able to related to the containers of bad and ideal feelings without having the integrity of the latter threatened by the former, the ego splits itself into a 'libidinal' and a 'destructive' part: that is, 'the early ego splits the object and the relation to it in an active way, and this may imply some active splitting of the ego itself' (Klein, 1946, p. 5) – a version of things quite similar to that postulated by Fairbairn. So, schematically, what has occurred is *first*, projection of destructive and good impulses on to an external object, *second*, the splitting of that object into 'bad' and 'good', and *third*, the introjection of those objects to form split ego–object relationships within the psyche. This is a description of the formation of the ego's structure in the very early months of life: it is organised around phantasies which in turn derive from the projected impulses of the child. Its characteristic defensive strategies, apart from projection and introjection which are more like the fundamental basics of mental activity than conventional defences, are splitting, omnipotent denial, idealisation, hallucinatory wish fulfilment – all prototypical 'schizoid' mechanisms. The primary anxiety is that of being annihilated by the Death Instinct; as the destructive feelings have been expelled from the psyche, anxiety is predominantly experienced as a fear of persecution. All this, it appears, is independent of the external world, except for the postulation that some object is necessary or the child would have nothing to use as the focus of her/his projections.

The paranoid–schizoid position is one which is held throughout life as a potentiality, and underpins adult schizoid functioning. The defences of this period also remain, developing into important forms of mental activity: for example, projective identification is the basis of empathy and symbol formation (Segal, 1973). But the paranoid–schizoid position is also a developmental state which is overgrown by further development. In the second quarter of the first year, according to Klein, the child gradually becomes more integrated and able to perceive the mother as a whole person, which in turn allows the infantile ego to become more integrated. The manner in which this occurs demonstrates the importance of Klein's idea that the good object is introjected in development (which contrasts with Fairbairn's view that it is only frustration which gives rise to an internal object world), and also reveals the subtle way in which environmental factors enter into the theory. Put simply, for the paranoid–schizoid position to be transcended in a reasonably unproblematic way, 'the necessary condition is that there should be a predominance of good over bad experiences. To this predominance both internal and external factors contribute' (Segal, 1973, p. 37). If all goes well, and is not disrupted either by excessively strong constitutional destructiveness or by a harmful environment, the child forms the belief that the ideal object is stronger than the bad object and, commensurately, that her/his own libidinal impulses are stronger than her/his destructive ones. This makes it easier for the ego to identify with the ideal object, in turn making the use of extreme mechanisms of defence less necessary. As the ideal object gains in strength, it is experienced by the child as in less danger from the bad object; this means that anxiety is lessened and hence the strength of the good object is reinforced. This again means that there is less fear of badness and less power attributed to the destroying object; the ego also is less depleted as projection is no longer as necessary as once it was. The final result of the beneficial cycle that is thus set up is that it becomes possible to integrate the persecutory and ideal objects in the confidence that the latter will not be destroyed by the former. Incidentally, this reveals again the importance of splitting: at the start of life, it is destructiveness that is paramount; it is only by splitting that the libidinal impulses are kept secure until their strength can be reinforced by good environmental experiences and by ordinary growth, so that this destructiveness can be contested. And it is good object *experience* that is also necessary; without it, there will be little opportunity for the ideal object to become a strong focus for the formation of a cohesive and integrated ego.

Given the situation described above, the integrative tendencies that are present in the early ego gradually achieve predominance and splitting ceases to be the characteristic mode of functioning of the child – although it remains an important defence which is always available. The experience of an integrated ego and the perception of the mother as a whole object is a considerable relief to the child, as persecutory fears lessen. However, a new problem is also created: because the mother is experienced as a whole object, not split into good and bad parts, she becomes the source both of gratification and pain, and the child's attitude to her is one of ambivalence. Thus, the good mother, from whom the child derives nurture and love, is no longer phantasised as separate from the frustrating mother upon whom the child's destructiveness is vented. The child is exposed to the feeling that s/he can damage or even destroy the mother with her/his destructive rage, and lose the most precious object. This gives rise to feelings unknown in the paranoid–schizoid position: mourning for the lost good object, and guilt over the way it has been destroyed (in phantasy) by the child's own aggression. In addition, because the mother is introjected, the destruction is also an internal destruction, leaving the child feeling wasted and empty. The mixture of feelings experienced at this point – love and hate, guilt and loss, the phantasised persecutors of the earlier phase – constitutes what is known as the 'depressive position'.

Despite the characteristically negative outline of the components of the depressive position, there are some crucial achievements under its sway. Dynamically, although the child is exposed to feelings of loss and guilt, the realisation of the integrated nature of the object produces a sense of optimism which can carry her/him to a triumphant working through of these more difficult feelings. This is because the badness of the object, and the destructiveness of the internal world, are now experienced as ameliorated by the goodness of the same object and the loving, constructive manifestations of the Life Instinct. In its integrated form, destructiveness is less threatening than in its split, pure form, and the child is thus more able to overcome it and become engaged in a benevolent cycle of depression and reintegration. In addition, a number of developmental achievements come about in this period. One is the enhancement of reality testing that occurs as the child begins to make a firmer division between internal and external worlds: for example, the mother's return after separations allows the child to calibrate the strength of her/his own instincts against the resilience of the object (Segal, 1973). The awareness of the split between self and other in fact only becomes possible once the integrity of the external object is recognised. Again, new psychological defences become available to the child, of which repression is the most important; this depends on the existence of a reasonably integrated ego. The Oedipus complex has its origin in the depressive position, depending as it does on an awareness of the existence of whole external objects which can form relationships with one another. The super-ego, which according to Klein has its first roots in the introjected ideal and persecutory objects of the paranoid–schizoid position, becomes more integrated and is experienced ambivalently, so that it loses some of its ferocious aspect and can come to represent elements of the loved, as well as the feared, parent/object.

Perhaps the most important new development in the depressive position is that of *reparation*, which has been taken up by some (e.g. Rustin, 1982) as the foundation of the prospects for a socialist –Kleinian theory. The idea is a simple one: reparation includes 'the variety of processes by which the ego feels it undoes harm done in phantasy, restores, preserves and revives objects' (Klein, 1955, p. 133). The concept of reparation transforms the idea of instinctive aggression from a deterministic principle to a complex containing positive possibilities: the formation of loving personal relationships out of a desire to 'restore, preserve and revive'. Reparation derives from the depressive position because it depends on the acknowledgement of the integrity of the good-and-bad object and the ambivalent instincts: something only needs to be made good if it is valued as well as hated; reparation is only possible if the ego contains good impulses as well as bad. The love immanent in reparation thus supports the integrating tendencies present in the ego; its 'building bridges' aspect also forms the basis of creativity (casting a different light on this from Freud's notion of sublimation), as the lost or damaged internal object is made good. Finally, the experience of reparation allows the depressive position to be transcended, as the child discovers within her/himself the resources to mitigate destructiveness, becoming more stable and also more realistic in monitoring the effects of her/his phantasies on objects. The significance of reparation places it in a special position with reference to other 'defences':

> Reparation proper can hardly be considered a defence, since it is based on the recognition of psychic reality, the experiencing of the pain that this reality causes and the taking of appropriate action to relieve it in phantasy and reality. (Segal, 1973, p. 95)

Intriguingly, what has begun as a theory emphasising the negativity of human experience, its fundamental destructiveness and the damage caused to self and others through envy and hatred, resolves into a precise and luminous celebration of making good, of forming personal relationships of the deepest kind on an image of concern and loving consideration. Despite all appearances,

Kleinian theory is not pessimistic. True, it does not advocate the basic goodness of all things, but then neither is it forced to assume the basic impossibility of the good environment to explain why this goodness is never realised. Instead, it begins with the concept of contradictory being, split in its essence as well as in all its relationships, and traces the manner in which integrity can be achieved. As such, it directs interest towards the specific kinds of social relationship that may be organised for full reparation to take place.

Klein's view of the fundamental contradictions of the human psyche is vitally important in the face of a romanticised notion of human integrity. The tendency of object relations theorists to postulate an initially integrated individuality which becomes split through experience is reversed in Klein, with the consequence that the possibilities for enriched relationships become emphasised and the trajectory of her theory is towards construction rather than withdrawal. The implications for political and psychotherapeutic work are significant. Instead of arguing for a return to a primeval state of goodness, wholeness and integrity, Klein's theory suggests that progress is an advance towards conditions which allow more stable and complete expressions of reparative urges, in the extended sense described above. Klein also provides a more complex account of both internal and external worlds – the psyche and the environment – which can be seen in her description of the early months of life. The psyche is made up of conflicting forces, the impact of which is to supply momentum for the generation of more advanced mental structures. In a parallel fashion, the external environment is also made up of contradictory elements – the breast is *in reality* both gratifying and frustrating – which the child has to deal with. Development in Klein's account is the gradual increase in the complexity and strength of the ego so that both these kinds of contradictions can be dealt with, meaning, not removed but tolerated. Hence Klein's deviation from a common tendency amongst psychoanalysts to describe the nature of the child in terms of certain structures: for instance, that s/he has a whole ego or a primordial id. Although Klein does discuss the id/ego issue, the basic material of psychic life in her theory seems to be the capacity for projection and introjection, for the mixing of external world and phantasy. She thus emphasises mental processes rather than structures: the activities by which a child comes to comprehend the ambivalence of the social world as well as of her/his own emotions, the links between these two kinds of ambivalence and the steps that must be taken to cope with them. From these processes, all else follows; in addition, it is only by understanding the real contradictions of the world, and tolerating them in an emotional sense, that it is possible to consider how to bring about change. Klein's theory is certainly limited by the biologism of its language and, more importantly in this context, its failure to deal clearly with the role of social events in development. But the principles on which it is based and the conceptualisation of development that it produces make it a dynamic theory in the full sense of the word: one that valorises internal forces and focuses upon the study of process. And the process which is emphasised is the intensely dialectical one of how the contradictions of the external world and the conflicts of the internal one meet, intertwine, and resolve.

Splitting and culture: Lacan

Whereas Klein's theory develops a notion of splitting as a defensive procedure undertaken by the ego as it faces up to the threat of the Death Instinct, Lacan makes splitting the fundamental developmental process. He does this, however, by employing a very different version of 'splitting' in which it functions as a developmental marker: the idea is that development occurs through a series of radical change points, fissures cutting the subject[2] off from its own history. More generally, Lacan focuses on alienation, on how the subject becomes formed in 'otherness', how identity is always produced by the insertion of the subject into something outside. Mitchell (1982, p. 4) states this succinctly:

> Psychoanalytic practice is in danger of seeing the patient as someone who has lost control and a sense of a real or true self (identity) and it aims to help regain these. The matter and manner of all Lacan's work challenges this notion of the human subject: there is none such.

As in Freud's most rigorous formulations, Lacan understands the human subject genetically: that is, there is nothing, not even the unconscious, that has pre-existent form as a germ of 'self' or 'ego';

rather, the subject is constructed through history, and that history is a sequence of alienations.

The work of Lacan and some of his followers will be returned to in the context of the feminist theories described in Chapter 7. The significant points to be dealt with here are those that exemplify Lacan's view of the nature and vicissitudes of the human subject. As a starting point, it is important to recognise Lacan's affinity with the philosophical school of structuralism, which emphasises the significance of the relationships between things over and above the things themselves. This is an approach particularly attuned to the study of language, where the work of Ferdinand de Saussure, in the early part of the century, laid the foundations for a theory of the linguistic 'sign' that stresses the arbitrariness of the links that are created between words and meanings (loosely, 'signifiers' and 'signifieds') and the way these links can be construed as a series of differences from other possible links. Psychoanalysis, because of its concern with symbolism and the distorted significations that arise through the effect of the unconscious on mental life, also lends itself to a structuralist reading: the interchangeability of symbols, the impact of processes such as condensation (the compression of multiple meanings into a single image) and displacement (representing a meaning by conversion into an analogy that retains its formal properties) and the therapeutic mechanism of transference, all allow scope for the virtuoso decodings of underlying relationship structures that characterises this approach. But Lacan goes further than simply to employ the methods of structuralism in psychoanalysis: he makes psychoanalysis a branch of structuralism, specifically structuralist linguistics.

For Lacan, the human subject is constructed in and through language. This does not imply that there is any particular preexistent subjectivity which learns to express itself in the words made available to it by language, but rather that the initially 'absent' subject becomes concrete through its positioning in a meaning-system which is ontologically prior to it and more extensive than it. The subject, the pronominal 'I', is created through an order that originates outside it, in the flux of intersubjective relationships that surround it and elect it to a place in their midst. Because of this, we are possessed and 'spoken' by language we do not own ourselves, but are constructed according to the possibilities offerred us by words.

> It is the world of words that creates the world of things – the things originally confused in the *hic et nunc* of the all in process of coming-into-being – by giving its concrete being to their essence, and its ubiquity to what has always been. (Lacan, 1953, p. 65)

This quotation makes it clear that Lacan is not just using the structure of language as an analogy for mental structure: he argues for the literal dominance of the 'word' over the construction of psychic organisation through the medium of pre-existent cultural categories. This actually raises a problem which will become clearer in the discussion of feminist psychoanalysis in Chapter 7: although Lacanians refer constantly to 'language', it is not always obvious what is meant by this. It sometimes seems that 'language' is being used in a very general sense to mean all symbolic systems (as in a passage shortly after the above quotation, where Lacan refers to the way 'Symbols in fact envelop the life of man in a [total] network' – Ibid., p. 68), whereas at other times it is precisely language itself – speech, in its narrowest formulation – that is taken to be determinant over psychology. The obvious difficulty with this narrow view is that language is a relatively late achievement in the life of an infant; if a broader view of language is taken, to mean all symbolic discriminations that surround a child, then what is being referred to is something more like 'culture', the relatively durable and pervasive symbolic categories by which a society expresses and perpetuates itself. It may be that culture in this sense has the same, or a similar, structure as language, but they are not the same thing. Nevertheless, it is through use of the wider formulation that Lacan's work seems to have most to offer, particularly for attempts to forge a social psychoanalysis. In this reading, Lacan's principal project is to show how what appears to be our central reality, our 'selfhood', is actually constructed through a series of shifts in which we become inserted into the symbolic order of culture. This process is in important ways one of alienation: in Poster's (1978, p. 89) gloss, 'What ego psychologists call identity, Lacan calls the imaginary. It is just that illusory sense of the self-centredness of desire in the ego which he tries to work against at all points'. A simplified outline of his developmental theory, in terms of the concepts added to those of Freud, will clarify this idea and its implications.

The subject is split during development through a complex process that separates it first from the sense of linkage with the primary object, the mother, and then from the illusory, narcissistic identification of the self as a perfect unity, until the subject's place in the symbolic world is found, and the unconscious produced. According to Lacan, the child begins life as an 'hommelette', her/his desires spreading in all directions, unfettered and unorganised. At this point, s/he is not a human subject, has no sense of the self as the central point of existence; there is no sense of difference, no boundary between desire and gratification. However, even at this stage the child is not immersed in 'the Real', Lacan's term for the unattainable objective wholeness of desire and gratification – a caveat which prevents his theory from proposing simply another version of the undivided ego of object relations theory, or of a romantic state of original bliss. Even at the start of life, the child is immersed in drives which are *partial*, in being already submitted to the possibilities allowed by her/his physical separateness from others, and by the restrictions of the immediate social world, for example, the way in which the child's own desires are already structured by the desire that the mother has formed for her/him before birth. Hence, from the start of life the drives are channelled into erotogenic zones and the child's body becomes divided up in relation to factors outside it. There is no absolute unity or primordial oneness from which the neonate proceeds: the impossibility of the Real is a representation of the notion that the infant is always cut off from the sources of wholeness, always experiences a disjunction between desire and the prospects of fulfilment. From the beginning, therefore, the child is constituted in relation to lack and to loss, and that loss has its form in the absence of the object of the child's desire.

The conversion of the primordial non-subject that is the 'hommelette' into the human subject involves two major splits, change points which cut the infant off from her/his previous position. First is the 'mirror phase' which introduces the child into the Imaginary order, the level of psychological functioning characterised by concern with the 'imago', the series of false images through which the child perceives her/his identity. Simply, the child's perception of her/himself in the mirror (that is, in the gaze or responses of the other with whom the child interacts) leads to a joyful but mistaken perception of bodily unity as the site of a unified self, a parody of all essentialist theories of psychology. Instead of being the subjective centre of the world, the ego in fact comes into being as an 'imaginary capture'; the moment of mistaken self-identification is the beginning of a permanent tendency whereby the subject seeks imaginary wholeness to paper over the conflict, lack and absence beneath. It is important to recognise the fantastic nature of this event: Lacan's image of the mirror phase is very different from the notions of other psychoanalysts. Rose (1982) points out the distinction with Winnicott and Klein: the mother does not mirror the child's actuality back to her/him, thus aiding the development of the true self, as Winnicott suggests, nor does she act as a receptacle for the child's projected drives, as Klein proposes. Rather, Lacan's use of the 'mirror' term has nothing to do with the reality of the child's inner drives, but describes a specious representation of false integrity, in which the mother presents her own vision *to* her infant. The child's perception of her/his 'specular image' thus produces a fiction: the fiction that s/he is whole and has a clearly ascertainable identity, when what is happening is really that the child is *identifying with* a vision that comes from elsewhere.

> But the important point is that this form situates the agency of the ego, before its social determination, in a fictional direction, which will always remain irreducible for the individual alone, or, rather, which will only rejoin the coming-into-being of the subject asymptotically. (Lacan, 1949, p. 2)

The mirror representation provides relief for the child from the tumultuous pressure of drives operating in fragmentation and disarray, and it also makes possible the distinction between self and other (having a view of the integrated self makes the postulation of another feasible) which is necessary for the insertion into the social world. At the same moment that the ego is created as an imaginary identification, it also brings into play one use of the rich Lacanian concept of the 'Other': the self that is thought of as the most intensely personal part of the individual is actually constructed by means of identification with something external, fundamentally other than the subject itself. Rather than being the source from which communications flow, the origin of meaning in a social world, the ego is created only in relation to something outside itself, it is 'inconceivable without the system, so to speak, of the other. The ego is referential to the other. The ego is constituted in relation to the other' (Lacan, in Macey, 1978, p. 116). Hence Lacan's antagonism towards ego psychology: the ego analysts operate to shore up and legitimise a structure which Lacan views as an 'imaginary capture' and a central feature of alienation; it is a fictional ideal serving to distance the subject and construct it in the gaze and order of otherness.

What the mirror phase achieves is an alteration of the infantile psyche from an immersion in fragmentary drives to the experience of integration and hence the possibility of recognition as an individual; the description here is of the origins of a narcissistic self, built on a failure to discriminate between self and other, apparently whole but in fact brought about through alienation. The limitation of this is precisely its narcissism: the imaginary absorption in the gaze of the mother does not allow for the kind of separation between subject and object upon which language is built. More generally, Lacan, following Lévi-Strauss, assumes that culture is defined by its structuring of the possibilities of the relationships between its members; it is only when the narcissistic relationship is interrupted that a fully social human subject is formed. It is the necessity to move beyond the Imaginary order, to encounter the full force of the cultural law, that brings about the second major change point in a child's development.

The second developmental split comes when the subject takes up its place as a member of a social order which predates and extends beyond it. This process is structured around the entry of the child into language, the method by which s/he takes up a position in a signifying chain: to speak, to be part of the language order, the subject has to move from the primary narcissism of the Imaginary to a position from which an outside other can be predicated and spoken to. In this sense language confers individuality on the subject, introducing the I–you dialectic by structuring its position with respect to culture (Macey, 1978). The 'Symbolic order', which is the order of the subject's full constitution as human, is thus the order under which the subject is positioned as a separate, speaking entity, with its subjectivity organised along specifiable routes, specifically those concerned with gender. Once again, this positioning arises from outside the subject, confirming its self-alienation: 'What I seek in speech is the response of the other . . . I identify myself in language, but only by losing myself in it like an object' (Lacan. 1953, p. 86).

The positioning of the subject with respect to language requires an encounter with otherness in a way that fractures the omnipotence of the mirrored 'I' in the Imaginary. If the Imaginary celebrates the fictitious identity of subject and ego, it is the tearing of this identity that produces the positioning of the subject in the Symbolic order, and at the same time constructs the unconscious by repression. For Lacan, the main centre of otherness is the father within the Oedipal situation, whose prohibition of the desire of the child in accordance with the incest taboo acts as the inauguration of culture by demanding that the child's libido becomes structured and also by initiating a series of differences along the male/female axis. The implications of this view for feminist psychoanalysis will be examined in Chapter 7; here, what is important is Lacan's emphasis on the presence of a third term to break the cosy mirror of the Imaginary, a third term which operates as a prohibition and a castration, and thus sets into motion the signifying activity of the subject's incorporation into culture. The incest taboo is not a law of nature, but a place where nature is tamed by culture, where desires that are biologically possible are made socially impermissible: 'The primordial Law is therefore that which in regulating marriage ties superimposes the kingdom of culture on that of a nature abandoned to the law of mating' (Lacan, 1953, p. 66). Human society is founded on the symbolic structurings of kinship patterns rather than the biological ones of procreation, and the positioning of the subject with respect to this structure takes place through the discovery of sexual difference and the repression of desire in the Oedipus/castration complex. Thus, the second 'split' in the construction of the subject is that of the castration complex, the enforced recognition of difference and the internalisation of a prohibition and a loss, which in turn constructs the unconscious. Hence the centrality of language as the communicative network which both insists on difference (or there would be no recognition of the possibility of communication) and provides the pre-given structures whereby relationships take place. Hence, too, one of Lacan's famous slogans: 'the unconscious is structured like a language', for the same processes that give rise to the subject who is part of the symbolic universe of language, produce the internal splits that constitute the unconscious (Coward and Ellis, 1977, p. 115).

The main concern of this section has been with the way Lacan emphasises the 'split' nature of the human subject, the sense in which it is constructed through a process of division, and gains its essential characteristics from this division. The subject can never be present to itself because the only formulation that can be made is through language, in which the subject appears as an alienated 'I', constructed in the discourses that surround it. More fully, the insertion of the human into language depends on an experience of otherness, of absence and of lack: it is only by the perception of a boundary between self and other, and hence of the impossibility of total fulfilment, that the child can formulate a communicable notion of the self; hence, in all its experiences in language, the subject is constantly reiterating its division from its integrity. The thrust of development is therefore not towards greater integration (as in Klein's work), but towards greater division, as the entry into the order of culture constructs the unconscious and sexuality in the awareness of a fundamental absence of gratification. So to Lacan's slogan, 'There is no sexual relation': Rose (1982) shows how this is because the unconscious divides subjects from one another even as it infuses them with the desire for unification.

The concern of Lacanian theory with loss, lack and the impossibility of unification – the impossible hunt for the Real – is exquisitely expressed in the notion of 'desire'. Lacan suggests that an object can only be perceived as such when it has become separated from the infant; that is, in order to long for something, one has already to have lost it. The longed-for object always, therefore, contains its own impossibility within it, a primeval loss which can never be made good. It is this which Lacan refers to as 'desire', this impossibility at the heart of satisfaction. Lacan formulates this as another indication of the significance of splitting in human existence, bringing with it the forlornness of the fiction of reconciliation. Pointing out how 'need' can be satisfied and 'demand' articulated. Lacan shows how sexuality can never be reduced to either of these terms, because it is based upon a desire that is only visible as an absence:

> desire is neither the appetite for satisfaction, nor the demand for love, but the difference that results from the subtraction of the first from the second, the phenomenon of their splitting. (Lacan, 1958, p. 287)

The contrast between this view and those of psychoanalysts who postulate a feasible return to integrity and wholeness could hardly be greater. Lacan's system knows no reconciliation; the Real, the romantic pre-social arena of immersion in full oneness, is always outside the subject, unavailable except through the fictions of the Imaginary. The subject is constructed within the system of social relationships, is never pure and whole, and is always alienated from its origins.

The politics implicit in Lacan's theory are provocative. Many have criticised Lacan for the totalitarian implications of his work: if humanism is a fraud and there is no fundamental human entity that is to be valued in each person, one is left with no way of defending the 'basic rights' of the individual, for the individual is apparently nothing more than her/his construction. The concept of the Real goes some way to alleviate this problem, but it must be admitted that Lacan's position threatens always to slip either into the essentialism it abhors (what is it that makes the 'specular assumption' of identity in the mirror? what are the exact ingredients of the 'hommelette'?) or into such a relentless structuralism that no content at all is allowed the human subject. The difficulties with this will become more apparent in the discussion in Chapter 7, but it can be argued that Lacan's insistence on the constructive primacy of language leads to a form of pessimistic determinism (the subject is fully determined by culture) and can also be used to legitimise oppressive practices (the Symbolic is structured by the Law of the Father, and one cannot escape that). In this respect, notions such as Klein's that the infant possesses directional drives which supply the raw material for constructivist processes, are both more appealing and more logically coherent. Nevertheless, Lacan's theory retains considerable interest, for a number of reasons. First, it presents a powerful assault on the view that the ego should be set at the centre of human psychology. Secondly, it articulates a theory of subjectivity which focuses on its structuring in accordance with cultural forces, and which provides an account of the way these forces operate at the deepest levels of the individual's experience. In Lacanian theory, the subject is never separate from the social world, is always thoroughly permeated by it and liable to the distortions inculcated by the predominant ideology. The subject is, in fact, structured in and by ideology, in the sense of the set of 'as if' formulations through which people comprehend their relationships with the world. These ideological relations are institutionalised in culture and manifested in linguistic practice; as such, they enter into the very centre of human consciousness. This idea, that subjective experience can never be a full encounter with the 'Real', but is always an 'Imaginary' relationship with a world that is socially organised, is an immensely productive one, and has had substantial effects on Marxists (for instance in the work of Althusser), and on feminists. Finally, although it is perverse and difficult, and despite the explanatory difficulties and questionable implications mentioned above, Lacan's theory presents the most radical critique from within psychoanalysis of essentialist assumptions of human integrity, and with this lays the groundwork for a provocative dismantling of the powerful assumptions surrounding 'human nature' with which we are saddled. Arguably, in this radical vision at least, Lacan's work is the closest that we possess to Freud's.

Part III
Psychoanalysis and Politics

Psychoanalysis has often been applied to social issues in a very crude way, effectively reducing social phenomena to psychology, or dismissing radical action as the product of neurosis. There are, however, some more sophisticated traditions which have attempted, with varying degrees of success, to explore the links between social oppression and psychological repression, and in so doing to build a bridge between Marxist theory (seen as lacking an adequate account of subjectivity) and psychoanalysis. Writers in these traditions have tended to take Freud to task for his notion that all societies are by nature repressive, and to argue that this is true only of some societies, that a utopian world can be envisaged in which the repressions will wither away and sexual freedom will be attainable. Chapter 6 discusses two of the most influential of these 'libertarian' approaches, found in the work of Wilhelm Reich and Herbert Marcuse, and contrasts them with some more recent ideas derived from object relations and Kleinian theory. The difficulties shared by the two libertarian accounts is that their biologistic reasoning and orientation towards the expression of sexual desire results in a loss of social perspective and a descent into individualism. The alternative approaches circumvent this problem by focusing on the quality of human relationships as their principal utopian vision; their difficulty is one of over-simplicity and a neglect of the importance of social structures.

Feminist applications of psychoanalysis, the subject of Chapter 7, have been available since the 1920s, but in recent years they have become particularly fruitful. There are two major strands which are compared in this chapter: the first deriving from object relations theory and the second from the work of Lacan. Each has advantages and disadvantages: for example, feminist object relations theory supplies a detailed account of gender-specific development but fails to confront the power of social and cultural structures; post-Lacanian feminism provocatively subverts patriarchal assumptions but risks slipping back into biologism. In the detailed discussion it is suggested that the latter approach may have more to offer a radical theory because it challenges the roots and structures of patriarchal law; whether it escapes that law is a more complicated question.

From Stephen Frosh
"The Politics of Psychoanalysis"
1987. Pub by YALE

6 Libertarian Freudianism

Freud's position on the relationship between individuals and society, expressed most fully in *Civilisation and Its Discontents*, is that the requirements of society are always opposed to the desires of individuals, with human instincts having to be controlled so that the collective can survive. In this view, it is inconceivable for a society to be based on principles of pure pleasure, the unfettered expression of sexual impulse; reality must enter into the organisation of the psyche, both to protect the social fabric against the destructive fury of people's desires and to ensure the mobilisation of psychological energy for the work of civilisation. Thus, a link is formed between the restrictions of society and the direction that repression takes within the individual mind. Through the experiences that the child has with the interpersonal world, such as in the trauma of the Oedipus situation and its consequences (for example, the formation of the super-ego), expression of basic instinctual desires becomes modified and inhibited, and a psychic structure is formed along lines which are compatible with the maintenance of social order. The impact of this process can be seen most clearly in the way the primitive possibilities of the new-born infant become organised around socially viable axes, notably those of gender and admissible sexuality. This is a description of how ordinary development takes place, but it is also, in Freud's hands, a statement concerning the limitations of any programme of social reform. For Freud, all attempts to theorise alternative social configurations must flounder on the necessary opposition of society to individual desires, because these desires are essentially anti-social, seeking pleasure for the individual in a blind and mechanistic way, or containing the potential for rampant destructiveness.

On the face of it, Freud's views are not particularly promising for socialists struggling to develop a view of progress and change: despite his support for reformism, all revolutionary activities are reduced by Freud to 'consolations'. This, amongst other reasons, is why Erich Fromm distinguishes between those aspects of Freud's thought which are liberal or reactionary, rooted in his society, and those more fundamental discoveries such as that of the unconscious which provide a continuing challenge to the bourgeois world (see, for example, Fromm, 1970). However, it is texts such as *Civilisation and its Discontents* that have provided the starting point for most Freudo-Marxists, who have consequently all had to struggle with the irreducible opposition between individual and society that is contained therein. The general line taken by many theorists is that whether or not repression is necessary and universal (on the whole, they think it not), its particular form and intensity will vary across different social systems, with those described by Freud being emblematic of a precise form of capitalism. Repression therefore operates not in the service of nature, but of particular patterns of domination; throwing off repression is thus a viable revolutionary goal. As will be seen, this approach has led to some invigorating theory and polemic, but also to a form of individualism in which it is assumed that at some point when unnecessary social shackles have been removed from the individual, her/his basic humanity can pour forth into happy fulfilment. Jacoby (1975, p. 74) points to the problem with such approaches: 'The various efforts to interpret Marx and Freud have been plagued by reductionism: the inability to retain the tension between individual and society, psychology and political economy.'

An alternative approach builds on another strand of Freudian thinking, the detailed developmental analysis describing how individuals are built up in layers around internalised social forms, themselves the product of history. This approach takes as its focal assumption the idea that individuality arises through a process of social construction, for instance, as described by object relations theorists. It is towards an account such as this that Part 3 tends, with a particular consideration in Chapter 7 of ideas that have been developed under the pressure of feminist theory. This chapter, however, looks first at two of the most influential writers on the liberational potential of psychoanalysis from the point of view of the possibilities for the release of repressed instinct – Willhelm

Reich and Herbert Marcuse. Although they have both been discussed elsewhere, their work retains a resonance with current psychoanalytic preoccupations that makes them important, and they also show in extreme form the consequences of adherence to the instinct theories that have been examined in Part 2. It is this aspect of their work that provides the focus of the account here, rather than a total exposition. In the latter part of this chapter, some recent attempts to sketch a possible approach towards a political psychoanalysis that employs concepts from the 'British school' (object relations and Kleinian theory) will be outlined as a way into the material surrounding feminism.

The Reichian revolution

One strand of 'Freudo-Marxism' originated with the extraordinary figure of Wilhelm Reich, at one time viewed as an outstandingly promising psychoanalyst, who took his search for the material basis of psychology into the realms of flying saucers and the universal substance, orgone energy, trappable in special boxes, agent of cancer cures, foundation of love. Reich's origins lie in the response to the failure of the revolutionary movement in Europe after the First World War: at the moment when economic and political conditions appeared right for socialist insurrection, the tide turned, and from the uncovered sands sprang fascism. Reich was amongst the earliest committed revolutionaries to perceive the relevance of psychological factors in these events, the sense in which subjective as well as 'objective' factors have to be favourable before change can occur. Where he differed from that earlier psychoanalytic socialist, Adler, was in the strength of his commitment (until the mid-1930s) to both the revolutionary and the psychoanalytic movements, and in his relentless, increasingly monomaniacal insistence on the primacy of sexuality as the mobilising agent of personal history.

In his practice and in his theory, Reich follows the line that ideology is a central component of social oppression. The task of psychoanalysis – a task still stressed amongst contemporary writers – is to give an account of the mechanisms by which the economic and political base of society could become internalised to form the set of unconscious beliefs and aspirations that so dominate individual life. It is not that there is some automatic link between economic structures and psychology, as is often taken to be implied in the traditional Marxist notion that consciousness is 'superstructural', following on from the determining structures of economic organisation. Reich clearly recognises the 'cleavage' between these two practices in his insistence on the importance of sexual revolution. Rather, the psychological processes of the individual are understood to intervene between economic structure and ideological superstructure to prevent such a simple relationship, and it is the task of psychoanalysis to trace this intervention. As Jacoby (1975, p. 93) points out, in Reich's approach this intervention has a negative character, suggesting that 'the more rational the behaviour, that is, the more in tune with class consciousness, the less the need for psychological interpretations'. The irrationality of personal psychology is itself, however, socially produced, in particular through family life; that is, there enters into each person a set of inhibitory and distorting factors which prevent a 'natural' response to instinctual impulses and social conditions. Psychoanalysis is therefore a process of undoing, of lifting the repressions and releasing the individual to act in accordance with her/his underlying desires – which are always, in Reich's view, sexual.

Reich argues that the primary life force, repressed with extreme viciousness in patriarchal–authoritarian systems, is sexuality, meaning the ability to express and experience one's true nature in (heterosexual) orgasm. It is here that Reich's attractiveness to the 1960s' libertarians resided, and it is also here that one of his most profound limitations inheres. Mitchell (1974) provides the best description and critique available, highlighting the tremendous emphasis in Reich not just on sexuality, but on a particular form of sexuality – genitality. Whereas Freud carefully delineates the various stages in the construction of adult sexuality (oral, anal, phallic, genital), Reich thinks only in terms of how society prevents the expression of something which is already natural and whole, the in-built, biological urge towards the heterosexual orgasmic embrace. The word 'biological' is important here: it is as if neurosis enters in with thinking, as if there is some automatic form of sexual expression which is biologically coded and necessary, and in which mental health inheres.

> My contention is that every individual who has managed to preserve a bit of naturalness knows that there is only one thing wrong with neurotic patients: the *lack of full and repeated sexual satisfaction*. (Reich, in Mitchell, 1974, p. 158)

All neurotics are sexually dissatisfied, all sexually dissatisfied people are neurotic. Fantasy, upon which psychoanalysis builds its expertise, is relegated to an epiphenomenon of repression in Reich's approach; it is the biological naturalness underneath, the bodily urge, that is primary and healthy, with fantasy only being its substitute. The unconscious, therefore, is not the repository of ideas, but only of instincts; ideas are a substitute for genital love.

> There is a sinister anti-intellectualism about Reich's theory of the origin of repression. Repression began the moment man made the mistake of thinking about himself, ceasing to trust his 'instinctual judgement'. (Rieff, 1966, p. 131)

Even in his early works, Reich's insistence on the primacy of genital sexuality above all things held the seeds of his descent into biological reductionism which, in turn, became cosmic biological mysticism.

Reich proposes not only that the economic process is coded in consciousness, but also that it is internalised in the character of the individual, using 'character' in the sense of the repressive armour which separates the socialised surface of the individual from the 'deep natural core'. The notion of 'character' has been an important one for Marxist psychoanalysts, particularly of the Frankfurt school, but Reich produced his own distinctively holistic version. For him, character referred to the regimentation of the personality in the light of repression:

> While the symptom corresponds essentially to a single experience or striving, the character represents the specific way of being an individual, an expression of his total past. (Reich, in Mitchell, 1974, p. 167)

Character, especially as 'character-armour', is the rigidified history of repression, defending against the inner rumblings of sexual desire and converting the natural human into the petrified automaton. This explains the apparently autonomous force of ideology: character structure is formed in childhood and therefore embodies the ideology of an earlier era, the 'force of tradition'. Because tradition is built into the personality of each individual, it is capable of maintaining a social order completely at odds with the logic of economic development and the reality of human needs: 'sexual inhibition changes the structure of economically suppressed man in such a way that he acts, feels and thinks contrary to his own material interests' (Reich, 1946, p. 66). It is the real needs, the 'deep, natural core' of the human, that must break through the repressive armoury of character if social change is to come about: 'the instincts and the proletariat must triumph together, or not at all' (Rieff, 1966, p. 126).

Reich articulates an important theme in radical critiques of Freud by asserting that Freud had been mistaken in believing repression to be an unavoidable consequence of any form of social organisation. In Reich's view, the confusion here is between that which is historically constructed and that which is natural: repression is not natural, but is a product of a particular form of society, the 'patriarchal–authoritarian' form. This has its central power base in the family, through which the oppressive injustices of capitalism are translated, in early experience, into the child's character. The Oedipus complex, for example, through which so much of the child's personality is organised, is produced by the structure of the family under capitalism and transmits to the child the (ideological) values of the parents, derived from their own position in the productive process. From the family and its repression of the natural instincts of the child, the perpetuation of reactionary politics is generated: for example, Reich argues that it was precisely the ruthless sexual repression to which the lower middle class Germanic child was exposed that created the authoritarian fixation upon which Nazism fed. Reducing the psychological essence of the child to her/his sexuality, Reich describes the formation of these half-people and their damaged society:

> The interlacing of the socio-economic structure with the sexual structure of society and the structural reproduction of society takes place in the first four or five years and in the authoritarian family . . . It [the family] becomes the factory in which the state's structure and ideology are moulded. (Reich, 1946, p. 64)

The patriarchal family's repression of the child's natural sexuality leaves her/him permanently maimed, submissive, apprehensive of authority and incapable of rebellion. Reich does not suggest, as some radicals have done, that more repression will produce more revolutionary fervour: sexual repression, because it withdraws sexual needs from consciousness and 'anchors itself as a moral defence' (Ibid.) prevents revolt against *both* economic and personal oppression. This is not, of course, an historically necessary state of affairs: with typical simplicity, Reich assumes that because patriarchy is reactionary, matriarchy must have been the original 'natural' and free form of social organisation. The replacement of matriarchy with patriarchy, epitomised in the institution of monogamous marriage, inculcates repression into previously free love; hence, overturning monogamy is a necessary step on the way to sexual and political freedom. More generally, any successful political revolution presupposes a sexual revolution, otherwise all the old authoritarian structures, embedded as they are in character and in personal relationships, will return. Translating this theory into practice, Reich established 'socialist' sex clinics giving psychoanalytic advice to the masses and aiming to arouse in them an awareness of the sexual reforms that must accompany a socialist revolution. He also worked out in detail such ideological weapons as legal protection for children against the sexual tyranny of parents, guaranteeing them the right to masturbate and play sexually with their peers, and encouraging adolescents to have sexual intercourse. Socialism would be built on the rock of these new children, free of the tortuous restrictiveness of socially induced sexual repression. Just as Reichian therapy was to be an active assault on all the rigidities of the character, as expressed in the body, so Reich's version of social rebellion parodies the traditional aims of therapy, at one and the same time ignoring psychoanalysis and reducing social revolt to sexual rebellion. Gradually in Reich's work, sexual revolt becomes not just a necessary concomitant of political revolution, but its essential component; in much of his writing it even appears as both a necessary and a sufficient condition for change. Remove the repressions that govern sexuality, he seems to be saying, and all the fundamental liberational drives of personal desire will be brought to the fore, which will blow away the old, dead world of character-rigidity and economic slavery, replacing it with a new order of universal embrace (genital only).

The strengths and weaknesses of Reich's position are fairly clear, and have been taken over into much subsequent work. On the one hand, he articulates the modern notion that political structures enter into the core of individuality, constructing each person's consciousness and creating personality characteristics around ideological axes. In so doing, he avoides the simple reduction of psychological phenomena to sociological ones that so plagues Marxist thought – the notion that consciousness is purely superstructural, determined entirely by the economic base of society. The reductionist view makes ideology a matter of only secondary significance, being little more than a misguided way of looking at things which is generated automatically by the individual's class position. Reich delineates a broader concept of ideology as something that determines not just a person's perceptions, but her/his character; thus, he moves rather close to the contemporary notion of ideology as a way of living in the world, of taking up a stance towards the fundamental structures of sociality which is in turn capable of influencing them profoundly. On the other hand, Reich's account of ideology still treats it as an error or distortion of reality, introduced to deny the individual access to her/his basic desires, which constitute her/his true natural core. Nevertheless, the manner in which Reich describes the insertion of ideology into this natural core is actually both subtle and helpful, particularly his account of the tendencies central to the patriarchal–authoritarian family.

The main difficulty with Reich's approach, then, does not centre so much on the details of his account of how society influences each individual's development, but on the *principle* that there is something fundamentally 'true' and healthy within the human personality, which is only waiting to recover from the assaults of ideological distortion in order to find its proper expression. This idea is always problematic, as it resolves into an appeal to 'human nature' which stands in danger of fixing the personality as unchangeable, as statements about the 'natural aggresiveness' of humans so frequently demonstrate. In Reich's case, the reduction is to a pan-sexual theory in which sexual energy is seen as the physically measurable natural driving force of the individual, to be liberated as part of a socialist revolution, thence to achieve satisfaction in an untrammelled playground of instinctual desire. It is in this sexual essentialism (the irreducible core of humanity is sexuality) that lie the seeds of Reich's later desertion of earthly politics for those of the universe: class, economic and political practice, as well as ideology – these are all concepts which become subservient to sexual desire. Even in his early works, where Reich avoids the simple reduction of politics to sexual liberation, it is clear that it is the latter that fascinates him, and which also prevents him from uncovering a path towards a genuinely socialist future. For whereas socialism is concerned with the possibilities of enriched relationships between people that are more egalitarian and less oppressive and limited than those available under capitalism, Reich has virtually nothing to say about relationships as such. His utopia is not concerned with a more developed network of social relationships; rather, it is libertarian in the most individualistic of senses, a system under which each individual's biological urges are to be played out in complete freedom. This form of politics returns to the individual rather than to the transformation of social structures which constitutes the progression to socialism. Consequently, and whatever the intent, politics is reduced to biology just as irrevocably and uselessly as mental life is reduced to attempts to achieve orgasm. By assaulting the entire concept of the mind, which is in the end the result of his programme, Reich removes all the subtlety of psychoanalysis' politics, leaving only sex (good) and society (bad).

Eros and civilisation

Much of the trouble with Reich's theory derives from his vision of the unconscious as a repository of repressed sexual instinct, this repression being a simple product of a specific oppressive form of society. Beginning with these premises, his radical vision could hardly be other than individualistic: throw off the repressions and humans will return to their supposed natural state, happily enjoying orgasm. While this may appear to be a particularly absurd instance of an off-the-rails theory, its fashionability is only just past, and always threatens to return as the glimmerings that people get of the alienations and distortions of their desires under capitalism push them in pursuit of the haunting, romantic mirage of their 'real' nature. This can occur even with theories that are sophisticated in their account of society and that avoid the Reichian descent into undifferentiated sexuality: all that is necessary is to fetishise the body in a way that is neglectful of social relationships. Marcuse's (1955) attempt to revolutionise Freudianism is an important case study in this regard. Denounced by the post-Freudians, particularly Erich Fromm, whose own 'cultural' endeavours he mercilessly dismantles, Marcuse's *Eros and Civilisation* was another key text for the 1960s, and remains a provocative and important document, as Jacoby's (1975) rewriting of it indicates. It has many attractions and excitements, and with Norman Brown's (1959) *Life against Death* presents one of the most fruitful advances towards a psychoanalytic theory of art and culture. With all this, however, *Eros and Civilisation* never escapes from the indictment that it has nothing to offer those who wish their revolutionary society to be one in which relationship values are prioritised and individual desire is put in the service of all. Painful as it is to accede to Fromm's strictures, for Marcuse has clearly revealed the paucity of the neo-Freudian's own attempts to add Marx to Freud, there is something to be said for his side of the vendetta:

> Marcuse's revolutionary rhetoric obscures the irrational and anti-revolutionary character of his attitude. Like some avant-garde artists and writers from de Sade and Marinetti to the present, he is attracted by infantile regression, perversions and . . . in a more hidden way by destruction and hate. (Fromm, 1970, p. 31)

Something, but not everything, for Marcuse's approach is an honest attempt to take Freudian theory and explore its own inherent radicalness, avoiding the portmanteau nature of most Freudo-Marxist endeavours. In his terms, the only departure he makes from Freud is to suggest that Freud's pessimism over the possibilities for a non-repressive civilisation is belied by his own theory, both inherently in that the logic of the theory is liberational, and extrinsically in that society has reached that point at which the revolutionary overthrow of repression is made viable. So whereas the neo-Freudians add bits to Freud to make his approach palatable, Marcuse argues that the historical substance of Freud's theories is to be recaptured through unfolding their own content, and that psychoanalysis is *essentially* an account of the repressions engendered within the individual by history; that is, it is a socially critical theory. The particular content he lights upon is that aspect of metapsychology most damned by post-Freudians – the theory of Life and Death Instincts, coupled with a radical revision of the notions of pleasure and reality principles.

Marcuse faces head-on the challenge of Freud's instinct theory, which is read by most people as being a hindrance to the development of a socially responsive account of human psychology. For Marcuse, much as for Reich, the existence of an instinctual component to mental life is a profoundly optimistic notion, because it suggests that whatever repressions may occur, however frozen through countless generations of oppression and dominance may be the possibilities for full existence, there is always an alternative, residing timelessly in the unconscious, plotting subversion. 'The *return of the repressed*', announces Marcuse, 'makes up the tabooed and subterranean history of civilisation' (1955, p. 16). Freud's concentration on the vicissitudes of the instincts allows one to build up a universal history of humankind, one that recognises that a repressive organisation of the instincts underlies all historical forms of domination, and hence that what we take to be the expression of our selves in ordinary life is actually a socially created distortion of the possibilities that lie inside us. All this is familiar from Freud's own account; where Marcuse starts to differ is in his view of the nature of the primary instincts. He takes seriously Freud's late theory of Life and Death Instincts (preferring the terms Eros and Thanatos), but he seems less clear about whether their apparent dualism is real or whether they represent a split in one major, primordial energic instinct. This is a significant issue for Marcuse because of his advocacy of instinctual liberation: if Thanatos is only destructive, its liberation can never do more than wreck the social world and individual life, and its constraint is always, consequently, necessary. In part, Marcuse's answer to this dilemma concerns the relative strengths of the respective instincts, with an Eros of renewed power having the ability to counter the force of destructiveness and overcome Thanatos (Robinson, 1970). Thus, for example, Marcuse describes how work of certain kinds derives its energy from Thanatos but, because it operates in the interests of culture, also strengthens and enhances Eros – an argument and attitude towards culture rather different from that of Freud.

> In attacking, splitting, changing, pulverising things and animals (and, periodically, also men), man extends his domination over

> the world and advances to ever richer stages of civilisation. (Marcuse, 1955, p. 52)

But he also expends some intellectual energy on whether there may be a monistic principle behind *both* instincts: for example, as Eros seeks satisfaction in the reduction of sexual tension, and Thanatos seeks it in the reduction of energic matter to rest, it seems possible that behind both instincts lies a common origin, and hence that Thanatos is always tempered by Eros, making instinctual expression without devastation a theoretical possibility. The problem of the aggressiveness implicit in the Freudian instincts is, however, never fully resolved by Marcuse and is a characteristic lapse in the libertarian position, which tends conveniently to overlook the pain involved to self and others in instinctual liberation.

Marcuse is more enamoured of Eros than Thanatos, despite Fromm's pillorying of him as nihilistic. He deals directly with Freud's idea that sexuality has to be repressed, both because it is inherently subversive and also because its energy has to be drained off to fuel the work of building civilisation. For Marcuse, Eros is only anti-social because it is distorted by the interests of domination: Eros pure and unfettered is constructive and unifying, and need not destroy society. Against the idea of an inevitable conflict between pleasure and reality militates

> the idea of the unifying and gratifying power of Eros, chained and worn out in a sick civilisation. This idea would imply that the *free* Eros does not preclude lasting civilised societal relations. (Marcuse, 1955, p. 44)

Psychoanalysis, of course, is the science of how this fails to come about, of how repression enters into the mind. The concept of repression is crucial here, forming the centre of Marcuse's account of the operations of domination and the possibilities for change.

Marcuse distinguishes between two forms of repression, 'basic repression', which is the constraint on instinct enforced by scarcity, and 'surplus repression', the intensification of that constraint by the hierarchical distribution of scarcity and labour. Intriguingly, he appears to have a positive view of basic repression. It is not simply that repression has been necessary to make possible the work of civilisation, which is Freud's argument, but that basic repression can act in the service of Eros by heightening the pleasure available to the individual through channelling instinctual drives into personally meaningful modes of expression.

> Such restrictions of the instincts may first have been enforced by scarcity and by the protracted dependence of the human animal, but they have become the privilege and distinction of man which enabled him to transform the blind necessity of the fulfilment of want into desired gratification. (Marcuse, 1955, p. 38)

In recognising the existence of *some* repression under all forms of social organisation, Marcuse draws attention to its historical components – not nature but *second* nature, the encrustations of the history of civilisation as they have been passed down across generations. But he also, as in the quotation above, revalues it as something producing particular human capacities for enjoyment and fulfilment; in a rare moment in which genitality appears to be approved of, Marcuse suggests that the progress to genitality through the 'containment' of partial sexual impulses belongs to this basic layer of repression which makes intensified pleasure possible. *Surplus-repression*, on the other hand, refers specifically to the restrictions upon the instincts that are compounded with basic repression in the interests of domination, and hence are always opposed to Eros. Surplus repression is not a simple addition, but in the history of civilisation has become intextricably entwined with basic repression, converting its positive potentialities into destruction and alienation, for example, by organising the conventional progress to genitality in such a way that the partial instincts are 'all but desexualised in order to conform to the requirements of a specific social organisation of the human existence' (p. 38). The addition of the concept of surplus repression makes repression a specifically historical notion, and one which depends on the organisation of any particular society: the necessity of repression varies with the maturity of civilisation, at least in terms of the extent of achieved mastery over nature through technology; given a constant level of repression, more will be 'surplus' in a culture of plenty than in one of scarcity. An assessment of the repressiveness of society thus depends on an analysis of human possibilities within a particular economic/technological structure; Marcuse's summary statement of all this makes it clear how this particular iron may enter the soul.

> Within the total structure of the repressed personality, surplus-repression is that portion which is the result of specific societal conditions sustained in the specific interests of domination. The extent of this surplus-repression provides the standard of measurement: the smaller it is, the less repressive is the stage of civilisation. The distinction is equivalent to that between the biological and the historical sources of human suffering. (Marcuse, 1955, pp. 87–8)

Here we have not simply an account of the vicissitudes of the instincts, but a 'standard' by which civilisation may be assessed. Characteristically, this standard is an individualistic one suggesting a rather specific view of what human nature might be: it is the treatment of the *individual's instincts* that is the measure of the quality of any social organisation – a different measure, for example, from one concentrating on the quality of human *relationships* that any society makes possible. Marcuse rarely moves into consideration even of two-person encounters; his concern is always with the liberation of individual desire. Be that as it may; having identified a standard, Marcuse uses it to measure contemporary civilisation and, not surprisingly, finds it wanting.

Marcuse places considerable emphasis on Freud's distinction between the pleasure principle and the reality principle, seeing the replacement of the former by the latter as 'the great traumatic event in the development of man' (1955, p. 15), even though this replacement is never secure, and leaves vestiges of pleasure within the life of the individual and in the artefacts of culture. Marcuse even adopts Freud's notion of the 'primal horde' and the killing of the father, using it as a myth containing important symbolic statements on the development of guilt and the general crime against the pleasure principle which ensues whenever successful liberation is followed by the restoration of oppressive authority. Where Marcuse differs from Freud, however, is in his reading of the particular contents of the reality principle. Opposing Freud's view that the reality principle is fixed by the facts of scarcity and the necessity to preserve society, Marcuse contends that there are numerous possible reality principles, the particular one employed being economically and ideologically determined. Just as the quantity of surplus repression marks the degree of repressiveness in any society, so the quality of that repression (i.e. the particular reality principle in operation) indicates the peculiar structure of domination characteristic of any society and of its history. In contemporary capitalist society, the prevailing form of the reality principle is the 'performance principle', under which society is stratified according to the competitive economic performance of its members. The performance principle is thus an instrument of domination rather than a 'natural' entity, and the repression it engenders is predominantly surplus, geared towards the reproduction of certain forms of power rather than the creation of the greatest possible residue of pleasure. In particular, the mode of existence characteristic of life under the sway of the performance principle is one of alienation, in the economic sense as one in which the ownership of the means of production is out of the hands of those who labour, and in the more profoundly psychological sense that all of life is reduced to a depersonalised hierarchy of useful performances in which one sells oneself as a commodity. Instead of expressing one's own desire in libidinally charged work – the work of Eros – under the performance principle libido is diverted for socially useful performances, 'useful' here signifying that which supports the interests of domination and expedites the conversion of body and mind into the instruments of alienated labour. Sexuality, too, is devastated by the activities of domination. Not only is all non-procreative sex suppressed so as to release energy for work, but the *organisation* of sexuality mimics the hierarchical and centralised organisation of social life under capitalism, for instance, by centralising the various objects of the partial instincts into one desired object of the opposite sex, or through the dominance of genitality over all pre-genital forms. Desires thus become alienated and organised in one fell swoop, signifying and expressing the repressiveness of society just as clearly as they indicate the poverty of individual living.

Marcuse has an almost eschatological view of how the repressiveness of life under the performance principle escalates in late capitalism. As technology advances, the potential for pleasure increases and more repression becomes surplus: there is no longer any need for so much repression from the point of view of the realistic limitations imposed by scarcity. But in the interests of domination, the repressed tendencies of the instincts cannot be allowed through; more energy is devoted to warding off the possibilities for rebellion by increasing the extent to which the productive capacities of the new technological society are turned *against* the individuals who might otherwise be liberated by its potentialities. This appears not simply in the grossest instances of state repressiveness and brutality, but more powerfully in the construction of an individual psyche which is a pure manifestation of alienation, from desire as well as the products of labour. Whereas under early capitalism the social focus on production at least allowed the worker her/his leisure time, however small, under late capitalism the urgency of consumption and the necessity for control of an otherwise restless stratum of desire has led to a stronger focus on the subjectivity of the worker, on manipulating her/his perception of needs until they match the requirements of sociality. This phenomenon is present in the manipulation of consciousness through the presentations of the communications media and in the valorising of empty pursuits – even including a sexuality laundered of its subversive possibilities by an absorption in gimmicky eroticism. It is also present in the decline of the family, the role of which is reduced to that of a symbol of the wider power of the administered society. Fathers are no longer dominating, threatening figures worthy both of terror and identification; instead, fathers are replaced by extra-familial impulses which propose identifications with the newest, emptiest and most confusing residues of banality and substitute excitement. *Eros and Civilisation* has been criticised for its neglect of the Oedipus complex as well as for an apparent nostalgia for the family (Poster, 1978), but Marcuse is making a significant point here about the incursions of administration into the individual psyche:

> As domination congeals into a system of objective administration, the images that guide the development of the superego become depersonalised . . . all domination assumes the form of administration. (1955, p. 98)

As alienation increases, the life-enhancing energy of Eros becomes more and more attenuated, human desires withering into apathy under the force of a totally administered society, itself consequently drifting towards a whimpering end. In this tale of woe, Marcuse paints as convincing a picture of contemporary society as any, and paves the way for the later work on narcissism of Lasch (1979) and others. On the other hand, whether his own recipe for the overturning of the administered society itself contributes to the advance of narcissism is a matter for consideration.

Given the power of Marcuse's description of the automatism of contemporary society, it is perhaps surprising to discover a strong strand of optimism in his account of the possibilities for immediate liberation (although in the 'Political Preface' to the 1966 edition of *Eros and Civilisation* he does not seem so sure). This optimism resides in part in a general tendency to locate the 'truth' of the individual in aspects of her/himself that lie outside performance, and that are somehow preserved in a personal core which is independent of the demands of the reality principle – another essentialist idea. More specifically, Marcuse places faith in the technological advances of capitalism, which have made it possible to envisage a world without scarcity (no Third World here) through what is in a sense *total alienation*: the replacement of all labour by machine work that then releases the individual to the world beyond the demands of production, in which it is free rather than labour time that defines the essence of a person's life, and in which play rather than work becomes the central activity. Under such conditions, the performance principle will wither away, and with it the organisation of the instincts, leading in the end to a gradual elimination of surplus repression and a strengthened libido that can absorb or neutralise destructiveness (p. 131). How is all this to come about? Through phantasy, polymorphous perversity and a new order of reality.

Phantasy (Marcuse's spelling) is given an important position in the Marcusian scenario, as 'one mental activity that retains a high degree of freedom from the reality principle even in the sphere of the developed consciousness' (p. 140). Phantasy, also called imagination, retains the tendencies of the psyche before it has been organised by the reality principle, and envisions the reassertion of the primordial oneness between playful pleasure and reality. As such, phantasy is not just a reminiscence of times past and lost, but also a probe into the future, a portion of hope that lives within us and attests to the reality of utopian possibility. Hence comes Marcuse's concern with the liberational possibilities of art: however much art reduces the power of its message through the appeasing reconciliations of aesthetics, it also presents for all to see an image of what is possible beyond the performance principle. Connected with this focus on phantasy is Marcuse's valorisation of 'polymorphous perversity'. If it is the performance principle that reduces the possibilities of pleasure to those of procreational genitality, it is in the interests of subverting the performance principle that Marcuse advocates a regressive liberation of pre-genital (or extra-genital) impulses to restore the primary function of sexuality – pleasure rather than procreation. The perversions are the revolutionary vanguard here: they 'express rebellion against the subjugation of sexuality under the order of procreation, and against the institutions which guarantee this order' (Marcuse, 1955, pp. 49–50). The perversions also present a danger to the revolutionary society, however: that in opposing procreation so forcefully they will serve the interests of the Death Instinct. Fromm (1970) puts this same point differently by accusing Marcuse, who glorifies the 'Great Refusal' of the order of procreative sexuality, of advocating a 'refusal to grow up, to separate fully from mother and soil, and to experience fully sexual pleasure (genital and not anal or sadistic)' (p. 32). Poster (1978), too, argues that because the perversions are repetitions of component instincts and childhood traumas, they cannot represent a real alternative sexuality: 'The way to affirmative sexuality, according to Freud, can only be through genital sexuality' (p. 60). But Marcuse's argument is that the subversion of genitality is to take place in the context of an overturning of the performance principle through social as well as psychological forces, and that the new order of reality that this will give rise to will be enough to restructure the significance of the perversions. Liberation of the instincts will have constructive consequences if it takes place once civilisation has done its work of producing the conditions for the overcoming of scarcity and for the formation of a humanity that can find its essence in sensuous play. The regressed libido will then spread to all parts of the body, libidinising it but not causing it to manifest destructive tendencies: the social transformations involved in this explosion of desire mark a crucial difference between promiscuity under the performance principle and true sensual liberation.

> The free development of transformed libido within transformed institutions . . would *minimise* the manifestations of *mere* sexuality by integrating them into a larger order, including the order of work. (p. 202)

Sexuality 'grows into' Eros; repressive reason gives way to 'a new *rationality of gratification* in which reason and happiness coverge' (p. 224). Finally, although the conflict between Eros and Thanatos remains problematic, Eros triumphs through libidinising all things constructively enough to serve its interests. For example, the obstructions and limitations placed upon Eros by internal considerations would enhance pleasure by 'swelling the tide of libido to its height'; individuals would face each other without the constraints of a reality principle imposed from outside, but in terms of their own internal needs and desires. And death, though retaining its eventual power, would lose its sting; the task of Eros would be both to struggle against death and to allow people to die with dignity.

> The necessity of death does not refute the possibility of final liberation. Like the other necessities, it can be made rational – painless. Men can die without anxiety if they know that what they love is protected from misery and oblivion. (p. 236).

A hint of humanism here, perhaps, in this most anti-humanist of writers? Certainly, there is no shortage of optimism, of faith in the benevolence of human nature and even (with ecological blindness) of the technology developed under capitalism.

Many aspects of Marcuse's theory caught the imagination of radicals in the 1960s and 1970s, and with good reason. As a critic of conformist tendencies he is without parallel; as a documenter of authoritarianism and bureaucratisation within the 'administered society' he is challenging and subversive. In addition, his use of biological concepts ('instinct') to subvert biological categories and demonstrate the confusions of 'nature' and 'second nature' which so support all reactionary ideologies is a powerful spur to liberational activity. But it was perhaps Marcuse's similarity to Reich which proved irresistible to the pleasure-seeking, individualistic 1960s, and which has hampered psychoanalysis from creating a satisfactory radical philosophy of its own. Where Reich sees revolution in the full genital embrace of orgasm, so Marcuse opposes the repressive structuring of the psyche with an exhortation to polymorphous perversity and the play of the instincts which, however dressed up in the guise of a new order of rationality, can only be individualistic and libertarian. Neither theorist has a detailed view of a society structured to allow a different order of sexuality which would be less repressive (to the individual) and oppressive (to others) at the same time. Instead, they paint a picture of a world in which there is no organisation, in which play is the highest good, sexuality bursting out libidinously and energetically, aggression conveniently having withered away in the process. There is *no* society in this view: social relations are reduced to pure, unproblematic and unmediated encounters between totally unalienated individuals. The problem here, in both Reich and Marcuse, is not just a failure to consider properly the institutions of a socialist society which might make possible improved conditions of individual existence, but a more pervasive failure to consider relationships at all. Theirs is a psychology which stops at the boundaries of the individual: it makes no difference where one's sexual desires are aimed, as long as they achieve expression. Marcuse's insistence that under a transformed society libidinal expression will always resolve into constructive and straightforward relationships is certainly utopian, and not just in the benign sense. It is also built on a neglect of the difficulties engineered into the psyche by the complexities of personal encounters in all envisionable worlds – a neglect reflected in his devaluation of the detailed psychoanalytic theory of how the axes of personality are formed through interactions with specific others, themselves the carriers of social and ideological messages. A radical psychoanalysis needs to deal seriously with these issues and to concern itself with the social structures that make the pains and confusions inherent in development manageable and constructive. Libertarian theory wishes away these difficulties in a utopian vision of how the existing patterns of dominance are to be swept into history; this vision is good for morale, but useless for strategy. It can, finally, never be a satisfactory psychology for any genuine attempt to build a world in which social relationships take a new, more progressive form.

Alternatives to libertarianism: revisionism

The best known criticisms of libertarian Freudianism, particularly as reflected in Marcuse's work, have come from those who might loosely be termed 'psychoanalytic humanists', but are more conventionally known as the 'cultural school' – particularly Erich Fromm. Opposing Marcuse for his individualistic and nihilistic leanings and opposing ego psychologists for their neglect of the unconscious and their concern with adaptation, Fromm proposes that psychoanalysis should become again 'a critical and challenging theory in the spirit of radical humanism' (1970, p. 45). Whereas ego psychologists have developed a psychology of rationality which threatens to obscure all radical impulses in Freud's work, Fromm's project is an 'id psychology' which extends psychoanalysis away from a limiting concern with sexuality.

> This revised psychoanalysis will continue to descend ever more deeply into the underworld of the unconscious, it will be critical of all social arrangements that warp and deform man, and it will be concerned with the processes that could lead to the adaptation of society to the needs of man, rather than man's adaptation to society. (Fromm, 1970, p. 45)

The regions other than sexuality into which psychoanalytic enquiry is to be extended are 'alienation, anxiety, loneliness, the fear of feeling deeply, lack of activeness, lack of joy' (Ibid). This list makes it clear that Fromm focuses on the problem of alienation, of the separateness that each person feels and attempts to deal with in their engagements with others. Here, he draws productively on existentialism: the fundamental truth of each of us is our aloneness, and it is the desire to overcome this that structures our existence. Healthy development depends on recognition of our separateness – that is, facing up to reality in an authentic and clear-minded way. The problem is that the potential that each person has for such authenticity is systematically distorted by society, which, in late capitalism, is dedicated to the production of certain kinds of character types (particularly those conducive to consumerism) that result in a stunting of growth and the perpetuation of specific forms of neurosis. In suggesting that there are distinct types of society which exploit people in different ways and develop varying patterns of repression and character type, Fromm is opposing the Freudian view on the fixed nature of repression and aligning himself with those who argue that it is historically determined. But Fromm is also against the pessimism of Marcuse concerning the possibilities for individual development within the pre-revolutionary world: whereas Marcuse argues that a total transformation of society is necessary for people to achieve their full potential, Fromm suggests that authentic living is always possible, once conventional neurotic responses to the aloneness of the self are recognised and surpassed. Marx and Freud together provide the analytical tools which make this possible, while humanism asserts the preciousness of each individual's being, and the potential that each person holds for a flowering of the personality in creativity and loving-kindness.

There is a certain amount that is of interest in Fromm's work – more than in the rest of the 'cultural school'. This particularly resides in his examination of some neurotic social tendencies, such as in his book *The Fear of Freedom* (1942), and in his own version of the criticisms of ego psychology, with which his antagonists have not always credited him fully. However, Fromm's concern with 'humanism' contains a drift towards moralism which cannot be said to be productive for radical discourse. His humanism reduces, as much humanism does, to the title of his 1956 book, *The Art of Loving*, and places the onus for change on individuals:

> I submit that if people would truly accept the Ten Commandments or the Buddhist Eightfold Path as the effective principle to guide their lives, a dramatic change in the whole culture would take place. (Fromm, 1968, p. 143)

This is the optimistic rhetoric that resides in much post-Freudian theory: focusing upon the way the individual's basic goodness is lost in society leads to a concern with individual change, whatever the socialist gloss. The suggestion is that humans are initially integrated and potentially good, loving and whole; it is different aspects of this essential perfection which are stunted under different social systems. Inherent in the individual is a potential for growth which can be activated by turning inwards (as in 'growth' theories such as those of Maslow and Frankl) and by expressing or discharging emotions. Marcuse (1955) and Jacoby (1975) have carried out an extensive hatchet job on this kind of thinking, with special reference to Fromm's work, so only the main points need to be reiterated here. Marcuse's is the more penetrating of the two critiques, with the most important argument contained early in his Introduction:

> In shifting the emphasis from the unconscious to the conscious, from the biological to the cultural factors, they [the 'neo-Freudians'] cut off the roots of society in the instincts and instead take society at the level on which it confronts the individual as his ready-made 'environment' without questioning its origin and legitimacy. (Marcuse, 1955, p. 6)

While this is somewhat neglectful of the distinction between Fromm's work and that of the ego psychologists, its thrust is accurate. Fromm and the cultural school advocate the addition of social values to psychoanalysis to make up for Freud's overwhelming concentration on the instinctual and (by implication) the biological. By doing this, however, they externalise social values so that the social environment appears as something ready-made, able to distort the consciousness of individuals, while the individual essence is also theorised as something prefabricated, and not constructed in and by social relations. This can be seen in the emphasis upon the 'total personality' of the individual, and in Fromm's belief that authentic living is possible in any society – a matter of choosing to live better and more honestly.

A perspective of this kind fails to examine the deepest levels at which individuality is created; it suggests that each person contains inside them some special spark which is not part of the social encrustations that define their immersion in a historical world. In addition, it turns attention away from the unconscious, the proper terrain of psychoanalysis, to that of the finished product of the 'whole personality', which only then interacts with the oppressive social world around it. Fromm eventually, as in the passage concerning the Ten Commandments quoted above, takes fully on board the reactionary imperatives of conformist society, without considering their relativistic and ideological determinants. Jacoby's (1975) critique is even more virulent and extensive than that of Marcuse, but does not add many substantive points to it. Aside from a cogent dismantling of the conformism of ego psychology and humanistic post-Freudianism, he again points out how the cultural revisionists introduce history from the *outside*, as something that operates on the already formed individual. The essence of Freudianism (and Marcusianism, in Jacoby's view) is how sociality is internal to each of us, undermining what we experience as the privacy of our selfhood with its constructing and organising imperatives. Failure to recognise this leads to a failure to distinguish between genuinely subversive concepts and those which contain the conformism of an alienated society: authenticity, growth, the 'art of loving'. In a sterling defence of the best elements in the critical theory to which Marcuse and Adorno adhere, Jacoby (1975, p. 88) destroys the revisionist appeal to the realisation of the personality:

> Against the neo-Freudians, who consider character a harmonious totality, Adorno interprets it as a result of a series of 'shocks' inflicted on the individual; it bespeaks oppression and violence, not growth, choice and values.

If one wishes for a radical alternative to the libertarianism of Reich and Marcuse, it is necessary to look further than Fromm.

Restructuring relationships

The sense of disappointment that arises from examination of the attempts to integrate psychoanalysis and Marxism is substantial, and legitimately so. Where such Freudo-Marxism has not drifted into conformism and insipid humanism, it seems to have created a monstrous vision of libidinal self-gratification which offers little but individualistic hedonism as its eventual goal. This is at variance with the project of constructing a society distinguished by both a profound restructuring of ideologically inscribed power positions and an enrichment of human *relationships*, which is presumably the source of energy for all socialist dreamers. As Rustin (1982) has suggested, such a relational view has to be rescued from the writings of the libertarians rather than being integral to them. But the attempt to employ psychoanalysis for the purpose of understanding the ideological construction of the individual and providing a programme for radical activity has continued unabated, fuelled by 'New Left' and feminist movements, which attempt to challenge the deep incorporation of subjectivity into the service of capitalism and patriarchy. These movements have recognised psychoanalysis' power to provide an account of the formation of the human subject within the context of specific social configurations, and in using it in this way have also reopened the possibility of a revision of both political and psychoanalytic practice. Two themes stand out in the recent non-Lacanian literature in this respect: a distrust of sexuality as the principal focus for socialist psychoanalysis, and an attempt to employ the language and concepts of object relations and Kleinian theory to emphasise the personal relations that might form the basis of a renovated society. These themes have a common origin in a general rejection of instinct theory as a basis for progress and its replacement with an object relational framework – a tendency which is commensurate with the wider arguments stressed throughout this book.

The sources of the defusing of sexuality as a fundamental concept lie in a rejection of libertarianism and in a revised characterisation of contemporary (late capitalist) human experience. The former has already been dealt with: the libertarians are now commonly seen as last-ditch adherents to an outmoded instinct theory which is capable only of producing individualism. The socialist Rustins could be the moralising Guntrip on this point:

> sexual well-being is likely to be an aspect, not a cause, of good relationships with internal and external objects. It is easy to see that much 'sexual liberation' has been a perversion of human sexual capacities. (Rustin and Rustin, 1984, p. 214)

Paralleling the trends described in Part 2, some of the most interesting attempts to construct a new form of socialist psychoanalysis use the relationship orientation of the 'British school' and take many of their images from theories of mother–infant relations. Rustin (1982), who adopts a Kleinian framework, supplies a particularly persuasive example of this tendency. He takes as his starting point the contrast between Freud's individualistic focus on instinctual gratification held back only by socially induced repression, and Klein's integration of desire within a framework assuming its *essential* relationship orientation – from the start of life, instincts are viewed as directed towards objects, however distorted they may be by projective mechanisms. In particular, Rustin emphasises the manner in which Kleinianism deals with painful feelings of various kinds and places them in a context wherein their overcoming is seen as operating in the service of enriched personal relationships rather than instinctual liberation. Because of this concern with the overcoming of destructive emotions, the argument goes, Klein is led to develop a theory that asserts a morality appropriate to socialist reconstruction, in which all things are made to serve the interests of doing good to others.

> Freud's super-ego is conceived as having a repressive and persecutory function, and Freudian analysis could therefore be understood as an emancipation from guilt, especially sexual guilt. In contrast, guilt in Klein's 'depressive position' is understood to arise from the recognition of the pain suffered by or inflicted on others, and as an essential part of relatedness. (Rustin, 1982, p. 81)

It is Klein's concern with destructiveness and the manner in which it can be dealt with or made good, that makes her theory an attractive basis for Rustin's attempt to outline a psychoanalysis with socialist possibilities. In refusing to idealise human nature, Klein presents herself with the problem of specifying the exact mechanisms by which people manage to overcome their dangerous emotions, so that they can live constructively with one another and develop their potential for fulfilling relationships. This is paralleled by one of the tasks of socialism: not just to remove the obstacles to better living (as if this would just occur naturally if the oppressive restraints of capitalism where smashed), but to develop the structures and strategies making enriched and egalitarian human relationships possible. If human nature is socially constructed, then socialist struggle involves articulating the ways in which a new and more gratifying 'human nature' can be produced – something which must include ways of overcoming the pains of separation, anger and envy, and of turning outwards from ourselves to find in others the fulfilment of our desires. Rustin's vision of the mechanism by which this might occur brings the Kleinian concept of *reparation* to the fore, in which people are judged and valued by the way they treat others.

> The relational focus of the British psychoanalytic school – the assertion that what matters most to human beings is whether they stand in loving and trusting relations to others – is the theoretical basis for a much enlarged concept of human development. (Rustin, 1982, p. 91)

Once again it is love that provides the subversive possibilities in a society that runs on greed and strangles nurture; only this time love means more than just the expression of instinctual sexuality. Just what it does mean is, however, problematic: the profound emphasis on the mother–child relationship that is present throughout the object relations and Kleinian literature and can also be observed in the writings on narcissism, always contains the danger of reduction of the social to the microsocial – of arguing that social changes come about through alterations in the interactions between individuals, rather than the other way around. This theme will be returned to in the next chapter, in the context of feminist object relations work, but the danger can be seen clearly in the romanticism that creeps into Rustin and Rustin's (1984) account of the revision of family life – for revision it is, with support for social reforms and an emphasis on the 'new compassionate family' (p. 215) to serve in the development of those 'altruistic capacities so important in socialist ideas of humanity' (p. 210). It is not that these ideals are incompatible with socialism; rather, it is that they are presented as the road to socialism, with little consideration for the structural components of the social world that militate against them. Although people's relationships can undoubtedly be improved, even under capitalism, they cannot be changed sufficiently to bring about radical social change; only social struggle can do that. To argue otherwise is, once again, to reduce politics to therapy.

A strand of recent psychoanalytically inspired thinking that is quite closely related to the views sketched above derives from the clinical recognition that the characteristic patient of Freud's, the sexually repressed hysteric, has given way to a new breed of analysand, the 'borderline', 'schizoid' or 'narcissistic' person who may have no particular symptoms, but who complains bitterly of the emptiness and meaninglessness of her/his life. In this clinical pattern, the individual feels unable to form relationships of any rewarding kind; s/he 'is "self absorbed" not out of carelessness, or an excess of conceit, but as the only alternative to the disintegration and emptying of the self' (Richards, 1984, p. 135). Lasch (1979, p. 74) lists the character traits of narcissism as 'dependence on the vicarious warmth provided by others combined with a fear of dependence, a sense of inner emptiness, boundless repressed rage, and unsatisfied oral cravings'. Sexuality becomes an item in this, used by the narcissist in the search for closeness, but also employed as a defensive manoeuvre against facing the emptiness that lurks within, and the recognition of the passing of youth and the reality of the contemporary taboos on ageing and death. The implications of this apparent shift in symptomatology will be discussed more fully in Part 4; here, the significant point is the manner in which it has been taken as characterising a particular form of personality which is both expressive of and produced by current patterns of post-industrial civilisation.

In the view of the most cogent and infuriatingly uncategorisable (except as 'New Left') of the prophets of narcissism, Christopher Lasch, this personality constellation is connected with the societal emphasis on consumption and manipulation, and reflects the destruction of the sources of inner direction – particularly the family – which provided the sense of coherence for other times. That one can read society's structure in the characteristics of individuals is taken as self-evident in this viewpoint, perhaps providing a measure of the extent to which the psychoanalytic notion of the construction of individuality through patterns of defence and repression has entered into the currency of cultural critics. In this case, the social structure revealed by narcissism is one of the manipulation of personal needs in the interests of administration and consumption, so that the individual loses all sense of her/his inner determinants and becomes a plaything on the breezes of the global market. In a world where oppressions of all kinds link with one another, nothing is felt by the narcissist to truly link with the self; the more acquisitiveness and consumerism take hold, the more the personality has to be sold rather than achieved, and the less is there any selfhood to return home to, when work is done. 'Selfhood is thus increasingly dependent on consumption and less so on secure intrapsychic identifications with other persons' (Richards, 1984, p. 134). The narcissist is a perfect product and customer for a world of schizoid pretences and lies.

Lasch (1979) places considerable emphasis on the destruction of the family, the 'Haven in a Heartless World' which titles one of his earlier books. This is not simply an extension of Marcuse's idea that the family has been replaced by a state-administered welfare which reduces the power of paternal figures and increases the direct hold of capitalism on the individual psyche. In fact, although Lasch does consider the absence of the American father to be an important feature in forming the characteristic narcissistic superego, full of punitive fantasies derived from very early life, his principal concern is with the distorted nature of mother–child relations under late capitalism. In essence, Lasch argues that the mother responds to the increasingly threatening nature of the external world with a desperate attempt to create an island of security in the family. Unable to provide full and spontaneous care, because of the entry of alienation into her soul and the 'invasion of the family by industry, the mass media and the agencies of socialised parenthood' (p. 291), the mother's attempt to become an ideal parent results only in smothering the child with solicitude. The coupling of this solicitude with a dearth of warmth produces the narcissistic character: exaggeratedly self-important but inwardly devastated. Here Lasch uses Kohut's (1971) notion of 'optimal frustration' (which itself is very similar to Winnicott's description of the good-enough mother's graduated failures), the regular experience of the mother's limitations which enables the child to relinquish the image of maternal perfection and take over many of her functions to provide for her/his own care and comfort (p. 293). The narcissistic mother's 'incessant yet curiously perfunctory attentions to her child interfere at every point with the mechanism of optimal frustration' (p. 294); the child is thence left with enormous fantasies of maternal possibilities, but no hope for their fulfilment, giving rise to the characteristic self-bolstering, self-avoiding pattern described above.

This admittedly schematic account of the use to which the notion of narcissism has been put demonstrates the absorption of psychoanalytically inspired cultural criticism with the impoverishment of human relationships in late capitalism, and particularly with the devastation of family life. Its interest derives from the manner in which it paints, with broad strokes, the characteristics of contemporary (American) society and then traces the impact of these characteristics on the interpersonal and private lives of individuals. This is in the tradition of all radical psychoanalysis: the *particular* attributes of a specific society give rise to certain personality characteristics and patterns of defence, rather than repression being fixed for all time by the nature of the instincts, as in Freud's original formulation. In addition, despite certain affinities that it has with Marcuse's ideas, particularly concerning the effects of bureaucratisation on the family, Lasch's account of how social attributes become formative of character are rooted in a reasonably subtle understanding of parent (mother)–child interactions, and it also deals in the relationship mode of thinking rather than with the individualism of instinctual desire. It goes further than much psychoanalytical theory, however, in drawing attention to the way these relationships are themselves determined by social forces: it is the nature of the surrounding social world (mass production and consumption, with its attendant fetishising of images and manipulation of democratic structures in the interests of bureaucratic administration, etc.) that gives rise to the solicitude/distance dynamic of mothering that in turn leads to the development of the narcissistic personality. The implication of this would presumably be that an overturning of the conditions of parenting is necessary for escape from narcissism, and that this overturning is a social rather than a psychological project. However, Lasch's own account is redolent of a nostalgia for traditional social forms and for family life: just as with the Rustins, the correct observation that the destruction of the family has left people with no roots from which to develop their personalities, is allowed to slide into the suggestion that a return to the family is the only way to restore human capacities. Lasch, in particular, is more sophisticated than to advocate this, but it is implicitly there in his documentation of the dismembering of culture and his failure to suggest any alternative direction in which to move. The libertarian excesses of earlier Freudo-Marxists have here been replaced by a relationship theory which remains tied to idealised images of family life, and which is simply opposed to the ravages of rampant late capitalist society.

The importance of these considerations can be seen from another contribution to the *Capitalism and Infancy* collection which includes the Rustins' paper, that of Kovel (1984). Where Kovel's approach is an advance on that described above is in his integration of pre-Oedipal and Oedipal levels of functioning with a more complex view of how the 'administered society' becomes internalised into everyday life. The use of the Oedipal concept is precisely attuned to the need to move further than the microsocial: in Laplanche and Pontalis' (1973) usage, it is always about how the two-person link between self and object becomes structured according to an overarching *law* which determines what is permissible and possible. Whatever the quality of the microsocial bond, the law (external world) has its say, and may distort or supplant it completely. Kovel contextualises his account of subjectivity in a Marcuse-style notion of the bureaucratic 'administered society', which permeates the desires of the individual and aligns them with the requirements of consumption in the late capitalist world, so that one's subjectivity becomes integrated with the 'objective' demands of capital. Underneath this, however, resides what Kovel carefully calls the 'trans-historical substructure for the possibilities of domination' (p. 106); transhistorical rather than biological because it does not reduce to the biological in any simple sense. Hinting at a Lacanian understanding of development, Kovel emphasises the way something external always operates to give shape to the individual's desires: in early life there is an

> elementary contradiction between the nameless urging that stems from the activity of the infant's organism, and the named construction that stems from incorporating the other's recognition . . . the energy comes from within, the form from without. (Kovel, 1984, p. 107)

Underneath the verbalisable possibilities of the psyche lies a realm of necessity which is experienced as a demand suffused with 'desire for an outer source of power' (p. 106); this is a necessary state because it derives from the universal experiences of undifferentiation and then separation and object loss that characterise early life. The pre-Oedipal psyche always threatens to collapse into itself: the boundaries between self and other are obscure, the significances of loss and its attendant anxieties enormous. Thus, the three-person Oedipus situation, when it comes about, operates partly as a defence against pre-Oedipal longing, bolstering the psyche against dissolution by asserting and clarifying personal boundaries. Hence the Oedipus complex, which embodies patriarchy and operates to perpetuate it in the contemporary world, derives a substantial hold over the individual through also performing a defensive role, protecting her/him against fundamental anxieties. It is this linkage of Oedipal and pre-Oedipal that provides the transhistorical quality to the structuring of the infant's psyche: the Oedipus situation is historically specific, an 'inward reflection of the given historical state of the family and of relations of production in general' (p. 109), but beneath it is a universal need.

Kovel's analysis links with Marcuse's and Lasch's separate accounts of the dismembering of the family, arguing that the installation of the Oedipus complex contributes to the perpetuation of a patriarchal order which has in fact already passed away in reality, being replaced by bureaucratic administration. Like Lasch, he postulates that the destruction of the real family of earlier times has considerable consequences for personal desire, removing the possibility of achieving stability, albeit oppressed, through a network of relationships with real, distinct others against whom one could locate oneself. Under the administrative mode, the self is faced with an undifferentiated otherness which recreates the conditions of infancy where the child is involved in a dyadic bond with the outside world, not yet made distinct by the lessons of Oedipus. This produces intense desires and dissolution anxieties (the narcissistic configuration), and a search for protective others which plays into the hands of post-capitalist administration. With the demise of the powerful patriarchal family comes the post-Oedipal image of the pre-Oedipal world, the consumer narcissist faced with the feeding, invading, obliterating other which has no specific personality, but which creates desires in the same instant as it fulfils them, leaving the genuine needs of the individual untouched underneath. So patriarchy is perpetuated through the internalised lost structures of Oedipus, at least to the extent that they carry with them a yearning for authority (p. 115), but the administrative society operates more forcefully through its ability to protect people against their real (pre-Oedipal) desires by manipulating what seem to be their needs. This account is very much akin to Marcuse's, as is Kovel's suggestion that infantile wishes carry within them the seeds of subversion: 'it should be recognised that the disorders we may expect – the workings on a macrolevel of that part of us called id – are the well-springs of resistance no less than acquiescence' (Kovel, 1984, p. 118). Kovel is cautious about prophesying, but his postulation of a transhistorical substructure of desire acts both to explain the hold of consumerist capitalism, and to suggest a Marcusian residual optimism deep in the wells of the mind. 'Some portion of fantasy always escapes', he suggest, 'not at all necessarily for better things, but available for something unexpected' (p.119).

The parallels between the approaches of Kovel and Marcuse reside in their joint concentration on the administered society and their endorsement of the notion of underlying desires. But Kovel's represents an advance both in its use of the literature on narcissism and in its more subtle encounter with the contradictions between pre-Oedipal, Oedipal and post-Oedipal structures. Kovel, even in his description of the 'transhistorical' substratum of desire, deals with aspects of relationships rather than instinctual gratification; this enables him to formulate his theory in interpersonal instead of individualistic terms. In addition, his description of the collapse of Oedipal structures carries with it neither a nostalgia for the family nor an assertion that everything can be dealt with from inside the confines of the two-person, mother–infant relationship. Nevertheless, Kovel's account retains certain sources of difficulty: it is not clear whence rebellion comes nor how the relationship structures of socialism are to be constructed in the wake of bureaucratisation; there is little by way of a political *programme* to match the coherence of the analysis. It is also so concerned with tracking the deleterious consequences of the administrative state that it appears to suggest a dismantling of all social forms as a possible way out. But it faces up to a problem that has permeated all the work discussed in this chapter. We began with libertarianism, the assertion that a new society would be created on the basis of the unfettered expression of instinctual desire, a paradisial playground for happily libidinous infants. The attempt to use enriched *relationships* as the yardstick for socialism is an important advance on this position, but has tended to remain rooted in pre-Oedipal dyadic relations and to reduce too easily to microsocial encounters. Finally, the reintroduction of Oedipus in conjunction with an analysis of narcissism and of the particular social configuration of late capitalism adds to this perspective an important awareness of how mental life is constructed by broad forms of social structure, which retain a determinacy over what is possible in any particular interpersonal relationship. It is precisely here, on the terrain of mothering versus Oedipus, that some of the most important debates to arise within radical psychoanalysis reside; and it is in the context of feminist psychoanalytic work that they have been most forcefully argued.

7 Feminist Psychoanalysis

Probably the most significant recent advances in political psychoanalysis have come from theorists and therapists aligned with some strands of the feminist movement. These advances stem from feminism's concern with the relationships between gender-differentiated subjectivity and the structures of the external world, symbolised by the slogan 'the personal is political'. This concern has led many feminists to consider the conditions under which subjectivity arises and the possibilities for change, something which in turn has led to a critical engagement with psychoanalysis. But there also has been and remains a substantial feminist opposition both to Freud and to therapy, in the former case because of the way the reactionary elements in Freudian thought can be used to legitimise biologistic descriptions of women's 'inferiority' (particularly through the notion of penis envy), and in the latter case because therapy often operates to confirm women's subordination by endeavouring to reconcile female patients with their lot in life, and by reproducing in the therapeutic situation the oppressive machinations of patriarchy (therapist as 'the-rapist'). The crucial word in characterising the links between feminism and psychoanalysis is, therefore, 'critical': feminist writers both subject psychoanalysis to a far-reaching political critique and also employ its insights and methods to enlarge the scope of their own theories on gender.

Because of their opposition to Freudianism,the feminists of the late 1960s turned to humanistic psychology for guidelines in self-expression and personal liberation. In the heyday of the growth movement counter-culture, it was consciousness-raising through personal support and the use of expressive exercises that started to make women perceive themselves as agents in society, whose feelings and experiences could be recovered from the oppression of silence enjoined upon them by patriarchy. While these approaches are still used and retain their value (cf. Ernst and Goodison, 1981, for a feminist humanistic handbook of considerable popularity), it is fair to say that there has been an explosion of feminist interest in psychoanalysis in the last decade, initiated by Juliet Mitchell's remarkable book *Psychoanalysis and Feminism*, published in 1974. Two forces have combined to create this interest. First, many women expressed dissatisfaction with the degree of change possible using consciousness-raising techniques: the revelation that expressing feelings does not of itself necessarily make one able to master or alter them, led to a reconsideration of psychoanalysis, specifically for what it has to teach on the dominance of unconscious forces and for the conceptual tools it provides for exploring the internalisation of patriarchal ideology. More theoretically, a growing awareness of the importance of ideology and the interlinking of power and sexuality directed attention to psychoanalysis as the one approach to psychology that attempts to articulate these issues. Thus, despite its oppressive history,

> psychoanalysis, as a theory . . . is currently popular among feminists because it seems to offer us, through its account of the construction of the self in family relations and the unconscious mind, an understanding of how subordination can be internalised deep in our personalities. Moreover, it is centrally concerned with the forging of sexual identity and with the extreme importance of the sexual in all aspects of mental life. (Cameron, 1985, p. 117)

As this quotation makes clear, psychoanalysis' significance for many feminists lies largely in the account it gives of the construction of sexual difference; as will be described later, this leads directly into the Lacanian account of personality formation, and focuses upon the issue of female sexuality as that which constantly raises the question of the constitution of the human subject (Mitchell, 1982, p. 25). However, there are differences between different feminist theorists here, with some arguing that it is psychoanalysis' general account of development through object relations which creates unconscious structures that is the crucial element for understanding women's psychology. These theorists tend not to emphasis sexuality *per se* but rather to see it as an element in a general pattern of relating that is formed by experiences in the social world. Hence, Eichenbaum and Orbach's (1982) apparently straightforward statement that 'We see the unconscious as the intra-psychic reflection of our present child-rearing and gender relations' (p. 15) is an assertion of the importance of *actual* relational experiences in contrast to the symbolic–universal structures emphasised by Lacanians. As will be seen later, the effects of these different perspectives are to direct emphasis to varying aspects of development and to produce differing accounts of the possibilities and strategies for change.

Interest in femininity is not a new occurrence in psychoanalysis, any more than is the recognition that this is an area of important dispute and theoretical dissatisfaction. Freud himself, despite the polemical nature of some of his pronouncements, was willing to recognise the provisional nature of his understanding of femininity, and early on some major psychoanalysts (e.g. Jones, Horney, Deutsch, Klein, Lampl de Groot) were willing to risk this as an arena for dissension from his views. This opposition was ostensibly to Freud's androcentrism, particularly in relation to penis envy and the castration complex (see Mitchell, 1974, 1982, for overviews of these disputes). The characteristic feature of the opposition was to deny Freud's idea that femininity develops through a growing awareness of lack and absence in comparison with the male, an account which places at the centre of the female mind a desire to be male. Although Freud is correct in thinking that the first love-object of both sexes is the mother, this does not mean that girls are in fact 'little men' as Freud would have it; neither does his correct observation of the existence of penis envy mean that girls are necessarily different from boys in their ideas about loss and threats to their personality. Jones (1927), for example, suggests that children of either sex can feel threatened with the extinction of their sexuality; he proposes that castration anxiety is part of this wider, non-gender-specific anxiety, which he calls *aphanisis*. Horney and Klein emphasise the pre-Oedipal role of the mother in determining sexual development, and see this as originary even of the Oedipus complex. Thus, Horney claims that the notion that there is only one genital, the penis, which one either has or lacks is in fact a defence against the overwhelming power of the mother; Klein (1932) argues that the frustrations induced by the early relationship with the mother leads to a turn towards the father and an idealisation of the penis, and she states firmly that 'in my experience the women's penis envy can be traced back to envy of the mother's breast' (Klein, 1957, p. 199). Horney (1926) goes furthest in all this by suggesting that Freud's account of femininity is fixed at the level of the four-year-old boy who cannot bear to envision the reality of a girl's separate sexuality, but must defend himself by disparagement of her possibilities. This fixation, she holds, prevents Freud from recognising the specificity of female development and hence developing an adequate psychology of women.

The opposition to Freud in the 1920s and 1930s served a useful function in demonstrating the inadequacy of Freud's terms and in asserting the need for a psychology of women that does not treat them simply as castrated men. As Chodorow (1978, p. 116) notes, in Freud's account a woman does not

> want sex for anything except reproduction and the restitution of her narcissistic wound. In the Horney–Jones–Klein account, at least a woman does want (hetero) sex for its own sexual sake.

But despite the important distinction introduced by Freud between sexuality and procreation, a distinction which one would have thought was basic to psychoanalysis, all his opponents of that period were forced back into biologism as a way of defending their account of a distinct female sexuality. Chodorow (1978) and Mitchell (1974, 1982) have demonstrated the manner in which this occurred: in rebelling against the Freudian dogma that it is castration which distinguishes male from female, the opposition invented a history for women as independent of men; being independent, it assumes a separation between male and female that is *always present* and is not created by any particular event or complex. This assumption automatically falls into an account which makes psychological difference secondary to biological difference. Thus, Jones, Horney and Klein argue that the girl's turn to the father in the Oedipus situation is a result of *natural* heterosexual drives which then produce penis envy as a defence against the potential consequences of incestuous desire. Whatever its attractiveness in side-stepping the notion of biologically ordained penis envy, this version of development loses the radical impact of

Freud's theory by turning attention away from the question of how male and female sexuality become constructed. Instead, there is an assumption that the sexes are already distinguished biologically, and psychoanalysis becomes simply a description of the manner in which the pre-existent male and female develop their full adult nature. In addition, heterosexuality is assumed as a biological urge, rather than analysed as the uncertain outcome of a long process of libidinal vicissitude. As Mitchell in particular shows, whatever the reformist or progressive intentions of the opposition, their approach actually results in a dismembered psychoanalysis, reduced to a platitudinous common sense. Despite the defects in Freud's account of femininity, it provides a standard whereby others can be measured; this involves, especially, a description of how, from the bisexual human infant, masculinity and femininity become engendered in the social sphere.

Mitchell's (1974) *Psychoanalysis and Feminism* was a watershed for feminist psychology, revealing the essentialism and biologism in contemporary critiques of Freud and introducing, in a slightly obscured way, the possibilities of psychoanalysis for elaborating the available accounts of women's oppression. In retrospect, it now seems that the major contribution of Mitchell's book was to clear away the confusions that prevented advances in feminist psychoanalysis, by unravelling common mistakes in anti-Freudian criticisms and by revealing the dead ends produced by absorption in the ideas of Reich and Laing. In terms of the development of a positive theory of psychoanalysis, Mitchell's book is confused and unclear; it appears, for example, to assert the value of Lacanian theory while omitting any discussion of language and having recourse to a generalised appeal for the overturning of patriarchy. Since Mitchell's book, there have been a number of attempts to articulate more clearly what psychoanalysis has to offer to feminism. Very broadly speaking, the most important of these fall into two distinct groups: those that rely on an object relations position within psychoanalysis, and concentrate on the early relations between mother and child; and those which take their theoretical base in Lacanian thought, placing more emphasis on the castration and Oedipal complexes. In the remainder of this chapter, some examples of both these trends will be examined, focusing particularly on the work of Chodorow (1978), and the accounts given of post-Lacanian feminism by Mitchell and Rose (1982) and Gallop (1982).

Object relations theory: the recovery of mothering

The particular assertions of feminist object relations theory are familiar from the broader object relations position outlined in Part 2. Chodorow (1978, p. 157) makes a characteristic objection to Freudianism:

> Both Freudians and the Horney–Jones–Klein opposition remain bound to a theory of development and an account of the oedipus complex which stresses libidinal and instinctual shifts and biology even when emphasizing difficulties in the attainment of biological destiny . . . These theories see people (in this case women) as appendages of their drives and genitalia.

In contrast, object relations theory is based on the postulate that the defining drive of the human being is to make contact with others – to form relationships – and that it is in the context of this drive that each individual's psychological structures are formed. Through relationships with 'objects' and the psychological discriminations produced by separations, the child's self is formed in specific ways, with 'instincts' employed in the service of available relationships. The central attraction of object relations theory for feminists, however, is its reorientation of psychoanalysis' concern away from the father-centred Oedipus complex (which, if it is dealt with at all, is seen mostly as a *product* of earlier development or as the point at which specific identifications are formed) and on to the earliest pre-Oedipal periods, in which the child is absorbed in a dependency relationship, characteristically with the mother. Not that this is necessarily a radical position: as described in Part 2, traditional object relations theory commonly employs romanticised notions of mothering which have the effect of devaluing the legitimate interest of the mother in aspects of her world outside her infant, and hence of perpetuating the patriarchal discourse which makes women nothing other than carriers of babies. According to this view, women can only achieve fulfilment through absorption in their infants; the contextualising of mother–infant interaction in a setting of other social relationships is neglected as much as is all the non-maternal elements of the mother's psychology. In taking up the maternal focus of the object relations position, feminists attempt to distance themselves from its conformism by drawing attention to the ideological nature of the conventional discourse on mothering, and the way it serves to perpetuate women's oppression. Nevertheless, feminist object relations theory lives with the danger of collapsing back into biologistic categories forced upon it by its utter reliance on the formativeness of mother–child encounters. To investigate the extent to which this danger is averted, it is necessary to describe in more detail the account that is given of the particular nature of mothering, and its effects in producing and reproducing gender differentiations.

The central claim that all object relations theory, whether feminist or not, makes in this area is that the early mother–infant bond has a special quality which sets it apart from all other relationships, and which has formative significance on the psychology of the child. First, this primary relationship is a crucial one for the development of the child's self.

> The growing child's psychic structure and sense of self . . . comes to consist of unconscious, quasi-independent, divided experiences of self in affective . . . relation with an inner object world, made up originally of aspects of its relations to its mother. (Chodorow, 1978, p. 78)

The whole of the child's psychic organisation is influenced by the passionate intensity of her/his interactions with the mother, with the early absorption of the infant in her leading to a gradual cognizance of selfhood through the particular pattern of gratifications and frustrations that are encountered. This kind of relationship is different from that formed with the father: the child's love for the mother is not initially under the sway of the reality principle, but is dictated by the fantasy of total unity and perfect gratification, giving it an extreme degree of intensity and ensuring that the mother–child relationship will centre on the axis of separation/engulfment throughout life. The father, on the other hand, is conventionally more distant from the start, treating his child as separate and perceived as outside the boundary of the mother–child unit. So fathers are important figures in encouraging the ability to differentiate between self and others, and between people, and thus operate as representatives of the 'reality principle' in contradistinction to the maternal 'pleasure principle' encounter. The separateness of the father enables the child to treat him as a genuinely distinct object with attributes of his own, and to form a truly ambivalent relationship with him. However, in the pre-Oedipal period the father is held to remain peripheral: because of his actual and emotional distance from the child, he is not involved as strongly as the mother in the basic organisation of the psyche and the self.

Much of the child's relationship with the mother is held to be characterised by ambivalence: love and hate are confused in the difficulty of perceiving separateness. The mother is both all powerful and all engulfing, contemporaneously gratifying and frustrating. This, given specifically female mothering, leads to particular views of women, which arise from the experience of the intensity of the earliest relationship and which are shared by children of both sexes. Chodorow (1978, p. 83) lists some of these expectations as follows:

> Girls and boys expect and assume women's unique capacities for sacrifice, caring and mothering, and associate women with their own fears of regression and powerlessness. They fantasize more about men, and associate them with idealised virtues and growth.

Chasseguet-Smirgel (1964), on whose work Chodorow draws, goes further by proposing that boys and girls maintain 'a terrifying maternal image' in the unconscious, resulting from projections of impotence; common images of women 'as deficient, as containing a hole or wound' are read as a denial of the power of the original mother (pp. 112, 114). Dinnerstein (1977) also argues that the experience of the omnipotent mother in early development leads to a rejection of women by children of both sexes, perpetuating male dominance. All in all, the experience of being mothered solely by women is made to carry enormous weight in explaining later conscious and unconscious attitudes towards them.

The description of early development given by Chodorow is no different from that expounded by traditional object relations theorists, with their emphasis on 'natural mothering'. It has the same virtue of providing a theory of psychic construction which identifies social interactions as central, and it has the same drawback of reliance on a single explanatory dimension, that of the quality of mothering. Where feminism differs most from traditional theories is in its perception of patriarchy: that the positions of men and women towards one another are fixed by a social structure which stands outside them, and which is designed to obscure the conditions of its own existence, so that it *appears* natural. Traditional theorists are simply taken in (or are in league with) patriarchal ideology; feminism is the challenge to that ideology that explicitly articulates its sociality and the way it is founded on a set of constructed power relations. Chodorow supplies a significant addition to this feminist science by going to the heart of individual development and suggesting a point at which what is social and what is biological become confused, in the experiences that the infant has of father and mother. Through his separateness and, later, his Oedipal role, the father acts as an important image of the social, whereas the mother's dilemma is precisely that she is the nodal point at which biology and sociality become confused; that is, the mother–infant relationship appears in fantasy as total biological absorption, whereas it is already structured by pre-existing social constraints. These constraints are the political conditions which give rise to exclusively female mothering and brand it inescapable. From the start of life, in the muddle and intensity that surrounds the infant's immersion in the mother, patriarchy constructs and organises, obscures and misleads. Amongst its victims, this perception reveals, are those psychoanalytic romantics who supply virtuoso paeans to motherhood. So feminist object relations theory does manage to avoid one of the basic pitfalls of the orientation to the mother; it remains to be seen whether it runs into others.

Nothing in the account so far discriminates between the experiences of boys and girls, but this is an important element in feminist theory. The fact of the biological gender of the child does not determine what s/he will be like, but it does institute a systematic differentiation in the mother–infant relationship which will have characteristic effects on development. Significantly, the focus of feminist object relations work is the manner in which the *real* relationship between mother and child is influenced by the child's gender and what that signifies to the mother. The crucial belief from which all else seems to stem is that mothers experience and treat their daughters differently from their sons, because of the unconscious and conscious impact that the child's gender has on the mother. Object relations theorists concentrate specifically on the relative consciousness of separateness instilled in the male and female child by the mother, which, they suggest, then dictates the structuring of male and female personalities and their particular characteristics throughout life. Eichenbaum and Orbach (1982, p. 30) provide a summary statement which captures the main point:

> In mothering a baby girl a woman is bringing her daughter up to be like her, to be a girl and then a woman. In mothering her son she is bringing him up to be other, to be a boy and then a man.

These writers postulate several aspects of the mother–daughter relationship that make for the particular shaping of a girl's psychology. These are, first, that the mother identifies with her daughter and projects on to her the same feelings that she has about herself; she acts towards her daughter in the way that she unconsciously relates to the repressed 'little girl' part of herself, so that 'the little daughter becomes an external representation of that part of herself which she has come to dislike and deny' (p. 33). Secondly, the ambivalence created by this pattern of identification leads to a peculiarly staccato quality and possible inconsistency in the mother's handling of her child, creating the precise conditions of oscillating frustration and gratification that make a child feel overpowered and rejected. According to Eichenbaum and Orbach, the consequence for the daughter is that she recognises in herself the 'little girl' rejected by the mother and splits it off, hiding it through repression and relating to the world through a series of false personal boundaries. Most importantly, through identification with the mother coupled with the experiences of frustration by her, the daughter learns to lose her expectations of being nurtured and instead to become extremely sensitive to the needs of others, to develop emotional antennae: 'she learns to give what others need; she starts to give to others out of the well of her own unmet needs' (p. 38). The full consequences of this will be described later, but object relations theory is here postulating a specifically female pattern of 'normal' psychopathology which derives from the real pre-Oedipal relations formed between daughter and mother. This pathology centres on difficulties surrounding boundary-formation, separation and articulation of personal needs, and is a predictable result of the projection by the mother of her own internalised self-denigratory attitudes, inherited in turn from *her* mother and related to the position of women in society.

There are some significant problems with the account given above which are endemic to the object relations position. First, although the emphasis on the specific interactions between mother and daughter provides a description of a plausible mechanism whereby feelings and attitudes can be passed on, it suffers from a subtle form of determinism, suggesting that the systematic similarities between women is due to the similarity in the *actual* behaviour of all their mothers. Although such similarities exist, so too do substantial differences; the theory described above has difficulties in dealing with situations in which the daughters of mothers who behave differently towards them, or who are absent or working or feminist themselves, nevertheless inherit a female psychology which is invaded by the oppressions of patriarchy. It needs an account that goes further than the immediate real encounters between mother and daughter to explain this, something which deals adequately with the *symbolic* role of particular people, acting as carriers of wider social messages. Secondly, feminist object relations theory's account of the girl's pre-Oedipal development is concerned only secondarily with psychic structure; it suggests that certain maternal attitudes towards femininity give rise to particular sets of emotion which in turn lead into predictable patterns of difficulty or repression in the girl. It seems more likely, and more congruent with psychoanalysis, that it is anxieties and emotions of various kinds that give rise to particular attitudes, and not usually the other way around.

The account of the girl's pre-Oedipal development through her relationship with her mother is presented in contrast with that of the boy. There are two significant strands here. The first concerns the boy child's automatic experience of himself as separate and 'other' to the mother, simply by virtue of his gender. Chodorow (1978) argues that the boy forms an 'active attachment' to his mother which, however powerful she is experienced as being, places an emphasis on his sense of difference from, and masculine oppositeness to, her. This derives not from some in-built knowledge on the part of the child that he is biologically distinct from the female mother, but from her awareness of his difference, an awareness which under patriarchy is also imbued with a sense of value. The boy child is other than the mother, so not so vulnerable to the narcissistic over-identification that plagues the girl's attempts to differentiate and construct a self. He is also valued by her as a potential agent in the world, and is thus more likely to internalise a sense of possibility and power.

The second element in the boy child's relationship with the mother that distinguishes it from the girl's is its sexualised nature. Although there is an important degree of mother–daughter sexuality, this is of a narcissistic kind and reflects the mother's relationship with her own body – hence the adult woman's supposed confusion of sexuality and fantasies of merger. Because boys are experienced by mothers from early on as a male opposite, they are more likely to be experienced in a sexualised way which reinforces the phallic–masculine separateness of the boy's experience of himself as he begins to differentiate. This sense of sexualised otherness become embedded early in the triangular relationship in which the father appears as a sexual rival, and which again extends the sense of boundary that a boy child experiences. Thus, whereas the girl's personality is always in danger of falling into that of her mother, for the boy the difficulty is in ever feeling that sense of closeness and absorption which forms the conditions for later relationships.

It is clear from everything that has been said above that object relations theorists assume that pre-Oedipal development for both boys and girls presage the Oedipal period and influence it markedly. For boys, in fact, they seem to suggest that the Oedipal structure is present early on, inherent in the differentiations made by the mother and the sexualised context for her interactions with her son. Thus, the early relationship with the mother already creates the internalised object relational patterns which are described by classical theory as being the result of the Oedipus encounter. Gender identity is formed by the experiences of early infancy rather than by later identifications, although the father does have an important role as a genuine object of ambivalence helping the boy deal with the intensity of his desire for the mother and generate a sense of masculine identity. Nevertheless, the father is a relatively shadowy figure even for the boy – an aspect of traditional object relations theory taken over by its feminist revisionists.

If the father–son relationship is rewritten in terms of the importance of mothering, that between father and daughter suffers an extraordinary transmutation in this branch of feminist psychoanalysis. On the face of it, fathers represent patriarchy and consequently have a central cultural role, breaking up the feminine absorption of mother and daughter, but also offering possibilities of separateness and symbolising power, freedom and differentiation from the mother. However, the significance of the father is lessened by the emphasis laid upon the role of the mother in determining the progression of the Oedipus complex – in fact, in determining the whole nature of the relationship of daughter to father. The sleight of hand here is to explain the girl's turn to her father in the Oedipus condition as a turn *away from the mother*, dictated by the intensity and frustration of the bond with her. Chodorow catalogues and summarises the various descriptions that analysts have offered here, all of which locate the turn to the father in the context of the mother–daughter relationship.

> It expresses hostility for her mother; it results from an attempt to win her mother's love; it is a reaction to powerlessness vis-à-vis maternal omnipotence and to primary identification. Every step of the way, as the analysts describe it, a girl develops her relationship to her father while looking back at her mother. (1978, p. 126)

Chasseguet-Smirgel (1964) has articulated this view most coherently and influenced object relations thought, even though her own framework employs a more traditional instinctual model. In outline, her argument is simply that children of both sexes experience a 'narcissistic wound' at the hands of the mother, who is perceived as omnipotent, terrifying and frustrating. Both boys and girls realise that possession of the penis gives the opportunity for healing this wound and also revolting against the state of dependency on the mother. Boys receive the promise of phallic power through their already experienced difference from the mother and through identification with the father; in girls, the desire for a penis (penis envy) leads to idealisation of the father and rejection of the mother. Thus, whereas in Freudian theory the girl's castration complex centres on anger with the mother for having created her defective, in Chasseguet-Smirgel's view it contains a flight away from the power of the mother and is generated by the quality of the early mother–infant relationship. An alternative view, favoured more by object relations theorists, is that the girl turns to her father not out of hostility towards the mother, but through love for her. This story is based on the premise that the girl notices the preference the mother gives her father (and brothers) and assumes this means she prefers people like her father, who have penises. Her penis envy is in response to her desire to please her mother, and her turn to the father is a defence against the impossibility of obtaining the penis for herself. Once again, it is along the parameters of the maternal image that the girl's relationship with her father is formed.

The overwhelming emphasis of feminist object relations theory on the centrality of the mother has been stressed throughout this account. The criticism that it relies too heavily on the actual interactions between particular real people, and takes too little account of the symbolic structures which give rise to these interactions and go beyond them, has already been made. The concern with the mother cannot, however, be read as a simple attempt to balance out classical psychoanalysis' androcentricity. For one thing, the fate of mothering in traditional object relations theory is enough to demonstrate that theories concerned with the maternal role can easily be disguises for patriarchal ideology. In addition, feminist object relations theory does present a specific *critique* of the conditions of mothering that it describes, which locates it within the socially created configurations of patriarchy, and which takes its place as a specific, and very powerful, mode of domination. Most persuasively, this critique takes the form of an account of the maiming of personality to which exclusively female mothering gives rise – an account which makes it impossible to see this as any kind of oppositional matriarchal utopia.

The personality deficits that feminist theory describes apply both to men and to women. Men acquire power under patriarchy, it is true, but at a substantial cost. In direct contradiction of Freud's assertion that 'the little girl is a little man', Chodorow (1978, p. 181) argues that 'Masculinity becomes an issue in a way that femininity does not'. Because of boys' experiences with female mothering, masculinity is based on a disavowal of things feminine, and thus is always defined negatively and precariously. Hence, boys have greater difficulty establishing a firm gender consciousness and tend to fantasise and idealise the male role (aided by the propaganda of patriarchy); this also leads to the rejection of femininity which can be seen in male violence towards women and in men's inability to sustain fully equal relationships with them. In addition, the relational capacities that the absorption in the mother produces in girls are repressed in boys; their sense of separateness leaves them always looking for the ideal One who can create a sense of full connectedness, without allowing the development of the capacities that might make this possible. Finally, women's mothering of men produces in them not just the personality characteristics attuned to male domination, but also those which are required for submission to the dictates of capitalist production – denial of affect and affection, avoidance of intimacy, competitiveness and inner emptiness. This description has come under fire from some sources (e.g. Sayers, 1985), for not explaining how men might oppose the conditions of their work or struggle to change themselves, nor what happens to prepare women for work. Its power, however, is to be found in the convincing portrait it paints of the difficulties men have with intimacy in personal relationships, and it is significant that the men's movement, in Britain at least, has based much of its more psychoanalytic theorising on these premises (cf. Metcalfe and Humphries, 1985).

While men suffer under patriarchy, it is, of course, concern over the oppression experienced by women that governs the considerations of feminism. These generally follow directly from the acount given above of the difficulties encountered by girls in escaping the overwhelming and suffocating identifications imposed upon them by their mothers, with consequent problems in forming clear ego boundaries and sense of self. For example, Eichenbaum and Orbach (1982) focus upon the repression of the needy 'little girl' part of every woman, the denial of basic desires because of the experience and expectation that they can never be met, coupled with a desperate search for a nurturing relationship that will make her feel fulfilled. Chodorow also emphasises the prolonged nature of the girl's pre-Oedipal tie to her mother and its construction around the axis of identification–separation, which raises specifically female issues of boundary confusion, dependency and narcissism. Because of the overwhelming impetus of the mother–daughter identification process, girls have less clear (more 'permeable') ego boundaries and consequently tend both to define themselves more in relation to others and to be uncertain where others are differentiated from the self – hence constructing narcissistic personality conflicts. Grunberger (1964, p. 79) and others have described the conditions of female narcissism in some detail, conditions which centre on the mother's inability to confirm her daughter's sense of personal competence and integrity.

> A woman is narcissistic before all else . . . women live in, and by, love. Because they are deprived of adequate narcissistic confirmation from the beginning of their lives they project their badly integrated, unfulfilled narcissism onto their relations with their partners; in a sense their lives are the story of this projection, its partial and fleeting successes and its inevitable failures.

These failures are in large part due to the inability of men to provide intimacy, for the reasons given above. This is one source of the drive to have a child: the mother–child relationship recreates the intense primary link that women are always seeking to regain and that men cannot provide (according to Chodorow this is a more likely outcome than lesbianism because of internal and external taboos on homosexuality and because of women's isolation from one another, something one would think might change more rapidly than male psychology). Thus, the contradictions in heterosexuality help to perpetuate female mothering as women experience a lack where they had hoped for connection, and, seeking out a newly intense primary relationship to fill this lack, lay the foundations for reproduction of the deleterious factors in male and female personality. In addition, irrespective of the emotional capacities of the particular man a woman finds, an exclusive relationship with a man is unlikely to be fulfilling to a woman because of the perpetuated absorption in the mother that survives the Oedipus period and is the determining influence on the female psyche. So while men seek for the perfect woman to re-invent the mothering relation, women seek out themselves, embedded in their needs for relatedness and nurture. None of this is a recipe for fulfilment or enriched personal development; the argument is that patriarchy, through its insistence on female mothering, creates deformed and thwarted personalities both in men and women, and in the same act reproduces itself.

An important element in feminist work of all kinds is to design a programme to overturn or alter the conditions that perpetuate patriarchy. Unfortunately, in its object relations form, this programme reveals the inadequacy of any account which does not have a properly worked out notion of the social conditions giving rise to personal interactions. For feminist object relations theory, the damage wrought by exclusively female mothering points to the direction in which radical change needs to come about: simply, this is the institution of practices of *shared* child care, which will provide both sons and daughters with the conditions under which their relational capacities can become fully developed. A ray of hope in this, according at least to Chodorow (1978), is that all it takes to be a mother is to have experienced the relational intensity of mothering oneself, as all humans have, and to be able to regress to the psychological level of this experience while also remaining adult. Equal parenting, by removing the fearful and derogatory attitudes towards women described above, 'would leave people of both genders with the positive capacities each has , but without the destructive extremes these currently tend toward' (p. 218). Dinnerstein (1977), arguing from a more Kleinian point of view and distinguishing between the history-making but nature-assaulting world of men and the nature-embodying position of women, also argues for shared child care as the solution to the destructiveness of contemporary culture. If men and women participated equally in the public world and in the private world of child care, then the nurturing qualities of women would overcome the destructively maimed and assaultive distortions of male character, to change all aspects of our currently patriarchal and vicious society. One has to have doubts about this, both concerning its possibility within the terms of the theory (how can shared child care come about when women and men have their personalities shaped so radically towards divergent positions on nurture? – Sayers, 1985; can men ever have the *same* impact on their children as breast-feeding mothers can, if it is true that early infancy is crucial in personality construction?) and, more generally, concerning the impact that changes in individual behaviour can have on social organisation. If patriarchy is a social phenomenon, it operates at a level that is broader than the interactions between particular people, and it produces systematic patterns of experience and action – ideology, one might say. There are certainly important ways in which individuals can change what they do (it undoubtedly would be a good thing, for many reasons, if shared child care was a general phenomenon). But to argue that social structure alters when individuals change their behaviour is actually to obscure the distinction between feminist and traditional accounts, a distinction that depends on the idea that the interactions between individuals (such as mother and child) are structured by something social that has its origins outside them, and is given the name of patriarchy. As in individualistic philosophies of all kinds, the relative order of things is confused: patriarchy may be influenced by the attitudes people take up towards it, but it is more powerful than they are, and will be maintained unless changes at the 'microsocial' level are combined with direct assaults upon the structure itself. Ideological struggle is legitimate and important, but it is only one form of political activity.

The caricature given above of feminist object relations' views on how to alter the structures of society is really not so exaggerated, and reveals the crucial difficulties with this approach. These have been touched on at various points previously, but the two central criticisms are worth summarising. The first concerns the generation of the account of sexual differentiation. For traditional Freudians, male and female identity is formed at the time of the Oedipus complex, as a cultural act that occurs through the institution of a ban on incest which takes its particular form from patriarchal society. Whatever its validity, this at least is an account of the origins of gender dimorphism which is given in terms of the child's *desire*, and not her/his biology. Object relations theory does not discuss such an insertion of patriarchal law, but focuses on the anatomical gender dimorphism of male and female and then describes only how the culturally determined associations and expectations that go along with these particular identities become internalised. In doing so, the psychoanalytic conceptualisation of the unconscious as an arena of conflicting impulses and wishes is neglected in favour of a description of how the child comes to absorb a set of attitudes from those around her/him. In addition, the context for the organisation of the child's psyche is given as specific interactions with certain real people, whose personal attributes are of formative significance for the child. Although this approach provides useful descriptions of characteristic patterns of early social interaction, with their projective and indentificatory accompaniments, it also makes the *structural* determinants of desire (deriving from the organisation of society at a symbolic level that goes deeper than that which is under the control of particular individuals) subservient to the more or less observable actions of the parents to whom a child happens to be born. Hence the possibility of arriving at a theory of change which focuses on the gender of the people that 'mother' a child, rather than on the social structures which determine that mothering and its characteristics – despite all that feminist object relations theory has demonstrated concerning the internalised distress common to women and men throughout patriarchal society.

This raises a second, related point that is significant in the critique of this form of feminist theory, one which is painfully apparent in the guidelines for political change that it delivers. This is simply that in its fascination with mother – child relationships it cannot offer a full account of patriarchy as a social structure which operates over and above the interactions between individuals and which, indeed, structures those interactions. The fact of female mothering cannot hold all the explanatory weight placed upon it, because without a theory of the positioning of this fact it has no power at all. Patriarchy *means* the construction of social and personal relationships in line with a particular 'law', the law of the father which makes all else subservient to its ends. Although Chodorow and others try to show how patriarchal values influence the instance and content of female mothering, their virtual neglect of the symbolic position of the father leaves them with little more than voluntarism. Changing patriarchy involves more than changing the proportion of child care carried out by men and women; it involves changing the material and symbolic structures that determine how desire is socialised. To comprehend this, one needs a theory of the structuring position of the father, a theory which can explain how patriarchy operates as a formative *principle* in people's lives. In the search for such a theory, attention has recently turned to the work of Lacan.

In the name of Lacan

In the account of Lacan's developmental theory given in Chapter 5, stress was laid on how language is given a structuring role in each person's life, and how this serves to 'decentre' the individual, so that the notion of each of us having a unique 'self' which determines our personal meanings and desires is exposed as an illusion. It is these points that also serve as the basis for a feminist use of Lacanian theory, for they contain within them an aversion to the biologistic readings that infiltrate so much of psychoanalytic thought. The first crucial notion here is one introduced in Chapter 5, that of the 'Symbolic' as a set of meanings that define culture and are embedded in language, that lie outside the being of the individual child but represent an order of humanity in which each one of us has to take up a position, or risk psychosis. There is, therefore, no self-generated set of meanings, biological or otherwise: all readings of the 'truth' of one's nature come from outside and are in a sense instances of alienation, the positioning of one's subjectivity in a chain of cultural signifiers that make particular kinds of sense of the phenomena of experience. Here is already a substantial difference from the approaches outlined earlier: object relations theory implies that the particular experiences which a child has with specific adults leads to certain associations and characteristic behavioural and defensive patterns. The notion of the Symbolic opposes this with the view that meanings are not generated by one's own experience *per se*, but that we become subject to predetermined meanings when we enter into the cultural order. Lacan, for example, emphasises Lévi-Strauss' view of the role of incest taboos and the exchange of women to suggest how the network of experiences surrounding gender are generated from pre-existent structures rather than from the intentions or biological characteristics of individuals. This law of exchange, itself mythologised in the Oedipus complex that serves as an originator of sexual difference in the life of each individual, is something which stands beyond the experience of any person, but defines the possible expressions of one's position in the cultural world. More generally, the notion of the Symbolic opposes any absolute fixing of sexual category according to biological gender. Just as desire is something built on lack, on the impossibility of attainment of absolute gratification, so the perception of oneself as 'male' or 'female' is illusory, a fragmented and tenuous experience built on the insertion of the individual subject into a symbolic universe which then obscures the fact of that insertion. Masculinity and femininity are not absolute categories, but are fantasies to which the split and oscillating individual subject aspires; there is no absolute determination of gender identity any more than there is determination of sexuality – in fact, the unconscious continuously undermines all certainties and apparent biological facts.

Lacan, following Freud, does not view the social world as arbitrarily structured. Rather, it follows a specific law, the Law of the Father, which defines the positions taken up by all subjects within it. Here is another reason for feminist consideration of Lacanianism: it deals directly with patriarchy, and whatever the value position that it may take up, it never pretends that the patriarchal law does not exist and that men and women are 'really' equal. In fact, Lacan goes to the other extreme, asserting that culture is always patriarchal, that it is in the exchange structures described by Lévi-Strauss that the essential order of the Symbolic can be found. The Law of the Father is seen as being identical with the law of language, the symbolic order which has as its entry the Oedipus situation, and which structures all interactions – even those between mother and child, made primary by object relations theorists. It is because of the Law of the Father that biological differences between male and female come to be the principal axis along which development occurs; in other words, patriarchy institutes a chain of meanings which define the individual and into which s/he is inserted, but because patriarchy structures reality it appears to be all-embracing, 'natural' and biologically ordained. So all experiences between person and person, from the earliest mother–child interaction, are organised according to the law and its symbolism. The determinism here is very striking: Lacan's theory implies that the array of meanings available to each person are fixed by the cultural order, that each person's 'desire' is structured in accordance with an overarching, symbolic presence. The main problem here, apart from overinsistence on a linguistic determinism which is belied by the facts of psychology (see Cameron, 1985), is twofold. First, the individual subject is reduced to a cipher apparently produced *entirely* by outside forces; this is characteristic of structuralist theories, but raises inconsistencies even within Lacan's own approach, for example in the notion that access to the Symbolic represents 'alienation': if there is only external structuring, what can the subject ever be alientated from? Secondly, Lacan suggests that the Law of the Father is to be identified with culture *per se*, that is, that all cultures are patriarchal. This idea is at odds with the notion of the arbitrariness of the organisation of desire: if meanings are always fixed in the same way (always patriarchal) then something must be determining this fixity. The danger here is that of slipping back into biologism in an attempt to explain the supposed universality of patriarchal culture; the more immediate step – that Lacan seems to take – is to adopt those particularly ideological blinkers that refuse to admit anything but patriarchy as any kind of 'culture' at all.

If there are difficulties with the assumptions underlying some aspects of Lacan's theory, his description of the mechanisms by which gender becomes organised under patriarchy remains immensely provocative. Two aspects of this have generated most interest and abuse amongst feminists, both of which have reference to the paternal law: the castration complex and the use of the 'phallus' as *the* signifier of desire.

In the theories of feminine development proposed by the early Freudians, there was an aversion towards acceptance of the concept of the castration complex and a tendency to interpret it as an instance of a more generalised fear of loss. Lacan opposes this tendency, arguing that it loses the specific ability of Freud's position to explain the origin of sexual difference. For Lacan, as is evident in his theory of desire, subjectivity only arises through experiences of lack and absence – the human subject is created in the context of division, the principal one being that of castration. In fact, castration operates retrospectively by giving meaning to all other experiences of division and separation, it is *the* moment of humanisation of the child into the social world, the world in which the Law of the Father dominates. The castration complex is the instant at which the structuring power of patriarchy is imposed directly on the subjectivity of the individual, coming from outside, wrenching desire away from the Imaginary mother–child absorption with its fictitious promise of life outside the signifier, creating difference and separation. The detachment from the Imaginary that this produces is, as described earlier, supposedly essential for the individual to take up a position as a human subject, making possible relationships with others and the positioning of oneself within culture. Because of its power, castration – the symbolic value of having or not having the phallus – imposes itself on all other attributes, even those which have preceded the complex itself. In addition, because it is the structuring law of patriarchy, the division caused by the castration complex *creates* the distinctions between the sexes, forcing each individual to take up a position as male or female. Being constructed in the action of a division based upon a lack or the threat of a lack, such a position is arbitrary and tenuous, always threatening to dissolve and carry with it the differentiations upon which self-awareness is premised. 'The selection of the phallus as the mark around which subjectivity and sexuality are constructed reveals, precisely, that they are constructed, in a division which is both arbitrary and alienating' (Mitchell, 1982, p. 7). Sexual relationship thus becomes the relationship between divided entities, unable to reach and unite with one another across the fundamental chasm of castration. The subject enters the symbolic universe on the basis of division and absence, the fantasised possession or lack of a symbolic object onto which all meanings and differentiations are projected – the phallus.

Lacan is conventionally accused of being 'phallocentric', and with good reason. In some ways, the central element of his 'return to Freud' is the centrality he gives to the castration complex and to the role of the phallus as the signifier of difference and desire and the sole maker of the distinction between male and female. Gallop (1982, p. 18) presents at least one answer to those who criticise Lacan on these grounds:

> If feminism is to change a phallocentric world, phallocentrism must be dealt with and not denied. If Jones, through his outraged spirit of fairness, appears as woman's ally, we should beware his faith in the harmonious relation between the sexes. Of what use is that faith when it wants nothing more than to cover over the disharmony from which feminism arises and which it would change?

Whether this is a complete defence of Lacan is doubtful; as will be described, there are Lacanian feminists who challenge the paternal law in this respect. As noted above, for example, Lacan's identification of the phallus as *the* signifier of culture is so flamboyant as to make one question his motivation: is it absolutely obvious that the Symbolic is always patriarchal, by definition? Cixous (1975) argues that Lacan, like Freud, is tied to an account of gender that is too reliant on vision, on the 'specular' anatomical difference between male and female – 'A voyeur's theory, of course' (p. 95). Her suggestion, taken up by the celebrants of femininity to be discussed later, is that the true differences reside in sexual *pleasure* 'in as far as woman's libidinal economy is neither identifiable as a man nor referable to the masculine economy' (Ibid). This association of visual-centredness with a patriarchal 'perspective' is a revealing criterion for use in assessing the ideological biases inherent in Lacanian claims. Nevertheless, Lacan's interpretation of the Freudian idea of the phallus is important, for it centres on a view of its symbolic function as the creator and sustainer of a difference based on a power that is itself illusory.

The term 'symbolic' is important in understanding the Lacanian notion of the phallus. The phallus is not the penis, the biological emblem of the male, but a representation of the penis in which it is portrayed as the originator and possessor of a power which in fact is found outside the self, in patriarchal discourse. The phallus enters at the point of the castration complex, to subjugate both boys and girls, but also to hold out to the former the hope that accession to its power may become possible, that it is identical with the penis which he currently possesses. But the castration complex also solidifies an awareness of lack for both girls (an awareness of an absence which results in penis envy) and boys (discovery of the impossibility of Oedipal union with the mother). All sexuality is created in this lack, leaving male and female as partial beings and articulating a dimension of desire on which the phallus is placed. Because sexuality as division is incomplete, the phallus comes to represent that which stands outside it, which is whole and which can repair the damage produced by castration and instituted by the Law of the Father. So, the imagined phallus of the Father is introduced as the third term to break up the mother–child axis and to provoke desire and sexual differentiation. In doing this, it structures human relationships and acts as the dead letter of the law, the material force which subjugates and marginalises women, but which is also not simply in the hands (or penis) of any living male. The phallus represents the transfiguration of a trivial anatomical difference into a matrix of power, of which it stands as emblem.

This description of the role of the phallus reveals something about its nature. In one sense, it is absolutely material – the dominance of the patriarchal order and the Law of the Father. But in another sense, it is also totally illusory. For one thing, it is

Imaginary in the Lacanian sense, the site of an imagined unity where nothing really exists. It is an essential element in Lacan's theory that there is no complete unity or Otherness that inhabits the universe; there is only the search for this Other that reflects and constructs the absences each individual feels inside and which are fantasised as fulfilling the desires that have had to be repressed at the instance of the castration complex – the desire to be the object of the mother's desire.

> The fact that the phallus is a signifier means that it is in the place of the Other that the subject has access to it. But since this signifier is only veiled, as ratio of the Other's desire, it is this desire of the Other as such that the subject must recognise, that is to say, the other in so far as he is himself a subject divided by the signifying *Spaltung*. (Lacan, 1958, p. 288)

The fantasy of the phallus as *the* phenomenon of desire, the attainable instance of power, is perpetuated in the Imaginary by its absorption as a visual image: a visual distinction between the sexes is made to stand for all sexual difference, so that the complexity of human subjectivity is reduced to a particular image, standing in for the whole and appearing unified, but actually containing only a partial signification. Hence, it may be added, the interest that some feminists have shown in Freud's note in *Civilisation and Its Discontents* concerning the repression of the olfactory sense in favour of the visual mode. Identifying the 'female odour' as subversive of male authority, these writers suggest that its subjugation results in the discounting of female sexuality altogether – all sexuality becomes masculine, articulated in terms of the presence or absence of the male genital organ (see Gallop, 1982, p. 27). So the phallus holds out the empty image of an identity between maleness and ubiquitous power when in fact all that exists is a division, a Law of a Dead Father that holds all in thrall, male as well as female.

There is another sense in which the phallus is revealed to be fictitious. The symbolic order is entered by means of the castration complex; that is, for entry to occur the phallus has to be missing, cannot be possessed by either male or female. This again contrasts it with the biological penis: the point about the phallus is that is represents the human lot that desire is always unattainable, is in fact defined that way, as that which has been lost and never can be found. In the symbolic order, this recognition goes further than in the Imaginary, where it is still possible to fantasise wholeness in the position of the Other – an object which is outside the self, but full and complete. The Symbolic demands recognition that no such Other exists:

> Castration means first of all this – that the child's desire for the mother does not refer *to* her but *beyond* her, to an object, the phallus, whose status is first imaginary (the object presumed to satisfy her desire) and then symbolic (recognition that desire cannot be satisfied). (Rose, 1982, p. 38)

Safouan (1977) states that 'the phallus is the very point where the Other of Truth (capital T) is seen to be without truth (small t)' (p. 134) and Lacan refers to the 'barring' of the Other (Ø), all to represent the idea that the Symbolic order is premised on the recognition of the unattainability of desire, of the dissolution of the Imaginary. So to a point taken up strongly by feminists: if the phallus represents patriarchal power but is also fictitious, then that ideology which allows men to erect their privilege on the 'fact' of the reality of the phallus is itself a distortion and an injustice. Gallop (1982) begins the assault in a characteristic way with an analysis of the Name-of-the-Father, the word of patriarchal law which forbids incest and structures sexuality. The Name-of-the-Father attributed to a child, she notes, depends on the mother's word; it is both an articulation of the law inscribed in language, and a moment of weakness and uncertainty which delivers power to women. This leads to an issue to be returned to later, to the notion of there being a feminist practice that can oppose this law – in Gallop's case, the advised practice being infidelity.

In arguing that it is the primacy of the phallus which distinguishes patriarchal law, Lacan gives an account of women which makes them marginal, outsiders. This is not necessarily the same as arguing that women are inferior; rather it is a statement of their subjugation under the Law of the Father. There are important senses here in which women do not exist (the title of one of Lacan's papers is '~~The~~ Woman Does Not Exist' – see Mitchell and Rose, 1982). In a simple sense, this describes the marginalisation of women under patriarchy: the girl is a 'little man' with no existence in her own right, her designation as human arises through the imposition of the Law of the Father and is described according to a masculine lack, the lack of the masculine organ. The whole order of the Symbolic is instituted by the castration complex, which defines the female as the potential fate of the male, something outside and other. In addition, the otherness of the woman takes on a sexual aspect which is equally impossible ~~The~~ woman). Being the negative of the masculine, women come to represent to men the possible place of fulfilment of the absence which is encapsulated in their desire, originating in the castration complex which leaves the boy as incomplete as the girl. It is not simply, as in object relations theory, that women are desired because they seem to promise a return to the mother–son bond of imagined childhood; it is also that men fantasise women as the Other who can provide fulfilment in the place of the experience of lack which operates under the sign of patriarchal law. But this Otherness is impossible, for two reasons. First, it is precisely the characteristic of the phallic order that it prevents any sexual relation occurring, that sexuality is constructed as a division and separation, in which wholeness is prevented and the apparent unity and dominance of the Imaginary phallus comes to take the place of a possible heterogeneity of encounters. The phallus oppresses women, making contact impossible across the great divide of sex. Secondly, the creation of *any* absolute category, woman as much as anything else, is a fantasy: there are no absolute answers or places from which lack can be filled and desire attained. So '~~The~~ woman', an idealised Other divorced from the reality of particular women, exists no more than does the phallus. The function of this fantasy is to provide men with an idea of the possibility of their own coherence and the attainability of their desire in the unreality of ~~The~~ woman; subverting this fantasy should consequently be as much a feminist aim as a psychoanalytic one.

There are a number of substantial issues raised by these ideas with respect to the possibilities for a feminist psychoanalysis. One arises from a tension in Lacanian work between the strong statement just made, that there is no possibility of women's existence within patriarchy, and a tendency to place women's sexuality outside the phallic order, to make of it something different and other – something Imaginary, perhaps. On the one hand, it is a startling accusation against patriarchy that it can neither provide an account of feminine sexuality – witness Freud's own difficulties in this matter – nor supply the conditions under which sexual linkage can occur:

> The phallic order fails because, although unable to account for the feminine, it would, none the less, operate as a closure, attempting to create a closed universe that is thoroughly phallocentric. The sexual relation as relation between the sexes fails. (Gallop, 1982, p. 34)

On the other hand, it may be that the failure to attempt to account for female sexuality is itself a patriarchal ploy – saying that woman stands outside language may be a way of forbidding her a language of her own. This tension is apparent in Lacan's own work, as he raises the question of what the 'otherness' of woman might be, and speculates on the possibility of a 'jouissance', an enjoyment of the body that goes beyond the phallic order. But it is post-Lacanian feminists who have articulated a vision of an alternative female order more fully, valuing it positively instead of as an alienated impossibility, providing it with a cornucopian content to contrast with the Lacanian emphasis on lack.

Most of the theories in question here are based on a notion that the female body acts as an alternative framework to the masculine penis/phallus – that the rhythms and sensations of feminity present a subversive alternative to the dominance of the Name-of-the-Father. There is also a profound interest in women's relationship to language – whether there is some basic femininity which can forge its own relationship to language, or whether, as Lacan holds, language operates as a patriarchal organ to split and form the subject in a deterministic manner, outside of which there is no possibility of existence. Kristeva (1974, p. 137) is both accepting and challenging Lacan's values when she states, 'In "woman" I see something that cannot be represented, something that is not said, something above and beyond nomenclatures and ideologies.' This is an oppositional statement with respect to patriarchy: woman is both outside its system and also in an important sense *real* – 'The' woman does exist, but not within male-dominated language. This is a crucial point for many post-Lacanian feminists, whatever their precise standpoint: the idea that patriarchy is characterised by an insistence on the dominance of the phallus, on 'oneness' – one way of speaking, one mode of sexuality – while female opposition comes in the form of heterogeneity, multiple meanings and multiple sexuality. Lacan's reduction of woman to mere oppositeness is seen as a standard patriarchal ploy reducing the challenge that women's positivity poses to male dominance – it is still the female defined as the passive of the male, the aim of male desire, the hole for the penis. In opposition to Lacan, claims are made for the existence of a women's language, suppressed under patriarchy, which is related to the body and to sexuality, and which is expressed in syntactic differences and most of all in the multiple meanings with which words can be imbued. Women's speech is fluid and heterogeneous; similarly, women's sexuality cannot be pinned down, is neither purely homosexual nor heterosexual, and hence continuously threatens to subvert masculine authority. Irigaray (1977) clearly locates feminine multiplicity in the body, experienced as a mystery that is always plural – at least two, never subject to the singularity of the penis, always touching itself auto-erotically, the lips of the vagina rubbing and embracing continually.

> This woman does not have a sex. She has at least two of them, but they cannot be identified as ones. Indeed she has many more of them than that. Her sexuality, always at least double, is in fact *plural*. (p. 102)

The 'otherness' of woman resides in her inconstancy, her multiplicity and flux, which functions subversively to undermine masculine attempts at control, at holding things in their place.

Gallop (1982) extends this notion into an entire feminist system of unsystematicity: the feminist revolution is that which turns upside down all authority, which leaves up in the air all questions, which refuses to make pleasure into stone. Female sexuality is

> a '*jouissance* enveloped in its own contiguity'. Such *jouissance* would be sparks of pleasure ignited by *contact* at any point, any moment along the line, not waiting for a closure, but enjoying the touching. As a result of such sparks, the impatient economy aimed at finished meaning-products (theses, conclusions, definitive statements) might just go up in smoke. (p. 31)

Just as the infidelity of an individual woman can undermine the claim to paternity by any man, so the rigorous practice of infidelity – fidelity to infidelity, if such a thing is possible – undermines the

Name-of-the-Father and subverts patriarchy. In addition, and centrally, acceptance of infidelity frees women from their own desire for the phallus and hence from adherence to the patriarchal regime: infidelity means recognising the non-existence of something outside that possesses all the power, and that is whole, rigid and the Truth. In a sense, the practice of infidelity is a Lacanian practice because it undermines the Imaginary search for the complete Other. But where the ability to become infidels originates is not all that clear – perhaps again in some in-built possibility within the body of the female.

Gallop's insistence on the power of feminine infidelity is congruent with other post-Lacanian ideas, but misses the positive content of many of the theories. The idea of infidelity to all orthodoxies implies a complete dismantling of the phallus, not just of the penis–phallus link: that is, *all* forms of authority and power are subverted. This is not even completely representative of Irigaray's thought, and other feminists have been more willing to assert the positivity of the female alternative; that is, to make claims for a new, different form of power. Cixous (1976) supplies a paean to womanhood that celebrates its potential for creativity, and for taking on male practice (in this case, in writing) and overcoming it. Cixous asserts woman's libido as 'cosmic' and her unconscious as 'worldwide'; feminine capacities can undo and outdo patriarchy, given the breaking of controls and the expression of full multiplicity.

> Heterogeneous, yes. For her joyous benefits she is erogenous; she is the erotogeneity of the heterogeneous: airborne swimmer, in flight, she does not cling to herself; she is dispersible, prodigious, stunning, desirous and capable of others, of the other woman that she will be, of the other woman she isn't, of him, of you. (p. 260)

Femininity is also not content with possessing a discourse that is different from that of patriarchy: in Cixous' version, it is an enormous hunger and joyous activation of living and desiring. The traditional Freudian account and its Lacanian derivative, in interpreting female desire as penis envy, belittles not just womanhood, but life itself.

> I don't want a penis to decorate my body with. But I do desire the other for the other, whole and entire, male or female;

> because living means wanting everything that is, everything that lives, and wanting it alive. Castration? Let others toy with it. What's a desire originating from a lack? A pretty meagre desire. (p. 262)

Whereas Lacan emphasises the impossibility of desire, the cipher-like status of individuality, Cixous asserts its fullness, the strength and revolutionary fervour that derive from wanting and wishing. Lacanianism, by making development both fixed and universally alienating, provides analytic tools for comprehending the organisation of desire while at the same time belittling any idea of change – there is nothing outside signification. Cixous, in contrast, takes Lacan's account of language and opposes it with the body. Lacan makes little attempt to articulate the world of women in terms other than those of patriarchy – the whole of culture, in his view. Cixous leaves patriarchy aside, 'A pretty meagre desire'.

Finally along these lines, Julia Kristeva has articulated an alternative system to that of Lacan which takes the idea of a specifically feminine system still further. In her case, however, there is an explicit denial that femininity has anything necessary to do with gender; rather, it is related to the ability to subvert the symbolic order by absorption in a preceding 'semiotic' dimension which is produced by the oral and anal drives of the child in her/his relationship with the pre-Oedipal mother. This is an approach that differs from that of Irigaray by its acceptance of the phallic order: language and the Symbolic are necessary to create a division between child and mother. But, like object relations theorists, Kristeva denies that the phallic attributes of language are necessarily male: the phallic mother is more powerful than the phallic father, because more veiled and obscured. So Kristeva does not propose ignoring the phallic attributes of language; rather, she argues that its power must be used and subverted at the same time. The phallus is not necessarily male, but is available to women too; equally, the particular feminine attributes of the semiotic are available to all with bodies to feel. For the semiotic is a particularly physical system, dealing with those aspects of language that are not simply concerned with representation – rhythm, tone, slips and colour.

> The semiotic is a more immediate expression of the drives and is linked to the bodily contact with the mother before the paternal

> order of language comes to separate subject from mother . . . the semiotic is always traversing language, always a bodily presence disruptive to the sublimated symbolic order. (Gallop, 1982, p. 124)

The semiotic finds its clearest expression in certain forms of art – hence the revolutionary importance of art for Kristeva, and the optimism with which she can face patriarchy. Whereas for Lacan, the pre-Symbolic era is ruined by the insertion of language, and rightly so because of its illusory nature, for Kristeva the semiotic operates to subvert the Symbolic order, holding out the possibility of a radical break.

There are a number of difficulties with all the positions described here. The foremost one that applies to feminist theorists is the tendency to fall back into biologism. Lacan's system is explicitly concerned with describing the origins of sexual difference in the splits introduced by language; all his opponents seem to assume the pre-existent nature of the feminine, expressed in the woman's body and her subversive relationship to language. In displacing the phallus, it is possible that this approach will lead back to the unintended biologism and romanticisation of the feminine that was the fate of the earlier Freudian revisionists. If it is from the body that femininity derives its speech, then it is also limited and determined by the body – something which poses empirical problems (what is this special heterogeneity of the female body? is it present for every individual woman, under all social conditions?) and which threatens to destroy the precise arena in which psychoanalysis operates, the arena in which fantasy appears as the gap between physical reality and imaginative possibility. There is also considerable inconsistency between theories, with some writers lauding the specifically feminine, while others (notably Kristeva) take femininity as representative of potentials that lie within every individual – that people of either gender can be 'feminised' in a revolutionary fashion. Is this a disagreement over biology, or over history? Some theorists (again, particularly Kristeva) also allow their images of femininity and motherhood to merge, placing immense emphasis on the role of the pre-Oedipal mother and romanticising her in a way that threatens to fashion an alternative orthodoxy not unlike that present in object relations theory. Other writers oppose this tendency (for example, Irigaray sees the maternal as phallic, 'closing in on the jealous possession of its valuable product' – 1977, p. 104), but none provide the kind of detailed account of the social determinants of mothering that some object relations theorists have managed. But most importantly, there is a question to be raised concerning the distinctive feminine practice that all these writers invoke: heterogeneous, multiple, inconstant. Lacan's claim is that womanhood is not construable through the language of patriarchy; in opposing him, Irigaray, Cixous and Kristeva use just this language – albeit flamboyantly, shiftingly and sometimes incomprehensibly. The result is a picture of femininity that is not, in its detail, remarkably different from many conventional (male) images of women: inconsistent and intuitive, with a sexuality that is less clearly directed and more tactile than that of men. The feminist theorists value this image differently, as a sign of women's potential rather than their faults. But the 'marks of womanhood' are not radically different from those given by patriarchy.

Despite these limitations, Lacan's feminist critics do bring out real problems with his theory. A relatively minor point is that in employing Lévi-Strauss' notion of women as objects of exchange, he runs the risk of assuming what he is intending to explain – the origin of sexual difference. This is minor because of shifts in Lacan's later work, but it does reflect an attitude towards women which pervades all his formulations. Lacan's emphasis on the arbitrary nature of sexual division is an important attraction for feminist theory, because it provides the tools with which to challenge the biologistic reasoning that so often is used to legitimise sexist practices. But his casual identification of the Law of the Father with the whole of culture undermines this approach and with it his careful account of the construction of the subject within the symbolic order. This is seen most clearly in the discussion of the nature and functions of the phallus: it seems to be the Lacanian argument that the *arbitrary* linking of phallus and penis is what is primarily responsible for the ridiculousness of the claims that men make to dominance. Feminist practice under this view is to reveal the arbitrariness of the linkage, but the dominance of the phallus cannot itself be challenged because of its structuring role in the construction of the human subject. As Gallop (1982) argues, following Irigaray, this fails to acknowledge the conditions of power that actually surround human relationships. For example, the fact that it is the penis which gives shape to the image of power cannot be accidental, is not totally arbitrary; rather, it is either biologically determined or it reflects pervasive social arrangements which are built on underlying relations of force. Lacan's failure to consider properly the second of these explanations vacates the field for easy appeal to the first. Henriques *et al.* (1984) take this further in criticising Lacan for the use of a structuralist paradigm that gives his theory a tendency to 'collapse into an account of a universal, albeit contradictory, subject who is not situated historically, who is tied and bound by pre-existing language, and is incapable of change because of it' (p. 217). The point is not that the whole of Lacanian theory is worthless, but that his description of the construction of the subject in language needs to be contextualised by an account of those power relations which construct the system itself, which give rise to the order of language that centres on the phallus and that creates the human subject in accordance with a patriarchal law. Lacan's theory describes the operations of that law in a way that is proving particularly provocative and influential for feminists; but to be more sure of being able to change it, an explanation of the origins and determinants of the Law of the Father is required. It is probably the case, however, that such an explanation will be found only outside the boundaries of psychoanalysis, in social theory and action.

Part IV
Therapy and Cure

Many of the issues surrounding the politics of psychoanalysis take concrete form in discussions of therapy, the practical arena in which analysis operates. This is because in dealing with personal change, therapy raises the question of political change, in two main ways. First, the social world places limits on the extent of personal change that can be brought about through therapy: material circumstances will restrict the difference that even the most powerful of 'talking cures' can make. Secondly, if individuality is constructed in a social context, then therapy acts politically when it operates at the level of the basic 'building blocks' of personality. The processes by which this occurs, particularly the impact of power relations on the therapeutic encounter, thus becomes a central issue when examining how political and personal change might be produced.

Part 4 investigates the approaches taken by psychoanalysts to therapeutic interventions. In Chapter 8, discussion focuses on the aims of psychoanalytic psychotherapy, in particular comparing followers of the 'analytic attitude' which claims that no absolute cures are possible, with those that have attempted to ameliorate the apparent pessimism of this position. Arguments appear from both left and right: some theorists suggest that what is most potent in Freudianism is its analysis of the sources of distress, with therapy being a compromise of this radical vision; others regard Freud as too dismissive of the chances of bringing about lasting change. In general, Chapter 8 defends the analytic attitude against both these positions but also argues that it is important to move beyond the analytic attitude towards commitment to some particular directions for development. Therapy is politically valuable because it addresses the internalised structures that contribute to the perpetuation of oppression and distress, but it is not the whole story, it must work alongside social action if social change is to occur.

Chapter 9 moves on from these relatively abstract considerations to discuss the accounts that analysts give of the mechanisms of therapy, especially concerning the actions and role of the analyst her or himself. The politics of this are usually left unconsidered and implicit in analytic writing. But in this apparently technical material (dealing, for instance, with the nature of transference and the use of interpretations) is contained insights into some central assumptions, attitudes and possibilities for psychoanalytic activity. Most importantly, different analytic approaches show varying degrees of awareness of the power relations present in therapy, and of how these can and should be worked with. When these power relations are recognised and used to explore the *internalised* power structures that have been embedded in the client's personality, psychoanalysis begins to contribute to social change.

8 Psychoanalysis and Psychotherapy

In Chapter 3, stress was laid on Freud's therapeutic 'pessimism', his belief that the goal of psychoanalysis could not be to bring about a major transformation of the quality of human existence, only to change 'hysterical misery' into 'common unhappiness'. In general, as described in Chapter 1, Freud seems to have been far less interested in psychoanalysis as a therapeutic system than as an instrument of knowledge, of the archaeology both of the individual and of society. Freud's project was to *understand*, to develop a system of ideas that could make sense of people, in their individual psychology and in the structures that they create for themselves. Psychotherapy was a secondary project, undertaken 'to make a living', a nuisance to the extent that it called for the watering down of analytic severities in the face of the pragmatics of everyday life. 'Therapeutic zeal' was to be avoided because it interferes with the proper conduct of an analysis, the primary goal of which is knowledge and not cure (Segal, 1981, p. 69). The most enthusiastic supporters of Freudian pessimism, such as Marcuse (1955) and Jacoby (1975), have taken up precisely this point, that theory and therapy are not necessarily integrated concerns, and have given it a particularly political twist, arguing that it is in its theory that the radical contribution of psychoanalysis resides. In so doing, they have attempted to defend the radical tradition within psychoanalysis against the adaptationist compromises that always threaten to engulf it and make it a poor relation in the pantheon of medical treatments, a relatively ineffective item in the structures of diagnosis–treatment–cure.

The starting point for this chapter is the argument that psychoanalytic psychotherapy *is* capable of offering insights and experiences which are congruent with, and can contribute to, progressive political changes. This position derives from the discussions of earlier chapters, in which it was suggested that the various branches of psychoanalysis have supplied important concepts for furthering understanding of how each individual becomes constructed, and of the incorporation of social axes into the organisation of desire. This line of argument makes psychoanalysis an agency of criticism even when it restricts itself to the personal concerns of individuals, because at the heart of these concerns is a process of social construction. Similarly, just as personality is socially organised, so is personal distress; investigating the desires and anxieties of individuals leads irresistibly to social critique. Therapy is not, in this view, a temporary palliative to tide the individual over until social change comes about. Instead, it is seen as a part of the struggle for such change, a necessary part as without it progress will falter on the barrier of deeply entrenched, retrograde and conformist feelings and ideas. Through the intense relationships of early life, as psychoanalysis has demonstrated, the power structures of society are reproduced in each individual; in the intense encounter of psychoanalytic psychotherapy, often involving regression to, and always commentary upon and reworking of, those early experiences, these power structures can be confirmed, or demolished, or revised. Psychotherapy is not an irrelevance for political activity; it is a potentially crucial part of the endeavour to 'transform consciousness' which is entwined with all the other transformations that radical practice involves. It is not, therefore, just for its revelations about the links between internal and social worlds that psychoanalysis is valuable, but also for the directives for action that these revelations produce.[1]

The position taken here is that psychoanalytic psychotherapy can operate productively to interrogate and alter the internalised stance taken up by each individual with respect to the social world. It is from this position that the attitudes and assumptions of various psychoanalytic accounts of therapy are examined in the rest of this chapter, with focus resting particularly on the *aims* for therapy expressed by different theorists. This is because the pronouncement of aims often expresses an orientation towards questions such as the limits of therapy and its social role, either explicitly or implicitly through the kinds of attainable change that are envisaged. As in previous chapters, the main interest is in the work of analysts in the object relations and Kleinian traditions, who between them provide a set of coherent and instructive accounts of the purposes of therapeutic practice. By way of contrast, some notions derived from Lacanian work are used to present an alternative image of the 'political' possibilities of analytic practice, leading into a discussion in Chapter 9 of the roots and functions of power relations in analysis. But first it is useful to consider in more detail the general question that has been touched on above: of whether psychotherapy of any kind, but specifically psychoanalytic therapy, can ever be more than a palliative for common ills. To do this, the views of Marcuse and Jacoby are described (because of their significance for radical critics of psychoanalysis), and Philip Rieff's important distinction between 'analytic' and 'therapeutic' attitudes, is evaluated and employed.

Against psychotherapy

Marcuse (1955), one of the most eloquent supporters of psychoanalysis' radical vision, argues that psychotherapy must be recognised as a compromise with the forces of oppression that may be necessary to enable individuals to survive, but which is nevertheless a partial betrayal of the insights provided by psychoanalysis. As such, it has no significance for theory.

> While psychoanalytic theory recognises that the sickness of the individual is ultimately caused and sustained by the sickness of his civilisation, psychoanalytic therapy aims at curing the individual so that he can continue to function as part of a sick civilisation without surrendering to it altogether. (p. 245)

Psychotherapy thus represents 'a course in resignation'; true radicalness resides in psychoanalysis' devastating account of the damage caused by social repression, not in the exigencies of making people feel better. The danger, in Marcuse's view, is that the pragmatic concerns of therapy will be extended to debase the uncompromising vision of theory; the crucial point is to maintain the distinction between modifying distress and creating real change. In Marcuse's opinion, the promulgation of positive notions of cure always mean total conformism unless there is social change; hence his dismantling of the ideological underpinnings of

Erich Fromm's suggestion that therapy can realistically aim at the 'optimal development of a person's potentialities and the realization of his individuality' (p. 258). Marcuse asserts that if these attributes are defined in the context of contemporary society, their attainment would be 'tantamount to successful adjustment' – this being a term of abuse in the Marcusian lexicon. If, on the other hand, some transcendent quality of 'individuality' is being referred to, then it cannot be attained without the total transformation of the social world: today, the achievement of such a therapeutic goal 'would mean "curing" the patient to become a rebel or (which is saying the same thing) a martyr' (p. 258).

It is important to realise that Marcuse does not argue that no psychotherapy should be offered people in their distress; rather, his complaint is that pragmatic goals are mistaken in the post-Freudian literature for absolute ones, and that the real goals are only to be found in Freud's analysis of the social sources of personal oppression and disturbance. Twenty years after the first publication of *Eros and Civilisation*, this argument received an exact recapitulation in Jacoby's (1975) memorable *Social Amnesia*. Here again is the Freudian stress on the *necessity* of neurosis in an oppressive society, coupled with a defence of theory as the true endeavour of psychoanalysis, working to reveal the precise mechanisms whereby oppression takes its effect.

> *Psychoanalysis is a theory of an unfree society that necessitates psychoanalysis as a therapy*. To reduce the former to the latter is to gain the instrument at the expense of truth; psychoanalysis becomes merely medicine.(p. 122)

Psychotherapy is forced to operate within the ideological and political structures of society; of necessity, this means that it cannot stand outside these structures to offer new images of human capability. As long as this is recognised, in the Marcuse–Jacoby argument, no harm is done; once the heuristics of therapy are raised up as universal truths, psychoanalytic theory, which is, in principle, able to transcend social conformism, becomes contaminated and blunt. In an unfree society, the interpersonal sensitivity present in therapy can only be a palliative; Jacoby echoes Marcuse once again in stating that real sensitivity under such conditions turns out as 'revolution or madness; the rest is chatter' (p. 105).

There is considerable value in the critiques of psychotherapy presented by Marcuse and Jacoby, and taken up by other radical theorists. Many therapists have overgeneralised from their everyday practice with individuals or small groups to suggest that social change can be brought about by therapeutic means – that restructuring society reduces to altering the psychology of individuals. The radical critics effectively counterbalance this notion by distinguishing appropriately between levels: society stands over and above every individual, influencing her/him (psychoanalysis being the discipline that describes the mechanisms by which this is done), but not reducible to the individual level. Hence, there is a clear division between therapy and political action, and it is only the latter that can bring about social change. This is an important point that can serve as one yardstick of the social sophistication of psychotherapeutic claims: basically, it represents an understanding of the limits of psychology. However, where the radical critique is at odds with the position outlined at the beginning of this chapter is in its implication that however justifiable therapy may be in its own terms (for instance, supporting people through acute distress), it has *nothing* to do with political liberation. The appreciation that these critics have of the need for a radical psychology does not go as far as an appreciation of the potential for radical psychotherapy: from the truth that therapy can never on its own bring about political change and that the possibilities for therapeutic improvement are limited within the constraints of capitalism, Marcuse and Jacoby read off the false notion that therapy is irrelevant to political practice, and hence that all psychoanalysis' radicalness is confined to its theory. But it is precisely because psychoanalytic theory so convincingly demonstrates that social forces are internalised by each individual and live on inside to form the basis of personality, that it is politically relevant to develop ways of acting directly on these internalised forces, as well as upon the external structures which give rise to them. This is not confusing therapy and politics, but it is rescuing therapy for a potential role *in* politics, based on the idea that individual change is not completely determined by social change, and requires methods tuned to the uncovering of unconscious structures.

Analysis and withdrawal

The view that psychoanalytic therapy is inherently limited is not confined to those critics who regard the whole of psychotherapy as conformist practice. Many traditional therapists have also been wary of making claims for their practice that are too far-reaching or positive in implication. For example, Storr (1966), in an engaging commentary on the concept of 'cure' in psychoanalysis, takes the view that the psychoanalytic procedure is inherently impossible if it sets itself up to provide some new way of being that is genuinely 'mentally healthy' or 'cured'. For one thing, psychoanalysis is not particularly successful at getting rid of symptoms, and should not be approached with this notion in mind; it is refreshing to read an analyst willing to admit that 'the evidence that psychoanalysis cures anybody of anything is so shaky as to be practically non-existent' (p. 57). Symptoms are not the point, of course, as most people seeking analysis do not have any specific behavioural dysfunction, but are more likely to be suffering from a general sense of malaise, an uneasiness with themselves or their personal relationships. In this, they are no different from anyone else: 'Patients can only be distinguished from non-patients by the fact that they present themselves for analysis, and not because they are noticeably more neurotic than those who do not seek an analyst's assistance' (p. 59). Storr suggests that most analysts note with relief the point at which their analysands stop talking about symptoms and get on to the real stuff, the structure of their lives; analysis thenceforward becomes 'an end in itself, a journey of exploration which is undertaken for its own sake; not so much a treatment, more a way of life' (p. 53). This journey cannot have a goal, because all ends are undermined by the analytic process: as one reaches 'integration', analysis reveals it to be built on shaky foundations; there is always more that can be said.

In suggesting that psychoanalysis is never ending, a process rather than the production of a particular state, Storr's view is akin to that of the more theoretically sophisticated Rieff (1966), who presents a strong defence of the 'analytic attitude' outlined in Chapter 3, whereby no solutions to the conundrums of living are offered and the neurotic roots of all apparent salvations are exposed by analysis itself. In its structure and content, psychoanalysis is both a product of and commentary upon the fragmentation of contemporary civilisation, offering no roots, no place to take hold, its most potent symbol that of the refugee.

> Psychoanalysis is yet another method of learning how to endure the loneliness produced by culture. Psychoanalysis is its representative therapy – in contrast to classical therapies of commitment. (Rieff, 1966, p. 27)

To the extent that they remain true to the analytic approach, psychoanalysts are of necessity cultural critics offering only the hard truth – that there is nowhere to hide. In the face of this awareness, there can be no talk of 'cure', no search for some new meaning or message by which to live. Despite the apparent nihilism of this reading of psychoanalysis, Rieff does provide an image of reconciliation which is very much akin to Freud's emphasis on reason. In Rieff's view, the central twentieth-century skill is the ability to live in the knowledge that there are no solutions, to reconcile oneself to the awareness that all around is alienation, and yet to remain sufficiently detached and balanced to tolerate these uncertainties without collapsing into neurosis or religiosity. A curiously negative view, but one built on an image of the analyst at the centre of the psychoanalytic procedure: detached, critical, cool, aware of all possibilities, choosing none.

The position that psychoanalysis can offer no solutions or cures is to some extent at variance with the therapeutic endeavour inherent in most psychoanalytic practice. Storr (1966) for one does end up with a positive image of reconciliation between the individual and her/his 'actual nature', both in terms of knowledge and way of life. More centrally, his ironic notion that psychoanalysis 'becomes itself the disease of which the patient seeks to be cured' (p. 58) is in part a screen for the kind of use of analysis that Rieff implicitly criticises – as a replacement for religious salvation, a new 'way of life'. But Rieff's own argument falters on the image of analytic distance that it presents, even though the accompanying cultural analysis is of dazzling perspicacity. At times, the problem is a crude individualism in which what appears to be being advocated is withdrawal into the self, sometimes to the extent of total egocentrism or perhaps Machiavellianism.

> When Freud rejected the notion of psychoanalysis as a propaedeutic to accepting one or another religious community, he imagined an ideal patient, one so strengthened that he could tolerate a return to nothing more than an environment in which the ego could fight more capably for itself in the subtle and universal war of all against all. (Rieff, 1966, p. 28)

Whether this is Freud or Rieff is open to debate. Perhaps more perniciously, however, the kind of withdrawal that Rieff reads in the 'analytic attitude' is that of absorption in detachment, taking up a position equidistant from all possibilities and viewing the most radical social transformation as no less specious than the most rigid authoritarianism. The problem with this idea is that, like some forms of Eastern 'liberation', it is a recipe for individualistic quietism: if all actions can be analysed, then there is no point in following any of them with the hope that something real and new will be attained. There are no ways of genuinely changing painful circumstances, only a series of techniques for psychic numbing. But although in practice psychoanalysis does sometimes seem to espouse acceptance as its goal, it also possesses tendencies which continually challenge and undermine the quietist option. First, all psychoanalytic goals – even detachment – are intermediate, because the meanings of these goals can always be interpreted and reframed. Psychoanalysis is ironic: it purports to build certain positives (rationality, self-control, self-knowledge), only to subvert them in the same instant. Rationality is undermined by the irrationality of unconscious desire, self-control is rendered impossible by the vacuity of the self when faced with the determining principles of the unconscious and social structuring, self-knowledge is always out of reach, needing another attempt at 'working through'. But there is a limit to the irony and continuous analysis, because psychoanalysis does have a story to tell that means it can take up a stance and can be differentiated from positions which suggest withdrawal as the only appropriate response to the horrors of everyday life. This is the story, developed in detail in earlier chapters, of how the self becomes constructed and of the incorporation of social axes into the organisation of desire. Psychoanalysis takes a particular position as to what is true and significant in human affairs, whether it be the fate of the instincts or of fulfilling personal relationships. It judges success or failure in these areas (even if success can never be complete) and explores the contribution of social relations of various kinds. In so doing, it provides some criteria for assessment of the relative worth of current social relations and of alternative social configurations – it takes, in other words, a 'moral' view. 'Detachment' may make life more livable, but it too is a neurotic escape; psychoanalysis has its own imperatives, to act in line with the excavation of personal and social roots revealed by its investigations. This takes therapy beyond the analytic attitude and into something more committed.

Relative goals

The argument given above is that the goals of a social psychoanalysis must partially accept but also move beyond the 'analytic attitude', towards commitment to a system of relationship-enhancing values. As well as opposing adoption of a 'distanced' attitude towards the world as a final therapeutic goal, this view is also at odds with another strong tendency in some social and psychological theories, that of a relativism which states that any position is as good as any other. Relativism is also not Freud's point of view; at its purest, the analytic attitude may reduce all possible options to equal neuroticism, but Freud maintains a sense of what is true, if not always of what is good: the truth lies in the activities of the sciences, which was one reason for his insistence that psychoanalysis should rank as one. Some analysts, particularly those viewing analysis as a hermeneutic rather than a scientific endeavour, have not bothered to include ideas of more truthful perceptiveness in their catalogue of therapeutic goals. This is visible in work from across the political spectrum. Storr (1966, p. 73) suggests that '"To every man his delusional system" is a likely principle of human existence; and the evidence that psychoanalysis is more than just another delusional system is slender'. Identification with the analytic attitude would then become simply acceptance of a system which makes existence more viable, not necessarily one which is closer to the truth about the human world. This is a strange bedfellow of Storr's additional assertion that the therapeutic impact of analysis derives from discovering 'who one is and how one came to be as one is' (p. 73);

discovering who one is through the adoption of a delusional system seems an unlikely recommendation. Sandler, Dare and Holder (1973), in their influential dictionary, offer something similar, if less extreme:

> it would appear that therapeutic change as a consequence of analysis depends, to a large degree, on the provision of a structured and organised conceptual and affective framework within which the patient can effectively place himself and his subjective experience of himself and others. (p. 115)

Presumably this is not meant to be as intellectualist as it sounds; still, it begs the question of whether there is something special about the analytic framework, or whether any other persuasive framework would do equally well. Ingleby (1984), writing from an explicitly socialist position, ends up with a similar formulation, if more fashionable vocabulary:

> The discourse of psychoanalysis provides a framework of interpretative and implicit responses, in terms of which individuals may orient and articulate themselves; it thus gives them a 'position' within a discourse, in which to exist as subjects. (p. 52)

This is certainly true and may well be a reason why analysis is therapeutic – it makes people feel less lost, it gives them a sense of themselves as in possession of their lives. In the 'action language' of Schafer (1976), it makes intelligible the previously 'disclaimed actions' in a person's history and helps her/him acknowledge them as part of their own choices. But whereas Schafer unselfconsciously emphasises the analysand's growing appreciation of the *real* origins of her/his actions and the *real* choices available for the future, the formulation that Ingleby provides leaves us with the individual subject swirling around in a web of discourse, anxious for a place to stand, grateful for the apparent firm ground of psychoanalytic insight which in fact is no more than one of a multitude of possible frameworks. Therapy is an illusion if it claims to offer anything concerned with the 'truth' of the subject; in reality it is no more than another ideological stance, an 'as if' way of relating to the world which provides relief from confusion and personal emptiness because it happens to be relatively coherent.

There is a lot to be said in favour of this formulation, which is close to the Freudian analytic attitude in its rejection of salvational cures or commitments to any one system of belief as 'the' truth. As noted above, however, it differs from the Freudian view in not even being committed to psychoanalysis, seeing it only as another system of discourses which is relatively successful in aiding the individual in finding a creed to prop up her/his dissolving subjectivity. It is also politically pessimistic. The enormous contribution of psychoanalysis to social thought is to reveal the intricate interweavings of social and personal that take place in the construction of the individual, and hence to demonstrate the manner in which ideological relations enter into the depth of the personality and provide axes around which it is organised. Psychoanalytic theory in this area is a collection of *empirical* assertions, not just a story; if it is wrong, if, for example, consciousness really does follow automatically from economic conditions or people's personalities really are determined by their genes, then it loses its value. Divorcing these theoretical insights from the practice of psychoanalysis is to take up the Marcuse–Jacoby position criticised earlier, that therapy can neither contribute to political change nor offer the individual anything more than emergency treatment or consolation. Yet, if psychoanalysis is correct in its description of the way social structures enter into the individual, and if analytic therapy really is powerful enough to bring about deep-seated personality change, there has to be a way of conceptualising therapeutic goals which goes further than relativism. Ingleby's idea that psychoanalysis provides people with a 'position' within discourse is an important one, similar to saying that it provides them with a voice to speak and a mind to make sense of things; but what they say and what sense they make is also a therapeutic concern. Many psychoanalytic workers have recognised this and branched off into new directions; in what follows, some of the most provocative of these are surveyed.

Psychotherapeutic cure, or 'promises, promises'

The principal attraction of the 'analytic attitude' is that it stops short of offering any kind of cure as a possibility, instead limiting itself to the negative aim of revealing to the individual the sources of her/his personal distress and then allowing her/him to determine the stance to be taken up towards them. In this way, psychoanalysis is freed to remain as a critical theory, never to be pinned down except in terms of its own irony, an 'attitude' rather than a set of precepts. In going further than this, one has to be cautious not to lose the great attribute of the analytic attitude: that it resists conformist consolations and ideological common sense. Still, it is not hard to see why many psychoanalysts and other therapists have been appalled at the grimness of the analytic attitude and have attempted to construct manageable aims for therapy which appease the demand for increased happiness. Freud himself, on occasions, moved this way, with his espousal of the hope that the ego might colonise the id, that consciousness might dominate unconscious functioning. Fundamentally, the aim of 'strengthening the ego' represents a siding with the reality principle, in a manner leading to increased alienation from unconscious desire, desire which in other accounts (e.g. the Lacanian one) represents the 'truth' of the subject. Yet the bulk of Freudian psychoanalysis is geared towards resisting consolatory gestures, posing questions, pursuing analyses of defences, the analyst distant, reflective, questioning. A task that calls for patience, realism, a lack of romanticism about what might be achieved. Small wonder, perhaps, that many therapists, faced with the clamourings of their clients and the pressures of their own anxieties, have itched to move further than analysis into what Rieff (1966) dubs the 'ecstatic attitude', the 'triumph of the therapeutic'.

Various therapeutic aims have been presented as alternatives to those of Freudianism. Most of these hinge on commitment to some system of values, a positive goal which can be embraced not only to bring about the removal of symptoms but to provide some new meaning to life. On the whole, this is a subtle endeavour, with the positive goal being little more than absorption into social normality, or the creation of fulfilling personal relationships. Hence the traditional 'termination criteria' for the end of an analysis, listed by Segal (1981, p. 23) as 'the lifting of repression, insight, freeing the patient from early fixations and inhibitions, and enabling him to form full and satisfactory personal relationships'. As will be seen below, there are quite a few variants on this kind of formulation, which rely upon the plausibility of realistic ordinariness while obscuring the ideological components inherent in common sense – what price 'full and satisfactory personal relationships' in a society dedicated to their destruction? But in the history of psychoanalysis there have also been some more consciously provocative formulations, which usually have led their promulgators into dissension but which have also had a powerful impact on the ideals expressed by many branches of psychotherapy. In what follows the general orientation of these formulations is criticised not when they go beyond the analytic attitude – as suggested above, this is necessary if the insights of psychoanalysis into social construction are to be acted upon in a progressive fashion – but when the forms of commitment that they promote are the product of particular ideological assumptions, usually left unquestioned or unacknowledged.

Rieff (1966) is the most poetic chronicler of 'commitment therapies', focusing most cogently on the work of Jung and Reich. His project is to demonstrate the 'salvational' nature of the approaches championed by these charismatic figures, therapies oriented towards the replacement of a lost religious culture by something new to which the individual could aspire. Commitment therapies are criticised by Rieff as a return to faith motivated by an inability to sustain that balanced, ironic distance which is the only protection that the modern person has against the ravages of culture. So Reich, as discussed in Chapter 6, presented aims which appear political but mask a biologically inspired identification with the goodness of the instincts: the goal of revolution is a new, non-repressive society in which the sexual urge can be engaged in to the full. There is an exciting optimism in the image of the full genital embrace which will destroy the conditions for neurosis in one cataclysmic and exquisitely simple manouevre. Because neurosis is biological and monocausal, the strategies for cure are relatively straightforward.

> The severity of every form of psychic illness is directly related to the severity of the genital disturbance. The prospects of cure and the success of the cure are directly dependent upon the possibility of establishing the capacity for full genital gratification. (Reich, 1942, p. 96)

The enormous difficulties with this view have been detailed in Chapter 6; the relevant point here is the contrast that this kind of therapeutic programme makes with that of Freud. Rieff mostly takes up the mystical belief in full genitality that is evident in Reich's writings, his search for an ideal character, but his missionary zeal is also shown in his reductionist prophecies of revolution: sexual revolution is the way, genital orgasm the meaning of life.

Rieff reserves his most telling irony for Jung, whose enterprise he sees as fundamentally theological and reactionary. Rieff reads Jung as in direct opposition to Freud: where Freud wanted to free us from the dictates of unreason and the domination of outworn symbols, Jung wanted to reconcile us with them, to find cure in the acceptance of 'the eternal order, replicated within [us] symbolically . . . By re-adapting the patient to his dominant archetypes, Jung helps him to neutralise the neurotic component in them' (p. 76). Hence the notion of 'commitment therapy': Jung dedicated himself to the construction of a new 'myth' for living, to fill the gap left by the decline of religious mythology – a decline to which Freud had contributed with his picking over of the origins of religion and culture. The myth Jung created, through detours and obscurities, resolved in the end to one thing: an integrating anti-rationalism that espouses feeling as its dominant component, the basic component of a new faith.

> The Jungian theory proposes to every disaffected humanist his 'personal myth' as a sanctuary against the modern world. Against the vulgar democracy of intelligence, Jungian theory proposes an aristocracy of feeling. (Rieff, 1966, p. 102)

Cure resides in being able to live according to one's myth, thereby attaining integration on a scale undreamed of under the auspices of the analytic attitude. 'Saving nonsense' is Rieff's term for this: any tradition is all right as long as it is a tradition, as long as 'Modern Man in Search of a Soul' can find a place to hide.

As argued earlier, Rieff's advocacy of the 'analytic attitude' (continually contrasted with 'commitment therapies') has deep drawbacks, notably because it leads him to place all forms of commitment on an equal footing, biology no different from religion, which in turn is no different from radical activity. It is one thing to argue that the roots of any individual's commitment to any particular scheme are analysable; another thing entirely to suggest that all options are therefore equally neurotic. Nevertheless, Rieff's characterisation of commitment therapies provides invaluable guidance when picking through the minefield of therapeutic options. 'Humanistic' psychotherapists have been particularly adept at taking up some basic psychoanalytic observations and tacking on to them notions of better living. The 'commitment therapy' side of this work often stands out clearly, for example, in Frankl's (1967) 'logotherapy', which deliberately exploits the sense of meaninglessness pervading most people's lives to construct a therapy based on finding a purpose. In a revealing passage, Frankl exposes the moralistic conformity of his approach in a way which is particularly poignant because it centres on the question of consolation, on which subject Freud, too, has something to say.

> It is not the least task of psychotherapy to bring about reconciliation and to bring consolation: Man has to be reconciled to his finiteness and he also has to be enabled to face the transitoriness of his life. With these efforts psychotherapy indeed touches the realm of religion . . . while the doctor is not, and must not be, concerned with helping the patient to regain his belief in God, time and again this is just what occurs, unintended and unexpected as it is. (Frankl, 1967, p. 41)

If this neatly illustrates Rieff's notion of a commitment therapy, Freud's approach to consolation is equally expressive of analytic pessimism.

> I have not the courage to rise up before my fellow-men as a prophet, and I bow to their reproach that I can offer them no consolation; for at bottom that is what they are all demanding – the wildest revolutionaries no less passionately than the most virtuous believers. (Freud, 1930, p. 339)

Despite the obvious superiority of Freud over the humanists, there is a disingenuousness in psychoanalysis' denial that it imposes any system of values on the individual client which in some ways makes the openness of the commitment therapies quite attractive. In the very structure of analysis and of the analytic movement there is a demand for, and enforcement of, some quite specific commitments. Not only are clients provided with a linguistic explanatory framework that 'makes sense' of their experiences, but the power relations within the analytic setting and beyond that in the institutions of psychoanalysis (with their right of expulsion and excommunication of those who subvert their values) enforce its adherence. The training analysis, rite of initiation into the body of the movement, ensures the perpetuation of the values and words of the high priests of analytic doctrine – albeit not without dissent, especially between different training organisations and between those analysed by different training analysts. In being hidden and denied but also immensely powerful and domineering, the demand for commitment made by psychoanalysis can drift near to exploitation. Certainly, one cannot easily take up that distanced 'analytic attitude' towards the psychoanalytic world if one is to survive in it. The alternative therapies at least put their values forward explicitly, even naïvely, enabling them to be engaged with and rejected. But they also share significant difficulties which relate closely to their conformism and to the falsity of the 'cures' that they offer. They are almost all individualistic, embracing therapeutic solutions to socially induced agonies, and in doing so they venture the Scylla and Charybdis of, on the one side, political reaction and, on the other, a belief that the world will change if only the individuals within it would do so. They are exhortatory, preachy, sometimes judgemental; under many circumstances they reduce deeply experienced distress to consolatory moralism. They are fundamentally false not because they strive to make people feel better, but because they raise up ideological standards and, by forgetting to investigate their social component, mistake them for the truth.

Positive psychoanalysis

There are some distinctions to be made amongst the therapeutic followers of Freud. Most analysts have been content to be practitioners, renouncing Freud's philosophical aim for the more everyday ones of earning a living and developing a recognisable if not everywhere reputable career. The Freudian goal of relieving 'hysterical misery', or at least alleviating unhappiness, is not always the language that analysts use; very often they see themselves as absorbed into the medical discourse of therapy – treating illnesses or disturbances, aiming at mental health. This, too, is a kind of renunciation, in this case of Freud's wish that psychoanalysis avoid the use of medicine as its model and institutional home. His fear and astute premonition was that psychoanalysis would become reduced to psychotherapy, eventually only to be found listed under 'treatments' in psychiatric textbooks, somewhere around other quaint interventions such as hypnotherapy. Jacoby (1983) has documented the stultifying effect of medicalisation on American psychoanalytic theory, using the fate of Otto Fenichel as his case study and bringing out the more-or-less deliberate 'repression' of the radical elements of analytic thought that result from the adaptationist pragmatism of medicine in a conformist society. But Jacoby only really emphasises one side of this repression, the side which makes theory subservient to therapy and hence removes from theory its critical, cultural thrust. The tragedy of Fenichel, for example, is that whereas his seminal *Psychoanalytic Theory of Neurosis* (1945) is justly remembered and consulted today, his cultural and political writings – equally psychoanalytic in content – have been systematically hidden, accidentally forgotten and, above all, left behind by a form of psychoanalysis that barely understands theory at all. But Jacoby is an eloquent enough expositor of this trend. What he pays less attention to (though it is clear from several comments that he is well aware of this side to things) is that medicalisation also betrays Freud on the field of therapy itself. For example, seeing analysis as treatment results in therapies that are geared to the removal of symptoms or the more palatable management of everyday distress. Coupled with a neglect of theory this in turn results in the apotheosis of 'common unhappiness' as mental health, something which is then substituted for a genuinely critical vision of how society and individual intertwine. So instead of Freud's rancorous musings on the oppressiveness of society and the impossibility of any form of complete well-being, we have the marginal alleviations of individual distress held up as an image of fulfilment. Hence the kernel of truth in Richards' (1984, p. 123) unfairly overencompassing accusation that, 'American psychotherapeutic Freudianism . . . is a major historical example of one of the social roles of psychoanalysis, the familiar one of support for individualistic ideologies'. Adherents of the 'analytic attitude' maintain the individual in culture as their focus, aiming only to provide knowledge, however costly it may be. Medicalised therapists, in contrast, look no further than the fragmented and isolated individual who wants to feel better, live a little more easily and forget the more unbearable of her/his pains. There would be nothing wrong with this, except that it threatens to become the whole of psychoanalysis, and to accomplish exactly that reduction of analysis to just one among an array of 'treatments' that Freud so feared.

There have been a number of different formulations from psychoanalysts concerning the aims of psychotherapy, often connected with criteria for termination but also written as general pictures of what 'mental health' might mean. The conformism of many analytic aims, particularly those that focus upon the successful adaptation of patients to the demands of social living, is very transparent and need not detain us; Lacan's (1958, p.243) critique of American ego psychology expresses the point well enough.

> One cannot recall without a sense of shame the criteria of success in which their shoddy work culminates: the achievement of a higher income, and the emergency exit provided by the affair with one's secretary, regulating the release of forces strictly bound up in marriage, career and the political community, do not seem to me to be worthy of an appeal . . . to the Discord of the instincts of life and death.

Unfair this might be, but it is the unfairness of truth: in concerning themselves primarily with adaptation, which follows from their theories in the manner discussed in Chapter 4, the ego psychologists and others have relinquished any possibility of articulating a set of critical aims for psychoanalysis.

The views of object relations theorists are of more interest, mainly because, in their endeavour to describe the form and structure of 'mature relationships', they offer some possible guidelines for assessment both of the direction of therapy and the relative acceptability of alternative social configurations. In broad terms, the goals of object relations therapy are to free the individual from fixations created by bad relationship experiences and to encourage internalisation of the more nurturant and supportive possibilities experienced in the relationship with the therapist. In accordance with the notion that unconscious fantasies are the product of frustrations in (early) human relationships, object relations therapy is oriented towards encouraging 'mature dependency', a state or ability to relate to others in a caring and mutual way, based on reality and free of the distorting influences of identificatory and projective processes. This view is clearly open to criticism: Kleinians, for example, would presumably argue that a relationship without projection and introjection is inconceivable – the mind would have to be empty and the world would have to be uncomplicatedly lying open for inspection for the active, constructive phantasies through which people interpret events to disappear. But the goal of 'mature dependency' does have certain significant attractions. At its most modest, the idea that therapy can result in positive growth in the context of mature object relationships is strikingly different from the Freudian 'analytic attitude'. This is not just because object relations therapy attempts to go further than the baring of psychic conflict, operating with a specific vision of healthy relationships and a model of mental well-being towards which therapy aspires. It is also specifically because of its relationship orientation: the positive images of mental health that can be derived from Freudian psychoanalysis are couched in terms of internal attributes such as rationality, freedom from conflict and so on; the goals of object relations therapy include these internal states but subsume them under the more outward-looking ability to form fruitful relationships. One touchstone for a socially oriented psychoanalysis, as well as for a socially responsive politics, must be concern for the quality of human relationships: it is, for instance, the disfiguring impact of capitalism on personal relationships that is a major motivation behind attempts to create a more egalitarian social structure. In explicitly addressing this concern and making it the crux of its therapeutic endeavour, object relations theory does present a set of values which is an advance on the image of the distanced, uncommitted individual that arises from classical instinct theory.

If object relations therapy offers a set of aims that contribute helpfully to attempts to construct a social psychoanalysis, it also possesses tendencies which pull it in the opposite direction, towards conformism. These tendencies are linked with the more far-reaching and optimistic nature of the aims of object relations therapy when compared with those of Freudian psychoanalysis. Guntrip (1968, p. 279) is explicit on this point:

> Freud said that at best we can ony help the patient to exchange his neurotic suffering for ordinary human unhappiness. That, I believe, is too pessimistic a view, and the patient has glimpses of feeling the possibility of experiencing himself and life in a much more real and stable way.

This is to be achieved not just through the analysis of specific conflicts or fixations, but through 'regrowing' the basic ego or 'whole personal self' (p. 317), something which traditional analysis often leads on to. Guntrip's optimism is very strong: although he acknowledges the impossibility of a *perfect* result, his view of a 'really good result' is that it will lead the patient to feel happy and to have a 'genuine sense of gratitude and friendly feeling for the therapist, along with a quite realistic appreciation of him as a human being' (1968, p. 332). At its best, this state of mind becomes a form of functioning involving a synthesis of 'insight, integration, individuation and personal relationship' – something which is called '"mental health" from the psychiatric point of view and "peace" or "salvation" from the religious point of view' (1968, p. 356). Here is the exact language of what Rieff (1966) dubs the ecstatic vision – the language of religious salvation, of discovering a new meaningfulness in deliverance from distress by the priestly psychotherapist. In this case, it is achieved through the medium of a real relationship with the analyst, a reparative bond of the kind discussed in the next chapter, which leaves the patient able to free her/his shattered internal world from possession by evil spirits and reconsecrate it to healthy integration. The religious terminology is no accident here: the object relations view is that the distressed psyche is one poisoned by internalised bad objects, from which it must be delivered. Hence Guntrip's liking for Fairbairn's comment that 'psychoanalysis is not reinforcement of instinct-control . . . it is more like exorcism' (1968, p. 342); getting rid of the devils and absorbing the 'good object' of the analyst so that personal growth can be supported, is the eventual goal of therapy.

Feminist object relations therapy has taken a very similar set of goals, expressed in somewhat less eschatological language. Eichenbaum and Orbach (1982) emphasise the 'little girl', full of unfulfilled needs and terrified of dependency, that lurks behind the defences of women, having been repressed or left undeveloped through early experiences in the mother–daughter relationship. Although acknowledging the 'little girl' feelings is extremely painful, 'the cornerstone of feminist therapy is to bring this conflict into the open, for as it is gradually exposed, the woman will come to understand more about what it is she searches for in her relationships' (p. 57). Through providing support for the expression of dependency needs in the context of a predictable and understanding relationship, it is hoped that the woman will be able to accept the therapist's 'repair work', taking in a sense of being cared for to heal the hurt of the 'little girl' and gradually learning to incorporate the goodness of the therapist (p. 59). This should lead to a stabilisation of dependency needs and an increased ability to develop a sense of self which does not consist only in the reflection from others' eyes. All this will come about through the woman's gradual recognition of the realistic goodness of the therapeutic relationship, living on inside her and available for booster sessions even after termination.

A more detailed examination of the notion of 'reality' in psychoanalytic psychotherapy will be provided in the next chapter. The central point here is how the articulation of a positive image of mental health which is one of the attractions of object relations therapy, also opens the way to a drift into conformist ideology and false consolation which is hard to evade. Guntrip obviously and unapologetically falls into it in his discussion of religious salvation, but Eichenbaum and Orbach are not that far away. The issue is, that any espousal of positive aims is doomed to conformism if it does not explicitly theorise the limitations of these aims under particular social structures. It is impossible to form a fully 'mature' and giving human relationship in conditions where relationships are systematically distorted, as they are under capitalism and patriarchy. This does not mean that relationships between people cannot be improved, or that one should not strive to do so. However, building a theory of therapy which neglects the structuring factors that influence people's relationships and instead suggests that it is possible for the therapeutic bond to alter their *fundamental* quality, is to reverse the orders of causality present in the world, and to fall into the reductionist trap of reading the social order as produced by the free behaviour of individuals.

Kleinians have offered some quite explicit formulations on mental health and on the criteria for termination of analyses. In some respects, Klein remains close to Freudian pessimism in her ideas on what is possible: although she states that 'the ultimate aim of psychoanalysis is integration of the patient's personality' (1957, p. 231) she also agrees that 'complete and permanent integration is in my view never possible' (p. 233). Her formulations on mental health, in fact, make it clear that her notion of integration, even if it were attainable, does not mean freedom from conflict. Rather, in true Freudian style, it requires the ability to live in ambivalence, tolerant and aware of the conflicting forces that under different circumstances might tear one apart. In this account, mental health 'is based on an interplay between the fundamental sources of mental life – the impulses of love and hate – an interplay in which the capacity for love is predominant' (Klein, 1960, p. 274). Given the strong instinctual bias of Kleinian theory, this idea follows naturally: one cannot totally root out bad feelings and derive perfectly good relationships with the outside world; one has instead to learn to live with them, hoping that the goodness inside will make envy and hatred manageable. In emphasising this, Kleinians also assert the difference between their notions of analytic health and any superficial adaptation. Klein stresses deepening of the personality as an aim, with a particular focus on the development of a rich phantasy life and a capacity to experience emotions, and Segal (1981, p. 71) states explicitly that 'cure does not mean conformity with any stereotyped pattern of normality prejudged by the analyst'. Whether Kleinian analysts find themselves able to retain this non-judgementalism in practice is a moot point; ideally, however, their aims are to restore to the client 'access to the resources of his own personality, including the capacity to assess correctly internal and external reality' (Ibid.). In theory at least, this is rather like the Freudian view that the aim of therapy is to enable the client to see things clearly and to take up a stance towards them which is no longer distorted by unconscious conflicts. Segal does provide a place here for what she calls 'another aspect of cure, namely, better object relationships', but it is clear that this is to follow naturally on the attainment of internal balance. Significantly, 'correct assessment' of external reality is included in the paradigm without any implication of *acceptance* of such reality, hence opening the way for a reading of Kleinian aims that allows for a critical stance towards the social world. But there is more to Kleinian images of mental health than Freudian distance; they also stress the importance of working through the passions of early life to create tolerance of ambivalence and to enable rectification of hate by love. All this presents an image of psychological liberation that is very different from the Freudian one. Rather than freeing the instincts from repression, repression operates as a goal of sorts: it is a healthy, relatively mature defence when compared with the incapacities generated by splitting.

In a paper on the criteria for termination of psychotherapy, Klein (1950) likens terminaton to weaning, which itself is the prototype of bereavement and mourning. For Klein, the experience of psychotherapy is modelled on that of the first year of life; termination is thus possible at the point when those early conflicts have been worked through – specifically, when paranoid anxieties surrounding envy have been overcome and replaced by depressive feelings which in turn have been successfully integrated into the personality. The reduction of these basic anxieties requires the analysis of very early experiences in the manner described in Chapter 9; the central point here is that the analysis of early conflicts slowly leads to integration of the destructive aspects of the client's personality, resulting in increased feelings of responsibility and a more developed ability to experience guilt and depression. This helps bring about a strengthening of the ego, which lessens the threat posed by destructive impulses and makes it less likely that the defence of splitting will have to be used to ward off bad feelings. Instead, loving and reparative emotions gradually come to the fore, allowing more integration of ego and object and the slow working through of the depressive position. Eventually, at termination, the analyst/mother can be mourned in a way that is initially analysed and then left to continue to operate on its own; successful mourning of this kind explains improvements that take place after analysis has ended.

It is of great interest that Kleinians so stress the developmental nature of analysis: therapy mimics the original mothering relationship, with a shifting between paranoid–schizoid and depressive positions and, when things work out, the gradual overcoming and integration of destructive feelings through the introjection of a good object, in this case the analyst. Just as the infant has to overcome the splitting of the mother into good and bad parts, so the analysand has to reduce her/his idealisation and hatred of the analyst, fusing them into a whole which can be internalised and mourned during and after termination, leaving the client more integrated than before. Klein is actually very optimistic about this process: although she accepts that appalling early experiences cannot be made good by an analyst at a later date, she claims that 'the introjection of the analyst as a good object, if not based on idealisation has, to some extent, the effect of providing an internal good object where it has been largely lacking' (Klein, 1957,

p. 234). Analysis leads to a growth in integration which in turn leads to a strengthening of the ego so that it is able to recover good experiences and tolerate the recognition of the bad experiences of the past; hence also one source of the optimism that Kleinians have concerning the analysis of psychotics.

As was noted in Chapter 5 with reference to their general developmental theory, it is striking how positive the Kleinians' view of the possibilities for change is, even if it is also recognised to be difficult and painful. In addition, notwithstanding their virtually total neglect of social considerations, the image of the perfectly analysed person that they end up with is one that eschews adaptation and instead emphasises the importance of an inner acceptance of confiict which allows a balanced assessment of the world. A problem with the concern of object relations theorists with the formation of mature relationships is that they encroach on the social domain without theorising sociality, so that they are perpetually in danger of slipping into the conformist assumption that 'mature', whole relationships are possible without social change. Kleinians share this danger to the extent that they too deal in external social relationships, but their unrelenting absorption (for which they are often criticised) in the phantasy world of the individual also allows that distance from here-and-now reality upon which a critical analysis can be based. On the other hand, they have nothing direct to say about the terms under which such a critical analysis can take place; Segal's (1981) statement on the ability to 'assess correctly internal and external reality' makes no comment on what such a correct assessment might be – what criteria are being used for evaluation. With all their drawbacks, object relations theorists are clearer here; Kleinians share some of their notions (for example, a goal of reducing distortions in perception due to splitting) while rejecting others. And amongst their core concepts is one which makes a goal of 'correct assessment' of reality troublesome: the idea that projection and introjection, as basic mental mechanisms rather than products of environmental failure, always operate, even in the comparatively 'mentally healthy' individual. If this is so, then the world as perceived is always half-created by the perceiver; conversely, it always operates to infiltrate and construct the individual's psychic structure. In this idea, that social and individual development are dialectical, interpenetrating processes based on confiict and contradiction, resides much of the radical promise of Kleinianism; it also produces difficulties in attempting to outline specific therapeutic goals.

Interrogating power

There have been very few attempts to articulate a political role for psychoanalytic psychotherapy which go further than the idea that therapy aims to strengthen the individual so that s/he can become involved constructively in collective struggle. As described at the beginning of this chapter, some critics have suggested that therapy, being focused on the individual, can do no more than this, that the only legitimate source of political activity is in mass action. It has been argued above that this is too limited a view, as it ignores the manner in which social forces are internalised by individuals, supplying the axes around which personality becomes organised, but also sustaining an existence which is not directly determined by social events. Hence the relevance of specifically psychotherapeutic goals for programmes of social as well as personal change. The rest of this chapter has been an attempt to describe some such potential goals and their implications, with object relations and Kleinian approaches again looming large. This final section introduces the question of the power relations that operate in psychoanalysis, raising the possibility that interrogation of these power relations may be the basis for one set of 'radical' aims. This section thus also acts as a bridge to the fuller discussion of the analytic situation that is the core of Chapter 9.

The concept of 'power' is a complex and difficult one, but in this context it refers to the force by which the structures of an individual's subjectivity are produced (see Banton *et al.*, 1985, for a fuller discussion). Power is thus a positive as well as a negative concept: it is not just a repressive activity which prevents certain actions or desires from coming to fruition, but it is also an enabling process which constructs and organises human possibilities. In a broad sense, power relations are the means by which society enters into the consciousness of each person, both literally through internalisations of the actions and dictates of 'powerful' people (especially parents), and symbolically through incorporation of the broader imperatives of social structure. If it is a radical goal of therapy to examine and perhaps help alter those psychological structures which reflect the impact of social forces, then a means towards this may be analysis of the power relations which support them. This can have two aspects: questioning or subversion of dominant, taken-for-granted power relations, and exploration of alternative uses of the power that is available. Psychoanalysis can contribute here through its use of the power relations that appear in the therapeutic setting, both because of the analyst's presumed mastery and expertise, and because psychoanalysis involves exploration of the formative experiences in the patient's mental life. The Lacanian tradition addresses these possibilities, particularly the 'subversive' one, most directly. For example, Gallop (1982, p. 102) describes the power that arises through apparent possession of the 'secrets' of psychoanalysis and comments,

> Analysis, if it is not to be a process of adapting the patient to some reigning order of discourse, must include the risk of unseating the analyst. No one can be master of the unconscious, even those whose profession it is to seek it out.

In unseating the analyst, the implicit power relations of the analytic encounter are overturned, and with it wider assumptions of mastery and control. Schneiderman (1980) also emphasises how the analyst's task is to thwart the patient's attempt to make her/him the source of all knowledge, and to supply 'decoy answers' to the patient's questions which will serve the purpose of arousing 'the patients' opposition and will lead him to offer a new response to his own question' (p. 11). Not that there is any one response that is the truth – there is no absolute Other from which answers derive. Analysis is oriented towards disrupting all answers; including those that reside in the person of the analyst; the desire for total knowledge and cure is an unattainable as any other desire. Ingleby (1984) similarly holds that analysis aims to 'destroy the very scenario upon which it is built', revealing the impossibility of controlling the patient and, while articulating everything in family terms, 'to dismantle the familial scenarios which have previously dominated his or her life' (p. 50).

These ideas connect very closely with the question of the manner in which power relations are interwoven with the analytic encounter, a question that is considered more fully in Chapter 9.

The central point here is that they acknowledge the reality of that power, which derives from wider social relationships but which becomes focused on the analyst in the therapeutic setting. A goal for therapy may then be to allow the patient to explore power relations as they emerge in therapy and as they mimic internalised relations from the formative periods of her/his life. In encountering the vicissitudes, realities, illusions and potential of analytic power, the patient may be helped to explore how power operates and the extent to which it can be subverted or employed to alter and enrich all kinds of social relations – a quintessentially political progression. Therapy is not, of course, the only domain in which the interrogation of power might happen, but it is an important one, because within it the forces that construct the personality can be explored and renegotiated in a way that allows the 'subject' more control. Through the replication of deeply unconscious expectations and modes of experience in the analytic encounter, the ideological axes upon which these things are based can be questioned intensively and with a subversively dislocating impact. None of this, however, represents the end of politics. Dealing with power in psychoanalytic encounters cannot be used in any simple way as a model for larger scale political practice: it has been maintained throughout this book that although individual and social levels are interconnected, they are of different orders, and the potential of the former to influence the latter is limited. In fact, one thing that marks out a politicised therapeutic approach is its recognition of the reality of social structures which act over and above the material that is accessible to change within the therapeutic situation. But it is a starting point, and part of the struggle for change: to enable people to recognise, re-experience and remodel the internalised structures of power that they carry around, and to help them to reposition themselves with respect to the hidden forces of social life from which these structures derive. In conjunction with the ideas on 'mental health' that derive from object relations and Kleinian theory, this approach represents an assertion that it is possible both to analyse and to be committed, to reveal the underlying structures of things and to choose between them on the grounds of their worth.

9 The Power of the Analyst

The previous chapter was concerned with the way in which the aims of psychoanalytic psychotherapy express certain political assumptions, either through an explicit formulation of particular images of mental health, or through a more subtle neglect of the limitations placed by social structures on possibilities for individual change. In the final section, analytic practice which takes seriously the power relations that can be found both within and outside the therapeutic setting was advocated. These debates, which take as a starting point the 'analytic attitude' of distanced, apparently neutral commentary, are replicated in discussions of analytic technique and therapeutic mechanisms. As in the previous chapter, the general argument adopted here is that in the intensity of the personal exploration produced by psychoanalytic psychotherapy lies a potential for revealing and challenging deep-rooted personality structures that are themselves connected to social forces. However, not all psychoanalytic approaches have this potential to the same degree: they vary in their conceptualisation of the therapeutic process just as in their conceptualisation of therapeutic aims, with some approaches adopting more consolatory orientations while others are harsher but more challenging. This might appear to be due to differences in purpose, between those procedures with more pragmatic and those with more analytically investigative goals. However, while the balance between the necessity of easing the distress of an individual patient and raising social questions is clearly a delicate one, the two aspects of therapeutic practice are not completely at odds with one another: if psychic pain has even partially social roots, then it can be an analytic task to reveal and interrogate them. Central to this endeavour will be the relationship between analyst and patient, and the use to which the energy generated by that relationship – more specifically, its power – is put. It is, after all, in the analyst–patient couple that the structure and force of psychoanalytic therapy resides; so it is also there that its ability to put into practice the radical potential of psychoanalytic theory might be found.

This chapter presents a survey of the way in which some of the psychoanalytic theories introduced earlier in the book have conceived of the therapeutic process. In particular, the implied power relations of the therapeutic encounter will be explored through an investigation of the images of the analyst that are produced by the various accounts of the basic components of therapy, beginning with a discussion of the positions taken by 'classical' and Kleinian theories on the crucial concepts of transference and interpretation.

Transference and interpretation

Given the centrality of transference in the theory and practice of psychoanalysis, it is perhaps surprising to realise that there are substantial differences even of definition. Sandler, Dare and Holder (1973, p. 47), after distinguishing between the 'treatment alliance' (based on the patient's wish to co-operate) and transference, define the latter as

> a *specific illusion* which develops in regard to the other person, one which, unbeknown to the subject, represents, in some of its features, a repetition of a relationship towards an important figure in the person's past.

It is seen as more than a general tendency to repeat past relationships; rather, transference represents 'a concentration of a past attitude or feeling, inappropriate to the present, and directed *quite specifically* towards the other person or institution' (Ibid.). This is very close to Freud's original definition of transference as 'new editions or facsimiles' of impulses and fantasies derived from past relationships and directed, in the context of therapy, at the analyst. But it differs from the conception of transference advanced by other analysts, notably Kleinians, who have extended the concept to refer to *all* aspects of the patient's communication with the analyst – the 'totality of all intrapsychic components of the patient's fantasies about and reactions to the analyst' (Langs, 1976, p. 57). Glover (1937) has perhaps the most inclusive of all possible definitions: transference, for him, reflects 'the *totality* of the individual's development . . . he displaces on to the analyst not merely affects and ideas but *all* he has ever learnt or forgotten throughout his mental development' (in Sandler *et al.*, 1973, p. 43). In this formulation, it ceases to be possible to distinguish realistic aspects of the therapist–patient interaction from imaginary ones, for all reality is read through a fog of fantasy, and is half constructed as it is perceived. The analytic relationship becomes a field of fantasy; any discrimination between internal and external worlds is made fragile and unconvincing.

The differing definitions of transference relate to some important differences in accounts of the nature of the mechanism by which transference operates. At the core of the classical view is the notion of transference as a form of *displacement*: feelings that properly belong in one relationship, directed towards some particular person or persons, instead become concentrated on to the analyst. This happens, also, with the symptoms of the patient's neurosis: these, too, get directed towards the analyst, creating the 'transference neurosis' which can then be analysed and removed. Because this assumes the possibility of forming relatively coherent relationships, classical theory makes transference the product of a fairly late period in the child's life, when the ego is well developed and there is a clearly established sense of self and of the boundary between self and others. The therapeutic focus is consequently on an autonomous individual psyche which has become fixated in certain ways, but which is basically capable of forming relationships and of distinguishing between fantasy and reality – hence the reluctance of classical analysts to treat psychotics, who supposedly lack these capabilities. The analyst's task is to aid the process of reality testing by helping the patient identify conflicts as they are expressed in the transference, and refine her/his knowledge of their origin and the way they distort contemporary relationships. The analyst in this scenario is in many respects outside the interaction: the passive recipient of, or 'sounding board' for, the patient's impulses and fantasies, relatively unaffected by them but commenting upon them in order to sort out their sense. Hence, although the analyst's refusal to accept the fantasy role given to her/him by the patient is seen as one of the major techniques for revealing repressed material, there is no necessary consideration of the real interpersonal aspects of the therapeutic encounter; rather, all that is changed occurs inside the patient's head.

The emphasis in classical theory on the distanced stance of the analyst is also reflected in the account it gives of the second pillar of therapeutic activity, interpretation. Sandler, Dare and Holder (1973) list a number of ways in which the term 'interpretation' has been used in the analytic literature: to refer to the therapist's inferences on the meaning of the patient's communications; to refer to the therapist's articulation of those inferences; to refer only to verbal interventions which have the aim of bringing about 'dynamic change' through insight; or to refer to *all* comments by the therapist. They also note that some analysts have rejected the notion of interpretation altogether: for instance, Menninger's (1958) view was that analysts should restrict themselves to being passive observers, occasionally commenting or *intervening* in what is going on. Nevertheless, following Fenichel (1945), Sandler *et al.* suggest a definition of interpretation as a communication from the analyst with a specific intended effect on the patient: 'all comments and other verbal interventions which have the aim of immediately making the patient aware of some aspect of his psychological functioning of which he was not previously conscious' (p. 110). This broad definition has its roots in the classical idea that therapy operates by communicating a form of knowledge to the patient's ego. The assumption behind it is that this knowledge will strengthen the ego and give it more power to control the demands of unconscious forces, or to allow conflicts to be dealt with in consciousness. The strategy by which this takes place is a gradualist one. First comes a process of building up a working alliance with the patient, whose ego is led to side with the analyst by its desire for freedom from symptoms, and by the support that the analyst provides. Initially, acceptance of the patient's defence may be a necessary strategy, but this is followed by interpretation of defensive activity which moves from surface to depth, from anxieties and impulses that are relatively near to consciousness to those that lie far beneath. In the classical approach, this means working in an order that reverses the developmental stages: from reasonably integrated genital concerns to more distorted and primitive anal and then oral ones; from interpretation of defences to uncovering of unconscious content (Zetzel, 1956). The rationale behind this is that the analytic procedure can only be helpful if the ego can be protected against being flooded with anxiety generated by primitive impulses. As defences, anxiety and emotions are interpreted at each level, the underlying conflicts which they reveal can be dealt with under the gaze of a gradually strengthened ego, freeing psychic energy and making it possible to move deeper. In all this, the support offered by the analyst is a significant prop to the ego, allowing it to cope even with destructive emotions. Gradually, impulses become more controllable, and more basic conflicts are ready to be faced.

Langs (1976) points to a limitation of the conventional classical form of analysis: that it avoids regressive and primitive processes and ignores preverbal responses. Too easily, the slow work of supporting a gradually strengthening ego can slide into the conformist adaptationism characteristic of ego psychology at its most short-sighted. It is also possible that this mode of work is in part the product of defensiveness amongst analysts – fear of dealing with destructive material that might bring up uncomfortable feelings. For instance, the politically progressive feminists, Eichenbaum and Orbach (1982), are opposed to early interpretations that expose the patient's vulnerability and can 'sound like an attack' (p. 52); it may be that this is due to their understandable desire to offset the patronising and punitive elements involved in much therapy, but it could also represent a rationale for steering clear of painful emotions. Elaboration of interpretations that 'sound like an attack' may in fact be an effective procedure for investigating the ways in which the patient's psyche is, or has been, under attack from powerful and painful forces. In many respects, this is precisely the argument used by Kleinians in their thoroughgoing critique of traditional views on the appropriate structuring of the therapeutic process.

The contrast between the classical and Kleinian views can be concentrated into one distinction: whereas in the classical view the analyst functions as a mirror on to which the patient displaces her/his impulses, Kleinians describe the analyst as a receptacle into which internal figures and the feelings that surround them are projected (Segal, 1981, p. 82). The crucial word here is 'projection', especially as it is linked with the reformulation of developmental theory by Klein which makes projection and introjection into fundamental mental processes (see Part 2). So, Klein (1952,

p. 53) notes the connection between what occurs in therapy and what takes place in early life in the following terms:

> I hold that transference originates in the same processes which in the earliest stages determine object relations. Therefore, we have to go back again and again in analysis to the fluctuations between objects, love and hatred, external and internal, which dominate early infancy.

This view has a number of important implications. First, it is directly responsible for the widening of the concept of transference so characteristic of Kleinian thought. If transference is based on mechanisms which are fundamental in mental life, which form the foundations upon which all mental functioning is based, then every aspect of the patient's communication must be in some way linked to transference and hence to primitive material. Klein (1952) is explicit on this point: exploration of the unconscious content of every aspect of the interaction between patient and therapist will reveal the defences being employed to ward off the anxieties produced by the transference situation. Segal (1981) formulates this by asserting that all aspects of the patient's communications in the session contain 'an element of unconscious phantasy', even if they appear to be concerned with external facts; this is 'equivalent to saying that all communications contain something relevant to the transference situation' (p. 8). Hence, Kleinian technique centres on the interpretation *as transference phenomena* of the varied material produced by the patient. In itself this is simply an extreme version of an approach common to many psychoanalysts, although different schools vary in the exact weight given to transference. However, where the peculiarities of the Kleinian approach assert themselves most is in the content of transference interpretations, which focus upon the elucidation of primitive material. This stance arises from two considerations. First, the Kleinian idea that transference operates through projective mechanisms which are fundamental to mental life and which are particularly characteristic defences in the formative paranoid–schizoid period, leads to a concern with primitive anxieties and with splitting processes otherwise found in early infancy. Secondly, Kleinians argue that in order for unconscious material to be acceptable to consciousness, the anxiety that it generates has to be lessened at the same time as the defences are removed. Hence, they place at least as much emphasis on the interpretation of basic anxieties as on the interpretation of defences, and do not follow the sequence from genital to anal to oral described earlier. Rather, they hold that because the phantasies that give rise to transference are constituted by early anxieties and object relationships, interpretation of primitive unconscious contents and defences is crucial from the start of analysis.

Another directive of Kleinian practice arises from their insistence on the destructive aspects of early life, leading to a focus on the *negative* transference, the complex of hostile feelings which the patient may bring to bear on the analyst. As mentioned in the previous chapter, Klein argues that working through envious and destructive feelings in therapy is a necessary prerequisite for any integration of the personality; it is through the analysis of the negative transference that this comes about, something which again involves exploration of early destructive feelings.

> We can fully appreciate the interconnections between positive and negative transferences only if we explore the early interplay between love and hate, and the vicious circle of aggression, anxieties, feelings of guilt and increased aggression, as well as the various aspects of objects towards whom these conflicting emotions and anxieties are directed. (Klein, 1952, p. 53)

Klein (1957) argues that the fundamental task of analysis is to enable integration of the personality to occur through overcoming splits in the psyche which are perpetuated by unresolved primitive conflicts. The appropriate method is to analyse both sides of the early love–hate conflict as they are replayed in the positive and negative transference. Destructive and loving feelings can by this means gradually be brought together in the presence of introjection of the good analytic object, allowing splitting to be overcome and integration of the personality to begin. But Klein also emphasises the difficulty of all this: resistance to analysis of envy and hatred is even greater than resistance to analysis of Oedipal jealousy and hostility. This is because these envious feelings threaten the whole existence of the ego; they relate to the Death Instinct and repeatedly reconstruct the passionate anxieties of early life. In fact, because interpretation of early impulses is so threatening, primary envy and the defences against it may appear more forcefully after the start of analysis, resulting in a variety of negative therapeutic reactions. Klein warns that the process of integration has to be a gradual one, not in the sense of the classical analysts' surface to depth movement, but because of the need for repeated analysis of the envy–splitting–integration progression before the destructive aspects of the personality can be accepted and, tempered with loving feelings, lay the foundation for improved stability.

Much of what has been described above comes together in the Kleinian concept of projective identification, which seems to have become acceptable as an explanation of the process of therapy to many analysts who would not otherwise hold with Kleinian concepts. In its 'pure' form, projective identification appears to be a wholly negative procedure; it is defined by Laplanche and Pontalis (1973, p. 356) as 'a mechanism revealed in phantasies in which the subject inserts his self – in whole or in part – into the object in order to harm, possess or control it'. In therapeutic parlance, this notion is often modified to include positive as well as negative insertions, opening the way for consideration of how it can have beneficial effects. In this account, the *projective* aspect of projective identification involves placing parts of oneself into an external object either in order to deal with their threatening aspects (in the case of destructive elements) or so as to preserve something good and loving, to place it elsewhere for safekeeping. Developmentally, this occurs before the period in which there is a clear differentiation between self and object (or it would not be fully possible), but because of the persistence of infantile feelings and mental processes throughout life, it operates just as noticeably and powerfully in adults, whether analytic patients or not. The 'identification' aspect of the mechanism is the process whereby the patient feels her/himself to remain in contact with those parts of the self that have been projected into the object, hence creating phantasies of control of the object by the self, or vice versa. In the analytic situation, projective identification involves interpellating into the analyst aspects of the patient's inner world, thereby influencing the analyst's emotional state. It is

> a means by which the patient induces in the analyst all sorts of feelings, such as helplessness, rejection and lack of understanding,

> based on the fact that the patient has projected into the analyst the child part of himself, with all of the related feelings. (Langs, 1976, p. 470)

As well as changing the analyst, however, the projected parts of the patient also undergo alterations while held by the other. These are then re-experienced by the patient through a parallel introjective mechanism, whereby parts of the analyst (which may originally have been projected by the patient) are internalised and alter significant aspects of the patient's psychic world. In this way, the patient not only internalises the analyst as a 'good object' who can make possible the integration of destructive and loving feelings, but also takes back aspects of her/himself which have been contained and altered through the analytic experience.

All this makes the representation of the analyst very complex in Kleinian thought: as Langs (1976) points out, the analyst can represent parent figures, as in classical theory, but also internal objects and part objects or even aspects of psychic structure, such as the id or super-ego. For example, in a seminal early paper influenced by Klein's work, Strachey (1934) suggests that in the course of therapy the patient sets up the analyst as a kind of super-ego or ego-ideal; s/he projects on to this 'auxiliary super ego' archaic objects which become refined by the transference interpretations provided by the analyst and which are then reintrojected and identified with to create a more realistic and moderated internal world. The analyst is thus involved in the patient's psychological processes in an intimate way: s/he becomes an internalised object bringing about changes in the structure of the mind. Consequently, the analysis of transference leads not just to an unearthing of past relationships, but also to an exploration of the 'current dynamic state of the patient's internal objects and unconscious fantasies' (Langs, 1976, p. 57). Overall, this also results in a much firmer focus on the interpersonal components of the therapeutic situation than in classical theory: the therapeutic situation is a ground on which the interplay of projection and introjection operates in relation to the presence of the analyst, who acts as the container and transmuter of feelings and parts of the patient's psyche, rather than just as a mirror to help the patient see her/himself more accurately.

The Kleinian approach contrasts with that of classical analysts in a number of ways. At the most schematic level, there is a difference in the focus of analysis. Where classical analysts concentrate on uncovering defences, on ego analysis, Klein's is very much an 'id psychology', dealing directly with primitive unconscious emotions and employing the analyst as an object to be introduced into the patient's unconscious world. The therapeutic mechanisms are projection, introjection and projective identification; change does not come about through increased knowledge becoming available to the ego, which can then control conflicts more effectively, but through repairing splits at an unconscious level, aided by the internalisation of the analytic object. Hence, the value of interpretations is that they feed back to the patient the projected elements in her/his personality, invested with the qualities of the analyst; as in Strachey's account, the process of change is one of identification and integration, not just greater control over impulse. Other analysts have often criticised Kleinian work on a number of grounds: for example, that their emphasis on interpretation of primitive feelings often operates to the exclusion of anything else, including recognition of the occurrence of real events; or that the manner in which they launch into depth interpretations at the earliest possible moment can lead to overwhelming anxiety or the raising of destructive defences which can then not be overcome. Kleinian analysts often seem to present themselves as omniscient and rigid, using the same techniques for the analysis of all problems, as everything is seen as referring back to basic infantile anxieties. In practice, some of these criticisms ring true, but where Kleinian theory repeatedly reveals its superiority is in its recognition of painful feelings, its refusal to turn away from despair and destructiveness, and its insistence that if one is able to face squarely up to this in an interpersonal encounter allowing modification of unconscious structures, it becomes possible to build a new integrity and stability. Pain is not celebrated in this approach, but it is recognised and employed in the vision of a completed personality. Insight is based on the renunciation of omnipotent phantasies and the integration of unconscious impulses as they are experienced through the medium of the analyst, modified through interpretation and through introjection of previously projected material. Reality *is* present here: conflicting feelings can be dealt with more appropriately, and the reintegration of the ego 'is inevitably accompanied by a more correct perception of reality' (Segal, 1981, p. 71). But the central political possibilities of Kleinianism are revealed in another statement of Segal's on psychoanalytic insight:

> It involves conscious knowledge of archaic processes, normally inaccessible to the most intuitive person, through reliving in the transference the very processes that structured one's internal world and conditioned one's perceptions. (1981, p. 79)

The Kleinian approach to analysis emphasises reworking the basic structuring principles of the personality, focusing particularly on the projective mechanisms which underlie the transaction between the infant's internal and external world. In so doing, it directly confronts the 'socialising' forces which construct the organised psyche and lead not just to psychological distress, but to the specific forms of psychic organisation prevalent within any social environment. Because of this attitude, Kleinianism has the potential to become a far more radical approach than those that take the ego for granted and aim only to strengthen it against the pressures of internal desire.

Schizoid phenomena and human relationships

The classic Freudian patients were hysterics and obsessional neurotics – people with relatively clearly differentiate symptoms who could be understood to be suffering from too much repression. They functioned on the ordinary human level which required recognition of reality and the ability to form relationships; in psychoanalysis, treatment was by uncovering repressed material through the medium of the transference. The end point of therapy referred to something like freeing the patient's ego from domination by unconscious forces, so that everyday life could be made smoother and richer. These classical neurotic patients, whose pathology was held to derive from Oedipal conflicts, were the bases upon which psychoanalytic theory was formulated and have dominated cultural images of analysis from the start, as well as dictating the therapeutic techniques employed. But over the post-Freudian period there has been a gradual shift in the nature of the typical analysand, from someone needing to liberate her/

himself from unconscious conflicts, to someone desperately seeking for a secure core of self.

> For perhaps fifty years, reports of analytic work have referred increasingly to patients who do not present with well organised neurotic symptomatology, nor with the massive disturbance of overt psychosis. Their malaise is profound but diffuse. Khan (1966) says: 'The schizoid character disorders are distinguished by the fact that the symptom lies in the way of being.' (Richards, 1984, p. 125)

Guntrip (1973, p. 148) provides a classic description of such patients.

> They are the people who have deep-seated doubts about the reality and viability of their very 'self', who are ultimately found to be suffering from various degrees of depersonalisation, unreality, the dread feeling of 'not belonging', of being fundamentally isolated and out of touch with the world . . . The problem here is not relations with other people, but whether one is or has a self.

The reasons for this change are debatable. For some, such as Fairbairn, it is a product of a recognition within psychoanalysis that the basic problems of all people are those of forming a self capable of relating to others: in his view, Oedipal neuroses of the classical kind do not exist on their own, and conflicts that appear to be concerned with drives and impulses are themselves based on more pervasive relationship difficulties. Others, such as the American critic Christopher Lasch, integrate their understanding of 'narcissistic' personality difficulties with an entire cultural movement fuelled by mass production and consumption, itself adding to the fragmentation of everyday life.

> A culture organised around mass consumption encourages narcissism – which we can define, for the moment, as a disposition to see the world as a mirror, more particularly as a projection of one's own fears and desires – not because it makes people grasping and self assertive but because it makes them weak and dependent. It undermines their confidence in their capacity to

understand and shape the world and to provide for their own needs. (Lasch, 1984, p. 33)

Although other writers paint a different picture of the contemporary world from that of Lasch – for instance, Jameson's (1984) evocation of 'postmodernism' draws much more heavily on Lacanian accounts of the psychotic experience – the theme of fragmentation, of being lost in a world of mirrors and insubstantiality is a common one, and may be persuasively linked to the clinical recognition of issues of personal relatedness as central psychological problems. This has led to some quite substantial alterations in technique which are of relevance to the general themes of this chapter, and which also reflect on the possibilities and limitations engendered by a 'culture of narcissism' (Lasch, 1979).

There are a number of alternative accounts (and terminologies) dealing with the kind of patients described above, who are variously called 'narcissistic', 'borderline', or (as here) 'schizoid'. While these accounts vary in their degree of allegiance to the Freudian instinct model (see Greenberg and Mitchell, 1983), there are substantial overlaps in their perceptions of the essence of the schizoid state, with all major theorists centring their ideas on analysis of disturbances in the healthy development of the 'self'. Kohut (1971) proposes that the central pathology of narcissistic patients derives from a maternal failure to support the infant's grandiose needs (akin to Winnicott's idea of infantile omnipotence – see Chapter 4) or allow it to dissipate gradually in the face of reality. The characteristic anxieties of the narcissistic personality follow from this: alternating between grandiosity and feelings of inferiority, the individual concerned is unable to form the kind of relationships through which a sense of self is cemented, and instead is prey to tremendous fears of engulfment and fragmentation at the hands of unmet internal needs. For Kohut, the pathological narcissism seen in analytic patients is a fixated form of normal narcissism: these people have never been allowed to grow up (Russell, 1985). Kernberg (1970, 1975) differs from Kohut on this issue, seeing narcissism as a product of a disturbed character structure that itself derives from failures on the part of the mother to supply the nurture and support that the infant needs. The inner devastation and feelings of envy and rage produced by this 'environmental deficiency' (again in Winnicott's terms) are so distressing that a grandiose self is formed as a defence against them. Underlying this grandiosity in the 'borderline' patient is a continuing rage which makes it impossible to integrate split aspects of self and object, leading to a weakened ego and an inability to form fulfilling relationships with other people experienced as whole objects. Thus, as in Kohut's theory, narcissism is an expression of a personality distorted by early maternal insufficiency.

The account of 'schizoid' states given by British object relations theorists is closely related to those of the American psychoanalysts mentioned above. For instance, Winnicott and Guntrip also suggest that the schizoid state is created by a specific interpersonal frustration, failure to provide the 'good enough mothering' conditions described in Chapter 4. This leads to an experience of devastating neediness and isolation and the construction of a 'false self' to defend the child's true self' from pain, with the true self becoming split off and hidden away as a regressed ego. The schizoid destruction is then created by the manner in which the false self can form only superficial and sterile links with others, while the true self withers away through lack of contact. The schizoid terror is of implosion: that real human contact will destroy the fragile integrity of the true self, which has nothing inside to bolster it up. On the other hand, inability to form relationships leads to a drying up of the self and the hiding away of its most vulnerable and needy part: 'the false self cannot . . . experience life or feel real' (Winnicott, 1956, p. 297).

All the accounts given above unite in emphasising the relationship problems of the narcissistic/borderline/schizoid patient. In terms of technique, this has led to modifications of, and also strong divergences from, the classical analytic procedure. The most traditional approach is offered by Kernberg (1976), who insists on the centrality of transference work and advocates thorough interpretation of the fantasies and defences that underlie interactions in the therapeutic setting. In fact, he lays considerable emphasis on the chaotic, intense and premature transferences characteristic of borderline patients, which create a particularly strong constellation of responses in the analyst. Kernberg's argument, which is akin to that of Klein, is that rigorous interpretation of the positive and negative aspects of the transference are necessary in order to expose the defensive functions of the grandiose self and to allow acknowledgement of the hurt and rage underneath. Only thus will it be possible for these feelings to become integrated with the healthier parts of the patient's personality: aggression and hatred must be analysed before they can be overcome. Kohut (1971) also recognises the transferences that occur during therapy, but he argues against the kind of interpretive activity characteristic of traditional psychoanalysis and advocated by Kernberg. This stems from his view of narcissism as an arrest in personality: the task of the analyst is to provide the conditions under which growth can begin again. As the original fixation was caused by rejection, the analyst endeavours totally to accept the patient as if s/he were an infant, creating a context of empathy and non-interference which mimics the supportive environment required in early life. Only gradually, as the analyst's realistic failures (e.g. due to separations during breaks in the analysis) appear and are worked through, is the patient's narcissism confronted, allowing her/him to develop a stronger sense of a self which can relate meaningfully with others.

Kohut's reformulation of the analytic process away from interpretation and towards the creation of a 'good-enough' relationship is striking, and is characteristic of the more forthright users of the insights of object relations theory. Winnicott and Guntrip are most significant here, the former suggesting a new set of procedures for use with schizoid patients, the latter reformulating the entire therapeutic process.

Winnicott (1955) makes a distinction between different kinds of patient which has been very influential amongst analysts. In the first group are those conventionally neurotic and 'normal' patients who function as whole personalities, with integrated enough egos to be able to relate to others as whole objects and to form transference relationships. For this group, Winnicott suggests that classical analysis, focusing on interpretation of the transference, is appropriate. Secondly, Winnicott draws attention to a group whose wholeness can only just be taken for granted; that is, they have entered into the depressive position, but precariously, making the survival of the analyst in the face of hostile feelings a crucial concern. So long as this focus is present in the analysis, Winnicott suggests that classical interpretive work remains acceptable. For the third group, the group of schizoid and otherwise regressed patients who are unable to form relationships (including transference relationships) with others, different procedures are required. For them, Winnicott (1955, p. 279) suggests something which calls into question the entire canon of received psychoanalytic technique:

> In regard to this third grouping, the accent is more surely on management, and sometimes over long periods with these patients ordinary analytic work has to be in abeyance, management being the whole thing.

The goal of therapy with schizoid patients is radically different from the conventional analytic work of exposing and sorting out conflicts under the aegis of a relatively integrated ego. Instead, it is more like re-mothering, taking a fragmented ego and providing the conditions of support and worth which allow it to begin to grow. *Management* actually means doing very little: a minimum of interpretation is provided, referring to the patient's basic sense of unrelatedness, but refraining from interrogatory or threatening comments. The focus is on the boundaries and consistency of the session: the presence of the analyst, reliable and accepting, who can begin through her/his predictability to make up for the absences and frustrations of the severely regressed patient's early life. Regression itself is seen as a productive mechanism under these circumstances: not only does it refer to the fundamental state of the patient's true self, but it also represents a normal healing process whereby the early 'failure situation' is returned to and repaired. The regressed state of the patient also means that everything that occurs in the analysis is experienced as if it were here-and-now reality; that is, analysis with such patients is not a process of making links between current emotions or perceptions and past experiences, but instead is a matter of *reliving* the past, of encouraging the patient to accept the security of the analyst's reliable presence to release, tentatively and with setbacks, the hidden 'true self' or regressed ego that has never been allowed to live. 'Management', therefore, involves doing everything necessary to provide the patient with a setting which allows nurture to be experienced.

The analogy of management and mothering pursued by Winnicott also produces a new attitude towards resistances, which are not analysed as aspects of the patient's pathology, as they would be with neurotics. Instead, with schizoid patients the analyst must interpret resistance as a sign that s/he has made a mistake, and must allow articulation of the reality of that error, so that the patient can experience realistic anger in the context of a relationship that continues to be secure. If the analyst defends her/himself, 'the patient misses the opportunity for being angry about a past failure just where anger was becoming possible for the first time' (Winnicott, 1956, p. 298). The 'negative transference' of classical analysis is thus replaced by objective anger about the analyst's failures; expression of this anger within the safety of the carefully managed setting allows integration of the self to begin to occur. Throughout all this, the metaphor of the maternal 'hold' is visible: the analyst supplies a safe and caring environment in which the patient can experiment with relationships, shaping her/his self in the light of the analyst's successes and failures, with the analyst offering support for the patient's gradually developing ego processes. Finally, Winnicott makes it clear that 'holding' of this kind is by no means passive; not only does it normally require careful monitoring and acute sensitivity to the patient's response to the setting, but with very severely regressed patients it can involve actively seeking out contact. In opposition to all traditional analytic practices, Winnicott (1955, pp. 281–2) states, 'In the extreme case the therapist would need to go to the patient and actively present good mothering, an experience that could not have been expected by the patient.'

It is interesting, if unsurprising, to note that Kleinians, who also work with severely disturbed patients, are often highly critical of the 'remothering' activities of object relations therapists. Segal (1981), for example, rejects the 'corrective technique' in which the analyst 'tries to be a good object to the patient rather than to make the patient aware as to why he is experienced in a particular way' (p. 80). Segal argues that such a procedure 'interferes with the psychoanalytic process and the acquiring of insight' (Ibid.). The active involvement of the analyst in supporting the patient's ego can, in the view of analysts from many schools, result in a collusiveness which is antipathetic to the critical distance necessary for therapeutic change to occur, and which can result in idealisation of the analyst which militates against the development of a reality sense. In defence of Winnicott, it can be said that his use of 'replacement therapy' is presented as an addition to classical analytic technique for use with a special kind of patient thought to be otherwise unreachable; in addition, his emphasis on the significance of the analytic setting and the congruence between his theoretical account and clinical recommendations has opened out for consideration a large range of interpersonal factors that might otherwise go neglected. But there are some important dangers with this kind of corrective work. First, it alters the stance of the analyst from that of critical ironist, revealing underlying conflicts, to that of rescuer and ideal – much as in the 'ecstatic' visions described in the previous chapter. In addition, its use of the maternal frame, both in theory and in practice, not only runs the risk of reducing to a procedure of attributing blame to 'not-good-enough' mothers, but also propagates a fantasy of omnipotence, that the analyst can be 'good enough' to make up for all the slings and arrows of fortune, however early they begin, however widespread they may be. Finally, there is a danger in all approaches that emphasise the supportiveness of the therapeutic relationship above its content, that there will be a drift away from exploration of the wider sources of an individual's pain, to a humanistic 'growth' encounter that submerges everything in an optimistic, but unrealistic, therapeutic 'love'. To see this more clearly, it is useful to consider briefly Guntrip's views on the centrality of the human relationship in therapy.

Guntrip takes up the Winnicottian notion of the analytic situation as a reparative one, emphasising forcefully its parenting components, the sense in which it is 'replacement therapy'. The therapeutic task with schizoid patients is 'how to start off the growth of an ego which has not yet properly begun to be' (1968, p. 359); this is linked to the patient's need for a relationship with someone 'who *in loco parentis* will enable him to grow' (p. 350). The analyst has to develop that sense of empathy with the patient that mothers have with their babies, that 'parental love, which the Greeks called *agape* as distinct from *eros*, the kind of love the psychotherapist must give his patient because he did not get it from his parents in an adequate way' (p. 357). Although this is similar in formulation to Winnicott's ideas, Guntrip extends the emphasis on relationship further than just the schizoid situation, and develops a harangue of the traditional psychoanalytic concern with technique. He is explicit on this point: classical analysis of transference can be helpful, but it often simply reveals the schizoid despair underneath, and anyway the active component of analytic treatment is always the relationship and not the techniques employed. 'Technique' is itself a dirty word in the Guntripian lexicon; not only is he critical of the 'objective' stance of traditional interpretive psychoanalysis because its unresponsiveness to the patient repeats the emotional traumas that presumably spark off schizoid conditions in the first place, but he is against the anti-humanist *sound* of the word. Technique refers to what the analyst *does*, but what matters is what the analyst *is* in the relationship with the patient.

> Terms such as 'analysis' and 'technique' are too impersonal. They remind me more of engineering than of personal relations. One can teach a technique, but cannot teach anyone how to be a therapeutic person. (Guntrip, 1973, p. 183)

In this view, therapy is the opposite of something technical, mechanical; it is the entry into a deeply empathic relationship which enables the patient to feel valued and held, perhaps for the first time, intuitively known and hence supported enough to allow change to be risked. Interpretation is 'simply the medium of an understanding relationship' (Ibid. p. 188); the crucial thing is to provide a new kind of relationship, a form of therapeutic love, which is the only possible context for genuine insight and change. Training of therapists is not a means of teaching them techniques, it is rather a process of drawing out from them the basic human capacities that are already there, helping them form better relationships with their patients and presumably with everyone else – not, it must be said, a notoriously predictable outcome of the conventional training analysis. There is, in fact, *nothing special* about psychotherapy; it is simply 'the application of the fundamental importance of personal relationships, in the sense of using good relationships to undo the harm done by bad ones' (p. 194). Entwined in this is a notion of how the therapist must become 'real' in the relationship with the patient: the analyst must genuinely care for the patient and be unafraid of a truly personal relationship with her/him; that is, the analyst must be a good object in reality and not just in fantasy. Sometimes what Guntrip means by 'real' seems to be 'empathic', but mostly he is referring to a relationship that is not built around the distance and fantasy-manipulation of other forms of analysis, but which represents the meeting together of two people in an ordinary, if intensely caring, way. The patient has needs of the therapist which go further than the interpretation of infantile feelings, and which involve a request for support in the real, everyday world. It may be that transference relations have to be worked through first, but these should eventually give way so that therapist and patient 'can at last meet "mentally face to face" and know that they know each other as two human beings' (1968, p. 353). It is never absolutely clear what such a meeting entails, but it seems that Guntrip is emphasising the ordinariness of the therapeutic encounter, seeing it as an interaction between two people trying to the best of their ability to get to know each other, but because one of them has had bad experiences in the past the other has to work extra hard at being caring and supportive enough for trust to develop. Whether the analyst should give advice or not is left open to the dictates of common sense; how much other active involvement in the patient's life is required is never specified.

Much of Guntrip's argument is familiar from other branches of psychotherapy, notably the humanistic school of workers such as Carl Rogers. In the humanists, too, there is an emphasis on the total personal encounter which allows the patient to retrieve parts of her/his self that have been submerged by painful or neglectful experiences in the past, thence to begin a process of 'personal growth'. Guntrip's discussion of 'reality' is also present in humanistic psychology, and has been taken up in some progressive ways, for example, in feminist psychotherapy where there is specific attention paid to dealing with the power aspects of the situation and with offering continuing support after the end of therapy (Eichenbaum and Orbach, 1982). There are substantial criticisms to be made of both these aspects of his work, however. Langs (1976) puts his finger on one of them in criticising the concern of Guntrip's mentor, Fairbairn, for the relationship between analyst and patient over and above technique: Langs argues that Fairbairn's focus on surface interaction leads to a neglect of the influence of unconscious fantasies and an avoidance of the analysis of basic intrapsychic conflicts (p. 232). This tendency is very noticeable in Guntrip's valorising of the 'reality' aspects of the relationship, especially as they are supposedly contextualised in wholly supportive and positive behaviour on the part of the analyst. Psychoanalytically, it is difficult to see how the painful feelings that the object relations theorists emphasise as being at the root of schizoid phenomena can be properly exposed and integrated if they are perpetually avoided – which is what appears likely to happen in relationships that prioritise here-and-now reality over fantasy, positive support over the analysis of destructive feelings. Politically, there are also some dubious assumptions in this approach to therapy which are familiar from the critique of object relations theory. It seeks to institute a replacement for the pains of the world in the rarefied situation of analysis, where it claims that a 'real' relationship is possible and that human love can overwhelm the damage of the past. This is neglectful of the structuring power of political relationships, suggesting that it is possible to experience some 'real' interpersonal encounter independently of the distortions induced by specific social forms. There is no way in which the destructiveness brought about through relationships embedded in certain social structures can be made good by a 'love' that stands outside them, and to suggest that such an artificial love can make up for the activities of the world is politically reductionist along the lines of the 'salvational' work described in the previous chapter – it makes social change a simple product of change at the level of individuals. If Lasch and other critics are correct in their linking of the increase of narcissistic character formations with changes in the social sphere, then to suggest that therapy can provide some *absolute* personal relationship is to argue that it can stand outside society, offering something which is pure and whole, uncontaminated by all the rest of the world. Whatever therapy at its best can do, it cannot do that.

The image of the analyst

The discussion of variations in classical, Kleinian and object relations approaches to therapy provides insights into their different versions of the 'image' of the analyst – the metaphorical position given her/him and the political implications that surround this. All forms of therapy involve power relations, both in the broad sense described in Chapter 8 and in the narrower sense that the relationship between the two participants (in individual treatment) is unequal. However supportive and egalitarian the therapist, the relationship is always an unbalanced one, its structure suggesting that the 'expert' therapist can deal with the patient's pain, can know more about the patient than the patient does her or himself. Psychoanalysts have traditionally claimed that they approximate in their sessions to a 'blank screen' on to which the patient displaces her/his underlying conflicts. In part, this is simply meant to allow the patient's fantasies free reign: 'By being nobody, the analyst can seem to be anybody; an enigma on which the patient can play variations' (Storr, 1966, p. 78). The analyst is a 'sounding board' against which the patient can 'test out the nature of his alientation' from self and others (Ibid.); the distance of the analyst from the patient and the lack of reciprocity in the therapeutic situation contributes to the productivity of this 'enigma'. Sandler *et al.*

(1973) also emphasise the importance of the 'professional attitude' of the analyst which allows her/him to maintain a certain distance from the patient and hence 'allows analysts to understand material in their patients which has not been adequately analysed in their own training analysis' (p. 69). Anna Freud's (1936) notion that the analyst 'take his stand at a point equidistant from the id, the ego and the super-ego' (p. 30) is a variant of this, as is Strachey's (1934) insistence that the analyst must at all costs avoid behaving in reality in line with the unconscious fantasies or introjects of the patient. But in classical analysis the exhortations to distance go further than that which might be expected if maintenance of neutrality were all that was at stake. This is apparent, for example, in Freud's 'rule of abstinence' which, as Ingleby (1984) points out, makes the relationship between patient and analyst less than a reciprocally human one. This rule is that according to which

> the analytic treatment should be so organised as to ensure that the patient finds as few substitutive satisfactions for his symptoms as possible. The implication for the analyst is that he should refuse on principle to satisfy the patient's demands and to fulfil the roles which the patient tends to impose upon him. (Laplanche and Pontalis, 1973, p. 2)

Whether it is intentional or not, this emphasis on neutrality and distance actually has the effect of enormously accentuating the power asymmetries present in the therapeutic encounter. The structure of the psychoanalytic situation is not simply one in which one person unavoidably has some power over another; everything that is done therein serves to increase that power. The analyst remains mysterious while the patient discloses the most intimate recesses of her/himself; the analyst is silent while the patient speaks; the patient is observed and the analyst invisible; and everything that the patient says is scrutinised for hidden meanings, so that even criticism of the analyst is interpreted as belonging elsewhere. The analyst can never be confronted, s/he epitomises that subtle power that slips away, unspoken but dominant. In theory, as everything that occurs between patient and analyst is analysed, the uses of power may itself be examined; but this is always in the terms defined by the arc of psychoanalysis itself. All this suggests that the apparent non-interference of the traditional analyst is a charade built upon a denial of politics: being neutral, passive, reflective is in many ways a means of avoiding articulation of the actual power relations that psychoanalysis produces and thrives upon.

Much psychoanalytic literature on the activity of the analyst has centred on the concept of 'counter-transference', a concept which expresses well the variations in attitude towards the analyst displayed by different theories. Laplanche and Pontalis (1973) define counter-transference as 'The whole of the analyst's unconscious reactions to the individual analysand – especially to the analysand's own transference' (p. 92), while Sandler *et al.* (1973) suggest that the 'most useful view of counter-transference might be to take it as referring to the specific emotional responses aroused in the analyst by the specific qualities of his patient' (p. 68). Although these two formulations are in substantial agreement with one another, there are some subtle and important differences. In the former case, counter-transference refers to something equivalent to the patient's transference: the analyst has certain unconscious feelings of her/his own which are experienced or manifested in the context of exposure to the patient. This is much like Freud's original view of counter-transference as a kind of resistance in the analyst, deriving from the arousal of unconscious conflicts by the patient, a notion which has been taken up in various forms by later analysts and has often resulted in an argument that analysts should strive to divest themselves of counter-transference feelings. Thus, in the classical tradition, the view is taken that the analytic encounter is one in which the analyst functions as a kind of blank screen upon whom the patient transfers fantasy material, which is then interpreted and clarified by the analyst acting in an emotionally neutral capacity, oriented towards reality. The operation of unconscious, 'neurotic' feelings in the analyst interferes with this process by influencing the patient's transference and by confusing the analyst's interpretations. Counter-transference is therefore something to be reduced to a minimum; it is not that the analyst should have no feelings at all for the patient, but that these should be both conscious and postponed during the therapeutic interaction. For object relations therapists the position is different but the attitude to counter-transference is similar: here it is regarded with opprobrium because it interferes with the formation of a real relationship with the patient, based on the specificity of that patient's needs rather than the unresolved conflicts of the analyst. Winnicott sees it as the therapist's 'neurotic features which *spoil the professional attitude* and disturb the course of the analytic process as determined by the patient' (quoted in Sandler *et al.*, 1973, p. 64), while Guntrip (1968, p. 333) suggests that counter-transference 'will be in proportion to the incompleteness of the analyst's own analysis'. Once again, it is only through clarity concerning the analyst's personal needs that those of the patient can be properly met.

Although Sandler, Dare and Holder (1973) derive their orientation from the ego psychoanalysis of Anna Freud, and hence are close to the classical position on most things, their definition of counter-transference leads into the major alternative understanding of the phenomenon, which is actually more characteristic of Kleinians. The important point in their formulation is that it refers to the *specific* emotional responses brought about in the therapist by the *specific* qualities of the patient; this in theory makes it possible to see these emotional responses as indicators of the peculiar nature of any individual patient. This is exactly what many theorists have argued: for example, Heimann (1950) suggests that the analyst sometimes unconsciously comprehends aspects of the patient's unconscious functioning, and that this meeting of two unconsciouses provides crucial information for monitoring of the therapeutic process. Greenberg and Mitchell (1983, p. 389) express the point most clearly:

> counter-transference provides the crucial clues to the predominant transferential configurations, since transference and counter-transference reciprocally generate and interpenetrate each other. Counter-transference is an inevitable product of the interaction between the patient and the analyst rather than a simple interference stemming from the analyst's own infantile drive-related conflicts.

The central point here relates to the different view of therapy put forward by those analysts working with an understanding of projective and identificatory mechanisms. Classical analysts emphasise the significance of interpretations based on an accurate perception of reality, thus viewing the analyst as standing outside the patient's pathology, commenting upon it in a clarifying way. In contrast, Kleinians and those influenced by their thought stress the way in which the analyst becomes a container for the patient's projected feelings and parts of her/his self and object world: the analyst is consequently involved in an interpersonal interaction that operates on several levels, including that of the interpenetration of the unconscious world of one participant by that of the other. The difference between analyst and patient is not that one has transference feelings and the other has not, but that the analyst has the emotional calibration to be able to use the feelings stirred up inside her/him to understand the patient's internal world. Hence, therapy becomes a two-way process whereby the working out of transference and counter-transference go on together, the analyst's awareness of this operating benevolently to provide new introjects for the patient to use. Langs (1976) extends this notion even further, if more formally, by using the concept of the 'bipersonal field' in which analyst and patient participate: in this view, transference phenomena

> have contributions from all parts of the bipersonal field, and can be understood and resolved only through the resolution of the pathology of the field – ultimately an inner resolution experienced by both participants. (p. 476)

The analyst is a full member of the field, contributing to it as well as acting as container and regenerator for the patient's projections. Changes that come about in the field affect both parties, although the major influences are always (in theory) on the patient. It should be noted that the structure of this position is more egalitarian than that of classical theory; on the other hand, the intensity of the interactions provoked by those workers concerned with projections and identifications is such that the power relationships present in analysis become accentuated rather than reduced. But the image of the analyst present in this version of counter-transference is as someone similar to the patient: wiser, perhaps, or more able to monitor and utilise emotions, but subject to the same processes and possibilities as the person with whom s/he is interacting. This mixture of egalitarianism and intense involvement of both parties raises some interesting prospects for examination and possible restructuring of power relations in therapy; such is not, however, the conventional focus of Kleinian analysis.

There are some alternative images of the analyst in psychoanalysis to the distant 'blank screen' of the classical school, mostly as a form of parent. As implied by all their metaphors of holding and 'management', object relations theorists concentrate on the role of the analyst as a maternal figure. Winnicott, in particular, provides an account of therapy as utilisation of an intuitive personal knowledge of the patient's needs that parallels the mother–infant relationship, or is even a deliberate imitation of the 'natural' response of a mother for her child. The analyst, acting as a 'good mother', makes it possible for the patient to take into her/himself those split-off, projected aspects of the psyche that are experienced as uncontrollable. Guntrip (1968, p. 360) formulates this idea in line with his own emphasis on the reality aspects of therapy:

> 'Analysing' is a male function, an intellectual activity of interpretation, but based on the female function of intuitively knowing experienced . . . through identification. Ultimately 'being there for the patient' in a stable and not a neurotic state is the female, maternal, and properly therapeutic function, which enables the patient to feel real and find his own proper self.

The assumptions in this passage concerning the essential differences between masculinity and femininity are fairly obviously ideological: that maleness is intellectual and analytic, while female means maternal, containing, loving. Therapy, already defined as a process of remothering, is also a 'female function', this being both a term of approbation and a use of conventional gender imagery. Leaving these assumptions unquestioned feeds into the creation of an analytic practice which supports patriarchal categories, even if the simple identity of these 'masculine' and 'feminine' attributes with actual men and women is avoided. It also, through a specious division of labour between male and female, avoids confronting the actual patterns of domination that appear inside and outside analysis. Nevertheless, this kind of language is taken up by many therapists without much consideration, including those troubled by the power elements of analysis described above. So Eichenbaum and Orbach (1982) emphasise the reality context of therapy as a way of reducing power imbalances, and also describe how the 'process of feeling that the little girl inside is accepted, understood and loved by the therapist is an extremely important part of the healing process' (p. 62). This kind of unquestioning modelling of therapy on an idealised maternal nurture is presumably what Klein (1957) is referring to when criticising analysts who fail to interpret their patients' longing for reassurance and appreciation and instead respond to it through identification with the patient's desire, with the result that they rush in and attempt immediately to alleviate anxieties instead of working with them. Nevertheless, Kleinians also use a maternal image of the analyst, albeit in a different way. Klein (1957) refers to the significance of 'repeated experiences of the effectiveness and truth of the interpretations given' as an analogue of happy infantile experiences of being fed and loved, both of them leading to the internalisation of the analyst/mother as a good object. More generally, the Kleinians' emphasis on projection and projective identification in therapy is an exact replication of their description of infantile development in the context of the interaction with the mother. It is not, however, that the analyst *replaces* the mother, as in object relations therapy, but that the processes exploited in analysis are the same as those in the infantile world, and act to install the analyst and – retrospectively – the mother as good internal objects. The 'analyst as mother' is more than a metaphor, but less than reality.

Oddly, despite Freudian patrocentricity and neglect of pre-Oedipal development, there is a far weaker theoretical tradition of 'analyst as father' than 'analyst as mother'. In practice, the history of the psychoanalytic movement itself attests to the sway of authoritarian figures over acolytes of all schools, but it has proved much more difficult to construct an image of the analytic role around maleness than around the more acceptable (in object relations theory) or basic (Kleinian) foundation of mothering. Rieff (1966) suggests the importance of having an 'exemplary figure' with whom to identify if cure of any kind is to be forthcoming; the dangers of authoritarianism are overt in his argument. However, in general it is not the explicit figure of a father that hovers over the analyst, but the implicit patriarchy involved in the manifestations of power present in the therapeutic setting. The way in which this infiltrates the classical notion of the analyst as a distant, neutral interpreter of psychic conflicts has already been described; the law-making paternal role provides an unarticulated substratum to this mode of practice. There is, in addition, a pattern by which analyst and patient perpetuate this patriarchal power by leaving it unquestioned, unanalysed. Fromm (1970) describes the 'gentleman's agreement' that often operates between patient and therapist so as not to challenge existing relations or bring up any substantially new experience, while Gear, Hill and Liendo (1981) suggest that the power relations inherent in 'therapeutic' relationships have a sado-masochistic structure in which each partner needs the other to continue in their respective roles. Ingleby (1984) points to the manner in which this avoidance of questions about the structure of analysis can prevent analysis fulfilling its liberatory potential. After noting the asymmetries of the power relations present in therapy, he suggests that it is an imbalance built into the very nature of psychoanalysis, which operates imperialistically on the values of both patient and analyst.

> What the patient submits to is not the rule of the analyst, but the rule of *analysis*, to which the analyst is every bit as subject. The real authoritarianism of psychoanalysis lies, not in the domination of patient by analyst, but in the domination of both by analytic doctrine. (p. 51)

Too simple, perhaps, and letting the actual person of the analyst off the hook too lightly. Nevertheless, Ingleby and others reveal what at least one necessary condition for a psychoanalysis that espouses a social practice must be: that it questions the conditions of its own existence, not just theoretically, but also in practice – fundamentally, in the overdetermined encounter between analyst and patient. Psychoanalysis is often contradictory in that it obscures power relations as well as dramatising them; examining the structure of the analytic situation as well as of the mind of the patient may help replace this obscuring function with a more genuinely *analysing* one. Especially, if this can be combined with the Kleinian-based insight that analytic practice is a meeting of two unconsciouses, then the exploitation of power may begin to be turned in the direction of challenge rather than conformity. Psychoanalytic theory does have some concepts that can help this to occur, as well as others that may get in the way.

The idea of analysing the structure of the analytic encounter is linked with a challenge to the 'mastery' of the analyst – her/his claim to knowledge or expertise over the patient's unconscious.

Perhaps not surprisingly, it is from feminism that the most astute attack along these lines comes. Gallop (1982) provides a dazzling critique of the authority structure of analysis, arguing that at every point that it becomes fixed in a claim to dominance or 'mastery', it also becomes patriarchal. This is linked with her own celebration of 'infidelity' as feminist practice, a notion questioned in Chapter 7, as well as to an opposition to Lacanian patriarchy that she articulates by reference to the Lacanian outcast, Irigaray.

> Irigaray's suspicion is that Lacanian discourse functions as some fundamental referent which any analysand's discourse can only 'translate', approximate to in some secondary, inadequate way. (p. 97)

Once again, this is a way of questioning the basic structure of psychoanalysis, its claim to have possession of a 'truth', a masterful practice, that is simply received and cannot be challenged. Gallop insinuates the continually subversive nature of the unconscious, the way in which no one can be its master; the analyst's position must always be undermined.

There is a difficulty and an irony with the argument just presented. The difficulty, which echoes one present in the substance of post-Lacanian feminist theories (see Chapter 7), is a danger that in opposing the mastery of Lacanian discourse a fetish of the irreducible mystery or desire of the individual will be set up – the idea that each unconscious is different, with its own determinants. At that point, all analysis disappears, replaced by an ecstatic vision of individual expression that loses the possibility of constructive social change. Secondly, the ironic twist to these theories is that although they are presented as a critique of Lacanianism, it is in Lacanian terms – as if the patriarch's word is prolonged in the arguments of his feminist opposition. Lacanian practice itself claims to be subversive, constantly upsetting the received wisdom of psychoanalysis. Elaborating the practice of Lacanian analysis, for example, Schneiderman (1980) emphasises how the analyst is 'a subjective participant in the experience of the transference', influencing what is said even though her/his intention is to let the analysand 'speak what had heretofore been unspeakable' – to find her/his own voice. This recognition itself moves some way towards demolishing analytic claims to truth: the analyst is not listening to the 'real' desire of the patient, but is participating in its creation. Just as the feminists suggest should occur, so the Lacanian enterprise claims to be directed towards subverting its own authority, revealing the manner in which there are no absolute answers to the patient's questions, no way of meeting her/his desire. Analysis in these terms has, indeed, the structure of patriarchy: there is mastery and phallocentrism, there is obedience to the word of Lacan. But it also contains, at times explicitly, an assertion that the end of therapy is the recovery of a voice for the patient's desire, and the dismantling of all claims to absolute authority. This is part game playing, part individualism, part nihilism – there is nothing to assert but the primacy of impossibility, the emptiness of desire. It cannot on its own provide an orientation befitting a social psychoanalysis which incorporates the kind of committed stance outlined in the previous chapter. For this to occur, something more akin to the Kleinian and even the object relations position is required: something which places an onus on the construction or reconstruction of personal and social relations of a high quality, deriving from an encounter that explores the deepest recesses of the personality. But where the ideas of Lacanians and others do contribute is in warning that the analytic encounter is itself structured by internal and external forces. This warning helps clarify the distinctions between individual and social levels, and also – through revealing and questioning the authority structures of analysis – provides a commentary on the links between power and change that operate in all therapeutic contexts.

Conclusion: The Politics of Psychoanalysis

Throughout its history, psychoanalysis has faced criticisms directed at its supposedly conformist nature. These derive from various aspects of its project. For some, the psychological orientation of psychoanalysis makes it irredeemably individualistic, a state of affairs aggravated by its adherence to a familial ideology, neglecting the way the bourgeois family serves the interests of particular power groups or modes of economic organisation. For others, the sticking point has been psychoanalysis' tendency to reduce what is social to what is individual, for example, by interpreting institutions or groups solely in terms of the psychological characteristics of their individual members. This tendency is also on view in the 'explanations' that are sometimes provided of revolutionary political activity as the product of psychopathological fixations. Feminists have been particularly scandalised by the biologism and paternalist or misogynist tendencies present in many psychoanalytic formulations, from Freud onwards. Finally, radicals of all descriptions have pointed to the therapeutic concerns of analysis and argued that at best they are irrelevant to political activity, at worst actively opposed to it, locating the sources of distress in individual pathology. It will be clear from the discussions presented in this book that all these criticisms have some force: in various ways, psychoanalytic theory has partaken of reactionary political assumptions, has joined in the chorus of voices raised against dissent, has supported the oppression of women and neglected the extent to which social behaviours and institutions are constructed rather than biologically determined. Psychoanalytic therapy has also frequently been conformist, either because of its underlying assumptions or despite them – for example, by virtue of its insistence on heterosexuality as the end-point of sexual development. The fact that most psychoanalytic practice around the world is private practice, engaged in by and for the affluent middle classes, has done little to enhance its political credentials.

All these criticisms, then, have tangible validity. All, however, are also overgeneralised, lumping together a wide variety of psychoanalytic approaches that actually have differing implications and political standpoints. More centrally, all the criticisms are inaccurate because they miss the most important point about the whole psychoanalytic enterprise: that its political significance arises from the focus of its analysis, the complex interweaving of what is external to the individual with what is experienced as most deeply private and personally formative. The argument in this book has returned several times to the idea that an important process by which society operates is to introduce into each individual its own ideological axes, which then become the generative kernels of emotions, attitudes and modes of relating to others – in other words, of psychic organisation. These axes are profoundly unconscious, entering into each of us through our early and most intense contacts with others who already bear the weight of ideology upon them. Their exact nature may vary according to experience, but these unconscious axes always exist, making it possible for us to take up a position with respect to the world, to perceive it and relate to it in particular ways. Because this is an unconscious process and not a simple matter of persuasion or conditioning, psychoanalysis is its science, for it is only psychoanalysis that is oriented totally towards the hidden recesses of psychology, the basic underlying forces that give us structure and momentum. Psychoanalysis is *always* politically relevant precisely because it always deals with the way experiences with the social become engaged with as if they are deeply personal, and because it searches out the unrecognised forces that give pattern to our desires, dreams and neuroses. And the politics of psychoanalysis always has a critical or subversive tinge to it, however obscured, because the project of uncovering the forces that underpin the individual personality is a radical one, akin to other attempts to show that what appears to be natural and inescapable is in fact socially constructed.

In answering criticisms of psychoanalysis' political role it is important not to go too far the other way. For one thing, psychoanalysis is not the whole of politics; it is simply the body of theories that deals with the formation of the unconscious, and hence with how social and personal worlds interpenetrate. In addition, as noted above, the criticisms presented by radicals do have force if distinctions are made between different schools of analytic theory. The main thrust of this book has been in this area: to juxtapose the most interesting strands of psychoanalytic thought in order to tease out their political implications. Only a few summary points need to be made here. First, it is worth reiterating the complexity of the situation: many psychoanalytic approaches have both progressive and reactionary components, or can be elaborated in either way. Thus, Freud's own work reveals how sexual identity is constructed out of bisexuality, but his assumptions about femininity act to produce an offensive account that is both biologistic and woman-hating. Freudian instinct theory, on the other hand, is obviously biological in its formulation, and yet contains the seeds of a radical understanding of the ways in which social constraints distort the possibilities inherent in individuals, alienating them from their own desires. Ego psychology appears to provide a descriptive framework in which the difficulties inherent in social integration are made explicit; yet, its concern with 'adaptation' eventually destroys its critical edge, reducing it to an account of how personal desires are managed in the interests of social cohesion. In a different way, object relations theory has been criticised throughout this book for its assumptions about psychic unity and its use of romanticisations of motherhood that feed into traditional patriarchal attitudes; in addition, its neglect of wider social structures is so complete that it hypothesises that the therapeutic relationship could remedy completely all psychic pain. Nevertheless, the firm orientation that this approach has towards relationships and its 'constructivist' account of development serve to open out psychoanalytic theory and to help make it genuinely interpersonal, shifting attention away from considerations of 'instinctual energy' and towards an understanding of the qualities necessary for human relationships to be rewarding.

Kleinian theory is perhaps the clearest instance of the difficulties involved in holding fast to general political evaluations. On the face of it, it is biologistic and pessimistic: the infant is born consumed by hatred and destructiveness, and there is nothing that can be done to remove these feelings. All activity reduces to the pressure of instincts, particularly the Death Instinct; the environment can only ameliorate this pressure, never replace it with something totally benign. In addition to this, Kleinian theory shows a virtually complete neglect of the social world: the mother–infant interchange is the entire limit of its political theorising. All this is true about Kleinianism, and yet the discussion in this book has revealed that it also has some immensely productive implications for progressive politics. Some of these stem from its concentration upon destructiveness, which enables it to avoid the utopian traps of object relations theory in which the whole of life is seen as a descent from the infantile Eden, and to direct its attention to the conditions under which the difficulties and pain inherent in human existence can be overcome or translated into something productive and 'reparative'. Additionally, although Klein relies heavily on a psychology of instincts, they are instincts that are always object oriented, making her theory one that centres upon the way relationships provide the structure for psychic organisation. The Kleinian fascination with opposed instincts also produces an intriguingly dialectical theory, in which projective mechanisms mediate between the contradictions that reside within each individual and those that exist without, until they are intertwined to such an extent as to be inseparable.

A final example of the difficulties involved in forming political judgements concerns Lacanian theory. This has been justly attacked for its obsession with the phallus, its obscuring of political choices and the authoritarianism implicit in its anti-humanist stance. On the other hand, it supplies the tools for an analysis of the way ideology, particularly patriarchal ideology, operates to construct the unconscious in particular ways, and it also produces an account of the aims and practices of therapy that contains a critique of its own claims to mastery, and that in some ways recommends subversion. Here again, ambivalence is the only attitude one can justifiably take towards this type of psychoanalysis: at the moment that it has most to offer, it is also most frustrating and dangerous. No general rejection or acceptance is possible, only a careful sorting out of elements and building on the basis of the contradictions that are revealed.

With the ambiguities and contradictions that surround psychoanalytic theories, is there anything general that can be said, apart from that such theories are politically relevant? There is no neat synthesis that can be made of the best elements in each approach: they are too fundamentally opposed, often in their basic assumptions. However, it is clear that positions which reduce psychic activity to the functioning of instincts tend to be reactionary, as do those that are directed towards the biological 'necessity' of adaptation to one's immediate social environment. Accounts of psychological liberation that go no further than the release of instincts are recipes for individualism, while those that deal only with two-person relationships have little to offer any general critique of social organisation or of the way ideology operates structurally to determine the possibilities available to individuals in their encounters with one another. On balance, Kleinian and Lacanian theories seem to have most to offer, largely because of their refusal to advocate simple consolatory responses to the difficulties of living. However, not only do both approaches themselves contain important lacunae and retrogressive elements, but they are also opposed to one another, for instance, in their formulations on splitting, on the role of pre-Oedipal development, and on culture. Kleinianism is strong in its account of mental mechanisms and of the manner in which disintegration and destructiveness can be overcome; Lacanianism takes up powerfully the issue of ideology, of how living in any society always involves alienation from certain personal possibilities. The choice between them is not easy, but nor can they be amalgamated; they simply have to be allowed to be, supplying different images of the human condition and alternative ideas for social advance. This may be a reflection of the inadequate state of psychoanalytic theory; it may also owe something to the contradictions inherent in contemporary society, and in the personalities of those who labour under it, the objects of the analytic gaze.

A final question raises its head, that of the implications of these psychoanalytic debates for personal and social change. It has been emphasised several times that politics cannot be reduced to therapy: however helpful or enabling the encounter between patient and analyst may be, it remains a microsocial event that on its own cannot alter the structural conditions of society. In the right form, however, it is an important element in encouraging progress: not only can it alleviate individual distress (which is likely to make someone more, rather than less, able to be politically effective), but it can also reveal the forces which have produced that distress in the first place. More generally, analysis can lay bare the conditions of a person's subjectivity – the generative axes around which psychic life is organised, that are themselves elements in an ideological space. This laying bare does not in itself amount to change, but it is an important step; reviewing and re-experiencing the formative experiences of one's life in the emotionally compelling setting of therapy is a profoundly disorienting and challenging activity. If the political Freudians are correct, such a form of ideological struggle is also necessary if political and economic change is not to be resisted by internalisations of the old, bad world. Psychoanalysis also provides a more general commentary on social change, however, that can be used as a yardstick of political development. This relies on the idea that a purpose of social action is to improve the quality of people's lives, to make the conditions of existence more egalitarian and fulfilling. This qualitative vision is one to which psychoanalysis can contribute, because part of its subject matter is the identification of the needs and desires that people have. For the libertarian Freudians, the vision is one of a playground of impulse, in which there are no constraints on sexuality. For object relations and Kleinian theorists, it is of certain forms of maternal nurture and support, allowing either for the growth of a whole psyche that can form mutually giving relationship, or for the overcoming of destructiveness in an integrated and creative way. For Lacanians, the image of the good society is much harder to pin down, because it is viewed as inherently impossible (another source of anti-Lacanian feeling); yet, their description of the operations of alienation and of the subversiveness of desire supplies some markers for progress. Again, it is important not to confuse levels. Psychoanalysis is neither a social theory nor a programme for revolutionary activity. Instead, it is a major tool for ideological struggle: it reveals the workings of society within each individual, it offers a means for directly confronting each person's subjectivity, and it supplies a set of criticisms of the distortions and despair that are suffered under conditions of domination. The politics of psychoanalysis are real and important, however ambiguous and partial they may be.

Notes

Introduction

1. The spelling 'phantasy' is a common one in psychoanalysis, but is problematic in that it is used to signify different things in different theories. In this book, its use is restricted to occasions when Kleinian theory is being discussed, as 'phantasy' has a reasonably specific sense there (see Chapter 5). In all other instances, the more conventional spelling 'fantasy' is employed.

4 Instincts and Objects

1. The term 'object relations theory' can be quite loosely applied to indicate any approach which focuses on the relationships between the developing ego and the 'objects' (people or parts of people) with whom it comes into contact. Here it is being used specifically to refer to the work of Fairbain, Guntrip and Winnicott; while Klein certainly dealt with ego-object relations it will be argued that her approach was significantly different from those of these theorists.
2. In Fairbairn's original (1944) formulation, it is only the *bad* aspect of the object that is internalised at first – i.e. the object is already split before internalisation occurs. However, in a 1951 addendum to the 1944 paper, Fairbairn acknowledges that this makes it difficult to understand why the good object is ever internalised, and alters his theory to suggest that the 'pre-ambivalent object' is first internalised because of its unsatisfying qualities, and then becomes split. It is this account that is followed in the text.

5 Splitting the Mind

1. Greenberg and Mitchell have clarified the sometimes confused Kleinian account of the role of reality by distinguishing four different approaches present in Klein's work. (1) A 'temporal layering sequence' in which the harsh early objects produced by the Death Instinct are overlaid by later images of the parents as helpful and kind; (2) an approach which suggests that the child's early objects are

derived from real experiences but become distorted by internal impulses; (3) a more fluid 'projection–introjection' mechanism whereby the internal object world is altered by incorporation of external objects which have themselves been the recipients of projected impulses; (4) an approach derived from work on the 'depressive position' in which it is suggested that internal and external object worlds derive from experiences with real objects, through a process of introjection and projection (Greenberg and Mitchell, 1983, pp. 134–5). As will be discussed more fully below, the emphasis on projective mechanisms apparent in approaches (3) and (4) present many possibilities for a social psychoanalytic theory.

2. The Lacanian terminology of the 'subject' is a confusing one, relying on a play between the linguistic idea of subject, the psychological notion of the individual human entity, and the idea of being 'subjected to' something more extensive than oneself. Its crucial argument, however, is that the subject is not something pre-given, but that it becomes formed through the process described in this section. Sexual division is one of the markers of the development of the subject; it is not inherent in it, but is given from the outside. Because of this, it is inappropriate to use gender labels (s/he, etc.), although the alternative 'it', adopted here for want of an option, is not a particularly happy one. Gender labels are retained in the text where the reference is to 'the child' or 'infant'.

8 Psychoanalysis and Psychotherapy

1. An extended account of the political significance of psychotherapy, and of mental health work in general, can be found in *The Politics of Mental Health* (Banton, Clifford, Frosh, Lousada and Rosenthall, 1985).

Bibliography

Wherever possible, references to Freud are given to the Pelican Freud Library (Harmondsworth: Penguin) (PFL), with the date of publication of the relevant PFL volume provided. Where the paper cited has not been included in the PFL (to 1985), reference is given to the *Standard Edition of the Complete Works of Sigmund Freud* (London: Hogarth Press) (SE), with volume and page numbers.

Banton, R., Clifford, P., Frosh, S., Lousada, J. and Rosenthall, J. (1985) *The Politics of Mental Health* (London: Macmillan).

Breuer, J. and Freud, S. (1895) *Studies on Hysteria* (PFL 3, 1974).

Brooks, K. (1973) 'Freudianism is not a Basis for a Marxist Psychology', in P. Brown (ed.), *Radical Psychology* (London: Tavistock).

Brown, N. O. (1959) *Life Against Death* (Middletown, Conn.: Wesleyan University Press).

Cameron, D. (1985) *Feminism and Linguistic Theory* (London: Macmillan).

Chasseguet-Smirgel, J. (1964) 'Feminine Guilt and the Oedipus Complex', in J. Chasseguet-Smirgel (ed.) *Female Sexuality* (London: Virago, 1981).

Chodorow, N. (1978) *The Reproduction of Mothering* (Berkeley: University of California Press).

Cioffi, F. (ed.) (1973) *Freud: Modern Judgements* (London: Macmillan).

Cixous, H. (1975) 'Sorties', in E. Marks and I. de Courtivon (eds) *New French Feminisms* (Sussex: Harvester Press, 1981).

Cixous, H. (1976) 'The Laugh of the Medusa', in E. Marks and I. de Courtivon (eds) *New French Feminisms* (Sussex: Harvester Press, 1981).

Coward, R. and Ellis, J. (1977) *Language and Materialism* (London: Routledge & Kegan Paul).

Deleuze, G. and Guattari, F. (1977) *Anti-Oedipus* (New York: Viking).

Dinnerstein, D. (1977) *The Mermaid and the Minotaur* (New York: Harper & Row).

Eichenbaum, L. and Orbach, S. (1982) *Outside In . . . Inside Out* (Harmondsworth: Penguin).

Ernst, S. and Goodison, L. (1981) *In Our Own Hands* (London: Women's Press).

Eysenck, H. J. (1985) *Decline and Fall of the Freudian Empire* (Harmondsworth: Viking).

Eysenck, H. J. and Wilson, G. D. (1973) *The Experimental Study of Freudian Theories* (London: Methuen).

Fairbairn, W. R. D. (1941) 'A Revised Psychopathology of the Psychoses and Psychoneuroses', in W. R. D. Fairbairn, *Psychoanalytic Studies of the Personality* (London: Routledge & Kegan Paul, 1952).

Fairbairn, W. R. D. (1944) 'Endopsychic Structure Considered in Terms of Object-Relationships', in W. R. D. Fairbairn, *Psychoanalytic Studies of the Personality* (London: Routledge & Kegan Paul, 1952).

Fairbairn, W. R. D. (1951) 'A Synopsis of the Development of the Author's Views Regarding the Structure of the Personality', in W. R. D Fairbairn, *Psychoanalytic Studies of the Personality* (London: Routledge & Kegan Paul, 1952).

Farrell, B. (1981) *The Standing of Psychoanalysis* (Oxford: Oxford University Press).

Fenichel, O. (1945) *The Psychoanalytic Theory of Neurosis* (London: Routledge & Kegan Paul).

Foucault, M. (1967) *Madness and Civilization* (London: Tavistock, 1971).

Frankl, V. (1967) *Psychotherapy and Existentialism* (Harmondsworth: Penguin).

Freud, A. (1936) *The Ego and the Mechanisms of Defence* (London: Hogart Press, 1948).

Freud, S. (1905) 'Fragment of an Analysis of a Case of Hysteria' (PFL 8, 1977).

Freud, S. (1913) 'On Beginning the Treatment' (SE 12, 121–44).

Freud, S. (1914a) 'Totem and Taboo' (PFL 13, 1985).

Freud, S. (1914b) 'Remembering, Repeating and Working Through' (SE 12, 145–56).

Freud, S. (1915a) 'Papers on Metapsychology' (PFL 11, 1984).

Freud, S. (1915b) 'Observations on Transference Love' (SE 12, 157–71).

Freud, S. (1917) *Introductory Lectures on Psychoanalysis* (PFL 1, 1974).

Freud, S. (1920) *Beyond the Pleasure Principle* (PFL 11, 1984).

Freud, S. (1921) Group Psychology and the Analysis of the Ego (PFL 12, 1985).

Freud, S. (1923) 'The Ego and the Id' (PFL 11, 1984).

Freud, S. (1925) 'Some Psychical Consequences of the Anatomical Distinction between the Sexes' (PFL 7, 1977).

Freud, S. (1926a) 'Inhibitions, Symptoms, Anxiety' (PFL 10, 1979).

Freud, S. (1926b) 'The Question of Lay Analysis', in S. Freud, *Two Short Accounts of Psychoanalysis* (Harmondsworth: Penguin, 1962).

Freud, S. (1930) 'Civilization and its Discontents' (PFL 12, 1985).

Freud, S. (1933) *New Introductory Lectures on Psychoanalysis* (PFL 2, 1973).

Freud, S. (1937) 'Analysis Terminable and Interminable' (SE 23, 209–53).

Freud, S. (1939) 'Moses and Monotheism' (PFL 13, 1985).

Fromm, E. (1942) *The Fear of Freedom* (London: Routledge & Kegan Paul).

Fromm, E. (1968) *The Revolution of Hope* (New York: Harper & Row).

Fromm, E. (1970) *The Crisis of Psychoanalysis* (Harmondsworth: Penguin).

Gabriel, Y. (1983) *Freud and Society* (London: Routledge & Kegan Paul).
Gallop, J. (1982) *Feminism and Psychoanalysis* (London: Macmillan).
Gear, M. C., Hill, M. A. and Lienda, M. (1981) *Working through Narcissism* (New York: Jason Aronson).
Greenberg, J. R. and Mitchell, S. A. (1983) *Object Relations in Psychoanalytic Theory* (Cambridge, Mass.: Harvard University Press).
Grunberger, B. (1964) 'Outline for a Study of Narcissism in Female Sexuality', in J. Chasseguet-Smirgel (ed.) *Female Sexuality* (London: Virago, 1981).
Guntrip, H. (1961) *Personality Structure and Human Interaction* (London: Hogarth Press).
Guntrip, H. (1968) *Schizoid Phenomena, Object Relations and the Self* (London: Hogarth Press).
Guntrip, H. (1973) *Psychoanalytic Theory, Therapy and the Self* (New York: Basic Books).
Habermas, J. (1972) *Knowledge and Human Interests* (London: Heinemann).
Hartmann, H. (1956) 'Notes on the Reality Principle', in H. Hartmann, *Essays in Ego Psychology* (New York: International Universities Press, 1964).
Hartmann, H. (1959) *Ego Psychology and the Problem of Adaptation* (London: Hogarth Press).
Heimann, P. (1950) 'On Counter-Transference', *International Journal of Psychoanalysis 31*, 81–84.
Henriques, J., Hollway, W., Urwin, C., Venn, C. and Walkerdine, V. (1984) *Changing the Subject* (London: Methuen).
Hirst, P. and Woolley, P. (1982) *Social Relations and Human Attributes* (London: Tavistock Press).
Horney, K. (1926) 'Flight from Womanhood', *International Journal of Psychoanalysis* 7, 324–339.
Ingleby, D. (1984) 'The Ambivalence of Psychoanalysis', Radical Science 15, 39–71.
Irigaray, L. (1977) 'Ce Sexe qui n'en pas Un,' in E. Marks and I. de Courtivon (eds) *New French Feminisms* (Sussex: Harvester Press, 1981).
Jacoby, R. (1975) *Social Amnesia* (Sussex: Harvester Press).
Jacoby, R. (1983) *The Repression of Psychoanalysis* (New York: Basic Books).
Jahoda, M. (1977) *Freud and the Dilemmas of Psychology* (London: Hogarth Press).
Jameson, F. (1984) 'Postmodernism, or the Cultural Logic of Late Capitalism', *New Left Review,* 146.
Jones, E. (1927) 'The Early Development of Female Sexuality', *International Journal of Psychoanalysis 8*, 459–72.
Kernberg, O. F. (1970) 'A Psychoanalytic Classification of Character Pathology', *Journal of the American Psychoanalytic Association 222*, 255–67.

Kernberg, O. F. (1975) *Borderline Conditions and Pathological Narcissism* (New York: Jason Aronson).

Kernberg, O. F. (1976) *Object Relations Theory and Clinical Psychoanalysis* (New York: Jason Aronson).

Klein, M. (1946) 'Notes on Some Schizoid Mechanisms', in M. Klein, *Envy and Gratitude and Other Works* (New York: Delta, 1975).

Klein, M. (1950) 'On the Criteria for Termination of a Psychoanalysis', in M. Klein, *Envy and Gratitude and Other Works* (New York: Delta, 1975).

Klein, M. (1952) 'The Origins of Transference', in M. Klein, *Envy and Gratitude and Other Works* (New York: Delta, 1975).

Klein, M. (1955) 'The Psychoanalytic Play Technique', in M. Klein., *Envy and Gratitude and Other Works* (New York: Delta, 1975).

Klein, M. (1957) 'Envy and Gratitude', in M. Klein, *Envy and Gratitude and Other Works* (New York: Delta, 1975).

Klein, M. (1960) 'On Mental Health', in M. Klein, *Envy and Gratitude and Other Works* (New York: Delta, 1975).

Kohut, H. (1971) *The Analysis of the Self* (New York: International Universities Press).

Kohut, H. (1977) *The Restoration of the Self* (New York: International Universities Press).

Kovel, J. (1984) 'Rationalisation and the Family', in B. Richards (ed.) *Capitalism and Infancy* (London: Free Association Books).

Kristeva, J. (1974) 'La Femme, ce n'est jamais Ça', in E. Marks and I. de Courtivon (eds) *New French Feminisms* (Sussex: Harvester Press, 1981).

Lacan, J. (1949) 'The Mirror Stage as Formative of the Function of the I as Revealed in Psychoanalytic Experience', in J. Lacan, *Ecrits: A Selection* (London: Tavistock, 1977).

Lacan, J. (1953) 'The Function and Field of Speech and Language in Psychoanalysis', in J. Lacan, *Ecrits: A Selection* (London: Tavistock, 1977).

Lacan, J. (1958) 'The Signification of the Phallus', J. Lacan, *Ecrits: A Selection* (London: Tavistock, 1977).

Langs, R. (1976) *The Therapeutic Interaction, vol II.* (New York: Jason Aronson).

Laplanche, J. and Pontalis, J.-B. (1973) *The Language of Psychoanalysis* (London: Hogarth Press).

Lasch, C. (1979) *The Culture of Narcissism* (London: Abacus).

Lasch, C. (1984) *The Minimal Self* (London: Picador).

Macey, D. (1978) 'Jacques Lacan', *Ideology and Consciousness 4*, 113–29.

Malcolm, J. (1982) *Psychoanalysis: The Impossible Profession* (London: Picador).

Mannoni, O. (1971) *Freud: The Theory of the Unconscious* (London: New Left Books).

Marcuse, H. (1955) *Eros and Civilisation* (Boston: Beacon Press, 1966).

Menninger, K. (1958) *Theory of Psychoanalytic Technique* (New York: Basic Books).

Metcalfe, A. and Humphries, M. (eds) (1985) *The Sexuality of Men* (London: Pluto Press).
Mitchell, J. (1974) *Psychoanalysis and Feminism* (Harmondsworth: Penguin).
Mitchell, J. (1982) 'Introduction – I', in J. Mitchell and J. Rose (eds) *Feminine Sexuality* (London: Macmillan).
Mitchell, J. and Rose, J. (eds) (1982) *Feminine Sexuality* (London: Macmillan).
Poster, M. (1978) *Critical Theory of the Family* (London: Pluto).
Rank, O. (1924) *The Trauma of Birth* (New York: Harper & Row, 1973).
Reich, W. (1942) *The Function of the Orgasm* (London: Souvenir, 1983).
Reich, W. (1946) *The Mass Psychology of Fascism* (Harmondsworth: Penguin).
Richards, B. (1984) 'Schizoid States and the Market', in B. Richards (ed.) *Capitalism and Infancy* (London: Free Association Books).
Rieff, P. (1959) *Freud: The Mind of the Moralist* (Chicago: University of Chicago Press, 1979).
Rieff, P. (1966) *The Triumph of the Therapeutic* (Harmondsworth: Penguin).
Riley, D. (1983) *War in the Nursery* (London: Virago).
Robinson, P. (1970) *The Sexual Radicals* (London: Paladin).
Rose, J. (1982) 'Introduction – II', in J. Mitchell and J. Rose (eds) *Feminine Sexuality* (London: Macmillan).
Russell, G. (1985) 'Narcissism and the Narcissistic Personality Disorder: A Comparison of the Theories of Kernberg and Kohut', *British Journal of Medical Psychology* 58, 137–48.
Rustin, M. (1982) 'A Socialist Consideration of Kleinian Psychoanalysis', *New Left Review* 131, 71–96.
Rustin, M. and Rustin, M. (1984) 'Relational Preconditions of Socialism', in B. Richards (ed.) *Capitalism and Infancy* (London: Free Association Books).
Rutter, M. (1982) *Maternal Deprivation Reassessed* (Harmondsworth: Penguin).
Safouan, M. (1975) 'Feminine Sexuality and Psychoanalytic Doctrine', in J. Mitchell and J. Rose (eds) *Feminine Sexuality* (London: Macmillan, 1982).
Sandler, J., Dare, C. and Holder, A. (1973) *The Patient and the Analyst* (London: Maresfield Reprints, 1979).
Sayers, J. (1985) 'Sexual Contradictions: On Freud, Psychoanalysis and Feminism', *Free Associations* 1, 76–104.
Schafer, R. (1976) *A New Language for Psychoanalysis* (New Haven, Conn.: Yale University Press).
Schneiderman, S. (1980) 'The Other Lacan', in S. Schneiderman (ed.), *Returning to Freud* (New Haven, Conn.: Yale University Press).
Segal, H. (1973) *Introduction to the Work of Melanie Klein* (London: Hogarth Press).
Segal, H. (1981) *The Work of Hanna Segal* (New York: Jason Aronson).
Storr, A. (1966) 'The Concept of Cure', in C. Rycroft (ed.) *Psychoanalysis Observed* (Harmondsworth: Penguin).

Strachey, J. (1934) 'The Nature of the Therapeutic Action of Psycho-analysis', *International Journal of Psychoanalysis* 15, 127–59.
Sulloway, F. J. (1979) *Freud: Biologist of the Mind* (New York: Basic Books).
Timpanaro, S. (1976) *The Freudian Slip* (London: New Left Books).
Turkle, S. (1978) *Psychoanalytic Politics: Freud's French Revolution* (London: Burnett).
Ward, E. (1984) *Father–Daughter Rape* (London: Women's Press).
Winnicott, D. W. (1950) 'Aggression in Relation to Emotional Development', in D. W. Winnicott, *Through Paediatrics to Psychoanalysis* (London: Hogarth Press, 1958)
Winnicott, D. W. (1955) 'Clinical Varieties of Transference', in D. W. Winnicott, *Through Paediatrics to Psychoanalysis* (London: Hogarth Press, 1958).
Winnicott, D. W. (1956) 'Primary Maternal Preoccupation', in D. W. Winnicott, *Through Paediatrics to Psychoanalysis* (London: Hogarth Press, 1958).
Winnicott, D. W. (1963) 'Communicating and Not Communicating Leading to a Study of Certain Opposites', in D. W. Winnicott, *The Maturational Process and the Facilitating Environment* (London: Hogarth Press, 1965).
Wollheim, R. (1971) *Freud* (London: Fontana).
Zetzel, E. R. (1956) 'Current Concepts of Transference', *International Journal of Psychoanalysis* 37, 369–76.

Index